The Bruce Lee Library

Bruce Lee

As revealed through the notes, letters, diaries, interviews, reading annotations, and library of Bruce Lee

The Art of Expressing the Human Body

By **John Little**

TUTTLE Publishing

Tokyo | Rutland, Vermont | Singapore

All photos appearing in this book are courtesy of the archive of Linda Lee Cadwell, the Estate of Bruce Lee, and Warner Brothers Films.

Published by Tuttle Publishing, an imprint of Periplus Editions (HK) Ltd.

www.tuttlepublishing.com

Library of Congress Cataloging-in-Publication Data
Lee, Bruce, 1940-1973.
    The art of expressing the human body / by Bruce Lee : compiled and edited by John Little
        256 p. : ill. ; 28 cm.—(the Bruce Lee library: v. 4)
        ISBN: 0-8048-3129-7 (pb)
        1. Bodybuilding—Training. 2. Physical Fitness. 3. Lee, Bruce.
    Lee, Bruce, 1940-1973. Bruce Lee library: v. 4.
GV546.5.L44 1998
613.7'1—dc21
98037849
                                          CIP
    ISBN 978-0-8048-3129-1

Distributed by:

North America, Latin America & Europe
Tuttle Publishing
364 Innovation Drive, North Clarendon
VT 05759-9436, USA
Tel: 1 (802) 773 8930
Fax: 1 (802) 773 6993
info@tuttlepublishing.com
www.tuttlepublishing.com

Japan
Tuttle Publishing
Yaekari Building, 3rd Floor
5-4-12 Osaki, Shinagawa-ku
Tokyo 1410032, Japan
Tel: (81) 3 5437 0171
Fax: (81) 3 5437 0755
sales@tuttle.co.jp
www.tuttle.co.jp

The Tuttle Story
"Books to Span the East and West"

Many people are surprised to learn that the world's leading publisher of books on Asia had humble beginnings in the tiny American state of Vermont. The company's founder, Charles E. Tuttle, belonged to a New England family steeped in publishing.

Immediately after WWII, Tuttle served in Tokyo under General Douglas MacArthur and was tasked with reviving the Japanese publishing industry. He later founded the Charles E. Tuttle Publishing Company, which thrives today as one of the world's leading independent publishers.

Though a westerner, Tuttle was hugely instrumental in bringing a knowledge of Japan and Asia to a world hungry for information about the East. By the time of his death in 1993, Tuttle had published over 6,000 books on Asian culture, history and art—a legacy honored by the Japanese emperor with the "Order of the Sacred Treasure," the highest tribute Japan can bestow upon a non-Japanese.

With a backlist of 1,500 titles, Tuttle Publishing is more active today than at any time in its past—still inspired by Charles Tuttle's core mission to publish fine books to span the East and West and provide a greater understanding of each.

Asia Pacific
Berkeley Books Pte Ltd
61 Tai Seng Avenue #02-12
Singapore 534167
Tel: (65) 6280 1330
Fax: (65) 6280 6290
inquiries@periplus.com.sg
www.periplus.com

Indonesia
PT Java Books Indonesia
Jl. Rawa Gelam IV No. 9,
Kawasan Industri Pulogadung
Jakarta 13930, Indonesia
Tel: 62 (21) 4682 1088
Fax: 62 (21) 461 0206
crm@periplus.co.id
www.periplus.com

16 17 16 15
26 25 24 23   1506MP

Text design—Vernon Press, Inc.

Printed in Singapore

TUTTLE PUBLISHING® is a registered trademark of Tuttle Publishing, a division of Periplus Editions (HK) Ltd

GET A CHECKUP FIRST

As with all forms of strenuous exercise, you must take note of one point before you start your training: You should go to see a doctor and make sure that you do not have any health problems such as heart disease or tuberculosis. If you unfortunately do have one, you'll have to stop your training and wait until you have cured it. Otherwise, the training will hurt you badly and may even result in death.
—Bruce Lee

To Terri Little and Bruce Cadwell—two wonderful human beings without whose patience, tolerance, understanding, compassion, support, and love this book would not have been possible.

CONTENTS

FOREWORD

By Allen Joe

When asked to write this foreword for one of John Little's definitive volumes on the life, art, and philosophy of Bruce Lee, I thought to myself, Where do I start?

How do I properly articulate the overwhelming emotions and warmth from my heart that I have for a man that I have known for over thirty years? How do I communicate the presence of a man that was—and remains—so influential in my life and so familiar to me and my wife Annie, that he is more like a family member? Indeed, Bruce Lee was a man who was such a good friend that I still keep a photo of him in my wallet—even more than two decades after his death. It is indeed an honor to be given this opportunity to say a few words about my friend, Bruce Lee.

I guess a good place to start is to answer the question I am most often asked: How did I first meet Bruce Lee? I met Bruce in Seattle in 1962 when my family and I were visiting to attend the World's Fair. James Lee, a friend of mine since childhood (and no relation to Bruce) had heard from his brother about Bruce and his martial art prowess and skill in cha-cha dancing. James asked me to check out "this cat" and see if he was any good. I was in for a surprise, to say the least.

I learned that Bruce was employed at a Chinese restaurant in Seattle called Ruby Chow's, so I went into the restaurant, ordered a scotch, and waited for him to arrive. After a little while, in walked a well-dressed young man; he was confident, almost cocky in his manner. So this is Bruce Lee, I thought to myself. After my introduction, Bruce asked me to demonstrate some of the gung fu that I had learned while in California. I performed a form from the *sam seeng kune* (three-line fist) style and Bruce remarked, "Pretty good, Allen." Then he asked me to try to throw a punch at him, and when I did, he simply grabbed hold of my arm and pulled me forward (utilizing a gung fu technique called a lop sao) so hard that I almost suffered a severe case of whiplash. That proved to be the beginning of a beautiful friendship.

I, of course, immediately reported back to James how impressed I was with Bruce's skill and ability. And James subsequently invited Bruce to Oakland (where we both lived) for a visit. I still have pictures of Bruce's visit to Oakland, when he first met James. On another visit, Bruce came to my house and we cleared the floor of all tables and chairs—not for gung fu practice, but for a demonstration from Bruce of cha-cha! Bruce definitely had rhythm and timing. After a few visits, Bruce decided to move to Oakland in 1964. He took James up on his offer to stay with him and his family. James's wife had recently passed away, so Bruce's new bride, Linda, took care of James's two young children.

In those days, James and I, along with Oakland student and friend George Lee, lifted weights to build our strength and muscle size. Before meeting Bruce, I had competed in body-building contests and trained under Ed Yarrick alongside some of the best bodybuilders and fitness buffs of the time—men like Steve Reeves, Jack Lalanne, Clancy Ross, Jack Delinger, and Roy Hilligan. When Bruce first moved to Oakland, he was very skinny. After seeing the size of our bodies—three "Chinamen's" bodies, at that!—I think Bruce's fierce competitiveness drove him to build up his own. I actually gave Bruce his first set of weights, and he tirelessly worked with them. By the results seen in Bruce's movies, I think it's safe to say that he was pretty successful with it.

Bruce and Linda's first child, Brandon, was born while they were living in Oakland. In fact, it was when Linda was pregnant with Brandon that Bruce had his famous altercation with the gung fu man who attempted to prevent Bruce from teaching his art to non-Chinese students. Although Bruce won the fight, he was displeased with his performance. (That was so typical of Bruce, to try to find ways to improve an already impressive level of expertise.) After it occurred, I asked Bruce about the incident and he commented that "it took way too long" for him to make the opponent submit. This marked the planting of the seeds of what would eventually blossom into his art of jeet kune do. From this moment on, Bruce constantly strove to improve himself both physically and mentally, and to research the mechanics and science of combat thoroughly in order to learn more effective and efficient ways to subdue an opponent. And, because he discovered that he was inordinately winded after this altercation, it was also at this point that Bruce increased the amount of hard physical training he performed.

After Bruce moved to Los Angeles a year or so later, he periodically came back to visit with us in Oakland, sometimes bringing his L.A. students Ted Wong or Dan Inosanto. And James, George, and I would also travel to Los Angeles for special events like Bruce's or Linda's birthday, thereby reuniting the "four musketeers" (Bruce, James, George, and I). I still remember the time we visited Bruce on the set of "The Green Hornet" and having to sleep next to Bruce's great Dane dog, Bo. Another memory is from the time when Bruce and Linda's daughter Shannon was born. By then, Bruce had really gotten into serious weight training and his body looked terrific. It was also during this visit that Bruce took me aside and showed me his now-famous "My Chief Definite Aim" statement, which he had written to help motivate himself.

Many people say that Bruce was way ahead of his time. But he was not so far ahead of his time as to seem eccentric or as though he did not belong to this world. I think a better description is that he was so finely attuned to himself and the world around him that he appeared to be ahead of his time. He dressed very well and related to all people and their situations. Bruce also knew exactly what he wanted in life. His focus and determination drove him to achieve the heights of success that he did in his short life.

I operated a grocery store in Oakland and Bruce often visited me there. I remember one time Bruce was at the store for eight hours, waiting to surprise Linda on her birthday. Using some butcher paper, he started sketching some beautiful gung fu drawings. At the end of the day, he just threw them away. I kick myself now for not taking them out of the garbage can! They would be priceless to me, not because of the frenzy of Bruce Lee–memorabilia collecting that has sprung up since his passing, but because of the memories they would now represent of the time I spent with my friend in the store that day.

Bruce used to tell me that he would become a common household name—"like Coca-Cola"—and so it has come to pass! In all my travels around the world, I have seen that the name *Bruce Lee* is known everywhere, from across North America to all parts of Europe and Asia. One must understand that it is quite an accomplishment to be recognized in countries, such as China, that have been repressed, and yet if I mention the name *Bruce Lee* in a city like Shanghai, a lightbulb comes on automatically within the minds of the native Shanghaiese.

In looking over some of these points, I realize just how easily my anecdotes of Bruce come to me. But that is the way it was with Bruce. Time would just stop when he was around. He was so inspirational and high-spirited. When I was down, Bruce would always lift my spirits and I would feel better. He could be a serious person one moment and a jokester the next. He never left our house without showing my wife how hard and flat his washboard stomach was. He would often leave us with knots in our stomachs thanks to his sense of humor and hilarious jokes. I hope that these few remembrances I share with you convey some impression of what Bruce was like and the excitement we had in knowing him.

I must give credit to John Little for taking on the tremendous task of documenting Bruce's body of work. John has sacrificed much in order to allow us to read and ponder what Bruce left behind. In this twelve-volume library, John shows us that Bruce truly was a Renaissance man— a thinker, a philosopher, an artist, a tremendous physical specimen, and an actualized human being. Bruce was multifaceted and multidimensional. John provides the opportunity to appreciate the many layers that comprise Bruce Lee. In many ways, with the drive and determination he has demonstrated in revealing the man who inspired him as child, John reminds me of Bruce.

I must also commend Bruce's wife, Linda. When Bruce and Linda were first married, she was just a girl in her twenties, who didn't even know how to cook. When they first arrived in Oakland, I showed her how to cook some of the Chinese dishes Bruce preferred. But she has blossomed into one of the most gracious women I have ever known. I know Bruce attributed much of his success to Linda. And it is with Linda's strength and perseverance that Jun Fan Jeet Kune Do was formed, an organization comprised of many of Bruce's direct students dedicated to the preservation and perpetuation of Bruce's art and philosophy. Bruce would be very happy about Linda's dedication.

Bruce and Linda's daughter Shannon was only a few years old when Bruce passed on. But with the formation of Jun Fan Jeet Kune Do, Shannon is learning more and more about her father through the memories of many of Bruce's students and close friends. And with Shannon's accomplishments, personally and professionally, Bruce would be moved, proudly hugging her and patting her on the back to acknowledge that she was always his little girl.

In closing, I suggest you read this book and use it to motivate yourself to pursue whatever goals you strive for in life. Here is the record of a man who had to overcome his own obstacles in life, and who achieved success because he believed in himself. Perhaps you can use this inspiration to achieve your own success. Even now, I feel Bruce's presence and he still motivates me to this day. When I'm lifting weights (which I still do two to three times per week), I "max out" my workout by doing one more rep for the "old man upstairs," and then do one more for Bruce. It never fails!

—Oakland, California, 1998

The Art of Expressing the Human Body

PREPARATION MEETS OPPORTUNITY

By Linda Lee Cadwell

Allow me to describe to you a particular day in Bruce Lee's life—a day when he failed to achieve the level of expectation he had set for himself; a day that became a turning point in his life.

The stage for the unfolding drama was the Jun Fan Gung Fu Institute on Broadway in Oakland, California, a training gym established by Bruce and James Y. Lee. Because I was about eight months pregnant with Brandon, I recall quite clearly that the events of this day took place either in late December 1964 or early in January 1965. Present to witness the historic milestone were Jimmy Lee and myself and several martial artists from San Francisco, whose names I never knew, although they appeared to be elder masters. The featured players were Bruce and a Chinese martial artist (younger than the elders), who undoubtedly had been picked to represent the interests of the San Francisco group.

Discussion of the issue that led up to this meeting could be an essay in itself, when viewed from the perspective of Chinese encounters with the West going back at least to the Boxer Rebellion. Suffice it to say that, in this instance, the traditionally trained gung fu masters did not look favorably on Bruce's teaching martial art to Westerners, or actually to anyone who was not Chinese. So strongly did they harbor this historically bound belief, that a formal challenge was issued to Bruce, insisting that he participate in a confrontation, the result of which would decide whether he could continue to teach the "foreign devils." Bruce's philosophy echoed that of Confucius: "In teaching there should be no class distinctions." Therefore, without hesitation or doubt, Bruce accepted the challenge and the date was set.

The fight that ensued is more important for the effect it had on the course of Bruce's life than for the result of the actual confrontation. However, here is a brief description of the physical action: Within moments of the initial clash, the Chinese gung fu man had proceeded to run in a circle around the room, out a door that led to a small back room, then in through another door to the main room. He completed this circle several times, with Bruce in hot pursuit. Finally, Bruce brought the man to the floor, pinning him helplessly, and shouted (in Chinese), "Do you give up?" After repeating this question two or three times, the man conceded, and the San Francisco party departed quickly.

The entire fight lasted about three minutes, leaving James and me ecstatic that the decisive conquest was so quickly concluded. Not Bruce. Like it was yesterday, I remember Bruce sitting on the back steps of the gym, head in hands, despairing over his inability to finish off the opponent with efficient technique, and the failure of his stamina when he attempted to capture the running man. For what probably was the first time in his life, Bruce was winded and weakened. Instead of triumphing in his win, he was disappointed that his physical condition and gung fu training had not lived up to his expectations. This momentous event, then, was the impetus for the evolution of jeet kune do and the birth of his new training regime.

Let me emphasize that, to my or just about anybody else's observation, in early 1965 Bruce appeared to be in superb physical condition. Growing up in Hong Kong, Bruce was not an especially genetically gifted youngster. In fact, his mother recounted to me that Bruce was a skinny little kid whose schedule of attending school in the day and (often) working on films late into the night did not foster a healthy lifestyle. However, from the age of thirteen, when he began to study Wing Chun under Master Yip Man, Bruce trained continuously and arduously on a daily basis, so that when I met him in 1963 he appeared to be in great shape. After the Oakland confrontation, this was not good enough for Bruce—he knew he had to do more and better to be prepared to realize his dreams when the opportunity arose.

For Bruce, it was not simply a matter of running extra miles, doing more reps, or increasing poundage in his weight training. He approached the resolution of the "problem" in a scientific manner: (1) Set new goals for fitness and health, (2) research the best ways to accomplish the desired changes, and (3) implement the new methods using a scientific approach, recording progress and modifying the approach when necessary. There was nothing haphazard about Bruce's training regime, neither was he particularly "lucky" in having started out with natural physical gifts. The greatest talents that Bruce brought to realizing his dreams were *intelligence* and *curiosity* (hand in hand, a powerful combination), *dedication* and *perseverance* (stick-to-itiveness even in the face of intervening obstacles), and *focus* (enjoying the journey as much as the destination).

Sometimes I am asked, How did he have the time to do so much training? The answer is simple—that was how he decided to spend his time. The choices he made in each of his 24-hour days included devoting several hours to training his body and mind in order to be the best that he could be. This is also where the wealth of his imagination came into play. In addition to regularly scheduled training times, it was "normal" for Bruce to be involved in several things at the same time: reading a book, curling a dumbbell, and stretching a leg, for example; or playing some kind of physical game with the children; or doing isometric-type exercises while driving his car. As a child he was nicknamed, "Never Sits Still"; he was the same as an adult.

The process that Bruce undertook to achieve his goal of superior fitness forms the contents of *The Art of Expressing the Human Body,* the title of which was so aptly coined by Bruce in describing his way of martial art. Bruce's martial art, jeet kune do, which is an all-encompassing approach to living life at the pinnacle of developed potential, naturally includes training the physical body to achieve its peak performance. A fitting description of Bruce's devotion to his art is to say that he attained the apex of functional beauty.

When reading this volume, it is more important that the reader recognize the *process* Bruce employed rather than dwell on the specific exercises and daily schedules. Rather than merely copy exactly what Bruce Lee did in his exercise sessions, one should take note of the numerous sources—both technical and through personal observation—Bruce employed in his research and seek to follow this scientific pattern of problem resolution. With the explosion of the fitness-health-wellness industries in the past several decades, there certainly is a great amount of information available to the inspired student. Bruce would have immersed himself in the new research and would encourage you to do likewise. Always improving, never arriving at the peak, but always undergoing the process, Bruce enjoyed the never-ending journey toward physical perfection. In other words, the means were as important as the goal, which was to be prepared when the opportunity arose to share his "art of expressing the human body." The record that survives of Bruce's *preparation for opportunity* consists, of course, of his classic films as well as the training notes he left, many of which are contained in this volume.

For myself, Bruce has served as a lifelong inspiration to be physically active and health-conscious. Throughout our lives together he was my teacher as well as husband, friend, and father of my children. I continue to rely on his example for daily motivation. Now, in the form of this book, an opportunity arises for the reader to share in Bruce's art and inspiration.

Paraphrasing Aristotle, the exclusive sign of a thorough knowledge is the power of teaching. It will become evident to the reader that Bruce had a thorough knowledge of fitness and training. Rather than clinging to the bits of factual information in this volume, it is more important to understand the method. We can all show our gratitude to Bruce for the example he left us by allowing the gift of Bruce's teaching to empower us to know "the way" to reach our maximum potential so that preparation will arise to meet opportunity.

PREFACE

All types of knowledge ultimately leads to self-knowledge. So, therefore, these people are coming in and asking me to teach them, not so much how to defend themselves or how to do somebody in. Rather, they want to learn to express themselves through some movement, be it anger, be it determination or whatever. So, in other words, they're paying me to show them, in combative form, the art of expressing the human body.
—Bruce Lee

For years there has been much speculation on how the great martial artist and philosopher, Bruce Lee, trained to develop his body. I say "speculation" for the simple fact that all accounts thus far have been largely anecdotal or secondhand, the result of asking only certain students (in some cases) decades after the fact to recall exactly how Lee trained in order to develop such a magnificent physique and how he was able to master the movement potential of his body to such an astounding degree.

The problem inherent in such a process is that (1) most of these students simply didn't pay that much attention to Lee's personal training methods, preferring at the time to focus more on his combative principles and techniques, and (2) not many of his students were actually given the opportunity to observe him train with any degree of regularity, as Lee preferred to train alone.

The problem is further exacerbated by the fact that Lee was constantly experimenting with new exercise apparatus and workout principles, so that even if students did manage to witness a workout, the most it would represent would be the cinematic equivalent of one frame out of thousands of feet of motion picture film. And, just as one frame could not be held up to represent the plot of any film, one vague memory of a workout performed over twenty years ago cannot realistically serve to frame the totality of Bruce Lee's training beliefs. As Lee himself once said, "There is no such thing as an effective segment of a totality."

Shortly after Bruce Lee passed away, when I was thirteen—an age when young males are seeking positive role models to whom they can look up—I recall being particularly impressed with Lee's physique and being equally frustrated with the lack of information regarding how he built it. Certainly he wasn't born with such a body, nor with such awesome physical ability. He must have created it—but how? If it was simply the result of his martial art training, then, by definition, anyone who practiced martial art—and Lee's martial art of jeet kune do in particular—would have a similar if not identical physique. And this clearly was not the case.

Pictures of Lee when he was in his teens and early twenties reveal that his body wasn't always so well developed—that is, it wasn't simply a genetic fluke. He had to have built it. Again, the question of "how?" arose. And again, no answer was forthcoming. The one field where I expected to find the answer—martial art—contained scores of magazine articles and even books written supposedly about Lee's "training methods," but they revealed nothing of substance about how he built his body. Any information they did reveal was vague and (I later learned) misleading.

People who knew Lee and even claimed to have trained with him revealed contradictory information, at best. One student recalled that Lee was "a five-mile-a-day runner" (he wasn't), while another indicated that Lee seldom ran more than "two miles a day." Then there is the subject of Bruce Lee's use of weights to build his body. For years the popular notion has been that Lee advocated the use of extremely high repetitions (i.e., upward of 25 reps per set) in his training, and yet in reading through his papers and personal training diaries while researching this book, I could find no evidence to support this contention (his own handwritten records reveal repetitions of a more modest nature, e.g., 6 to 12 per set).

Further, none of these so-called authorities seemed able to explain or clarify exactly what it was that Lee did to become what some have called "the fittest man on the planet." Simply saying that he "lifted weights and ran" was a woefully inadequate explanation. How could such a response (which was pretty much the word of the authorities) prove helpful to the individual interested in following Lee's conditioning methods? After all, such an answer is really no answer unless the "how" and "what" are addressed: How did Bruce Lee lift weights? What exercises did he employ? How many sets did he perform? How many reps did he perform? How many days per week did he train? And, most importantly, did Bruce Lee have any special training routines?

Finally, the answers are forthcoming. Twenty-five years after Lee's death, his widow Linda Lee Cadwell graciously opened the door to a heretofore unknown world of Bruce Lee. Private papers, essays, reading annotations, and diaries were revealed, containing information invaluable to all those wishing to know more about what Bruce Lee *really* held to be important and, by

omission, what he really *did not* hold to be important. In addition, Lee's papers, which frame *The Art of Expressing the Human Body*, finally allow us to view the *exact* methods that Bruce Lee employed to build, develop, and condition his incredible body.

Some individuals believe that unless you possess Bruce Lee's physical attributes, attempting his workouts and training methods is futile. I can only respond that this directly opposes Lee's own beliefs and, indeed, the laws of human physiology. The stimulus that resulted in a bigger, more defined, faster, and stronger muscle in Bruce Lee is the exact same stimulus that will bring about a similar response in you—such is the nature of human physiology.

Anatomically and physiologically every human being is essentially the same—something Bruce Lee was keenly aware of during his lifetime, and that is reflected in both his martial art and his personal training beliefs. And, while it's true that certain anatomical and physiological features may vary among individuals, such variations exist within a very limited and quantifiable range, without altering the fact that the basic governing principles are the same, and without altering the essence of our own distinctly human physiology.

All you have to do is be willing to take the knowledge made available to you in this book and actually make use of it on a regular basis. As Bruce Lee did. Indeed, don't expect Bruce Lee–like results unless you're willing to put in Bruce Lee–like hours to achieve them. As Lee himself said, "Knowing is not enough, we must apply. Willing is not enough, we must do."

Reviewing, collocating, and editing Lee's training and conditioning materials has been the culmination of a twenty-five-year dream for me. I've finally been able to obtain answers to questions that I'd long ago assumed would go unanswered. Fortunately for my own curiosity and for posterity, Bruce Lee was very meticulous about not only his training but his life, philosophy, and martial art.

The Art of Expressing the Human Body represents the formal presentation of Bruce Lee's authentic training beliefs. Each chapter contains material provided, not through hearsay or forgetful colleagues and self-styled "gurus," but rather by Bruce Lee himself, as revealed through his writings, reading annotations, letters, diaries, and interviews. Only in instances when there have been gaps in Lee's narrative have I found it helpful to appeal to those "who were there" or who trained alongside him and, even in these instances, I have solicited recollections only from those who spent the most time with Lee. Even then I felt compelled to check their recollections against known facts and, indeed, against the recollections of others who could either corrobo-

The Art of Expressing the Human Body

rate or refute their recollections. Where such recollections have been supported unanimously, I have given them credence. Where they have fallen short, they have been omitted.

The book's thesis is the acquisition of muscle and the strengthening of the body and all of its subsystems in order to cultivate a condition of total health and fitness. Since muscle is the engine that moves the body, it is crucial for individuals (martial artists in particular) to build as much of it as possible. Do not misunderstand this statement to imply that we all need to look like competitive bodybuilders, however, as this is not the case.

Muscles such as those that comprised the physique of Bruce Lee are the result of training for a functional purpose. That they also happen to look quite impressive is simply a side benefit. By way of contrast, muscles that are developed solely for the sake of appearance are seldom functional, aside from the training required to maintain their existence. So, unless your walk of life requires you to pick up heavy objects repeatedly (for "sets" and "reps") and then strike a pose, it is unlikely that you'll want to invest the time required to train "for show" as opposed to "go."

The information in *The Art of Expressing the Human Body* provides the potential to put you into the best shape of your life. You'll feel better, have tremendous energy, achieve a state of total fitness, and look great. And, on a personal level, I'm delighted to say that it should forever put to rest the misbegotten notion that Bruce Lee was somehow a "natural" who didn't have to work—and work hard and often—to obtain every ounce of muscle he developed. I hope to make it obvious that Lee had to research and apply a tremendously vast body of knowledge in order for him to have advanced to the level of conditioning that he did.

The thousands of hours that Bruce Lee spent training alone set an example that reveals to us the potential we all have to become better and more fully functional human beings. Moreover, it has endured beyond his passing. It has lived on through his written words, photographs, and the memory of his actions. Or, as Linda Lee Cadwell more succinctly put it in the inscription that is inlaid in a special book that resides at the foot of his headstone:

Your inspiration continues to guide us toward our personal liberation.

It is with the profoundest respect for the memory of Bruce Lee and what he accomplished in the world of physical fitness that I have undertaken the writing of this book.

—John Little
June 1998

WHAT PEOPLE ARE SAYING ABOUT THE "LEE PHYSIQUE"

I know that millions of his fans are convinced that Bruce was born with a special body; they have watched him exercise his extraordinary strength, seen his agility, studied him as he flexed his small but marvelously muscled frame. Many of them simply do not believe it when I explain that Bruce built up his outstanding physique through sheer application and willpower; through intense training.
—Linda Lee Cadwell

Bruce Lee had a very—I mean a very—defined physique. He had very little body fat. I mean, he probably had one of the lowest body fat counts of any athlete around. And I think that's why he looked so believable. There's a lot of people that do all those moves and they do have the skill, but they don't look visually as believable or as impressive as Bruce Lee did. He was one of a kind. He was an idol for so many. The great thing about someone like Bruce Lee is that he inspires so many millions and millions of kids out there who want to follow in his footsteps. They want to become martial artists, they want to go and be in movies. And so what they do is that they go out and they train every day for hours and hours. Someone like Bruce Lee provides a tremendous inspiration, which helps so many kids around the world. He had a profound and tremendous impact worldwide, and I think that he will be therefore admired for a long time.
—Arnold Schwarzenegger

Bruce took off his T-shirt, and I marveled again, as I always did every time I saw his physique; he had muscles on muscles.
—Chuck Norris, *The Secret Power Within*

He created himself. He sculpted himself; every one of his muscles was absolutely toned and tuned to whatever it was he was doing and totally functional. And the last time I saw him he was just in absolutely perfect condition; his skin was like velvet; it was smooth and he looked fantastic.
—James Coburn

He didn't weigh that much but he got the most out of what he had. He was very strong and the weight that he did have was all muscle. He was in very keen shape; very sharp.
—Kareem Abdul-Jabbar

When he took his shirt off—God!—he looked like Charles Atlas!
—Taky Kimura

The Art of Expressing the Human Body

INTRODUCTION

An anecdote has endured for nearly three decades concerning the muscles that adorned the physique of the late martial artist, actor, and philosopher Bruce Lee. It concerns a lady by the name of Ann Clouse, the wife of Robert Clouse, who was the director of Lee's last film, *Enter the Dragon,* for Warner Bros. It seems that Mrs. Clouse had ventured onto the set of the film and was absolutely mesmerized by Lee's incredible muscularity as she watched him, stripped to the waist and perspiring heavily in the hot and humid Hong Kong climate, immersed in choreographing the film's fighting sequences.

When Lee took a brief respite, she ventured over to the young superstar and asked if she could "feel his biceps." "Sure," Lee replied, responding to a request he'd received on numerous occasions. He tensed his arm and invited her to check it out. "My God!" she exclaimed, drawing her hand back instantly. "It's like feeling warm marble!"

It's fascinating that more than a quarter of a century has elapsed since Bruce Lee's passing in July 1973 from a cerebral edema, yet people are still talking about the physique of a man who stood but five feet, seven-and-a-half inches tall and weighed, on a good day, around 135 pounds. I say "fascinating" only in relation to the context of our Western culture, where our standard for a great physique has typically been some steroid-bloated linebacker who stands well over six feet and weighs in at nearly 300 pounds. Even more fascinating is the fact that almost everyone continues to derive something different from their encounters with Bruce Lee, whether in person or through the mediums of film, print, and video. Martial artists continue to revere his physical dexterity, power, and speed, as well as the genius he displayed in bringing science to bear on the world of unarmed combat; moviegoers are impressed with the man's animal magnetism and the fact that he single-handedly created a new genre of action film, opening the door for the Sylvester Stallones and Arnold Schwarzeneggers who followed in his footsteps. Philosophers are impressed with Lee's ability to have bridged the philosophical chasm that separated East and

West, and to have effectively synthesized what many had considered to be two irreconcilable metaphysical viewpoints.

And then there is another pocket of humanity—the bodybuilders and physical fitness afficionados—that sees something else in Lee. It's equally fascinating—and ironic—that, while Bruce Lee never considered himself a bodybuilder in the classic sense of the term, his physique continues to be revered by bodybuilders and athletes on numerous continents as one of the most inspirational of all time. Bodybuilders young and old know from a quick glance at his physique exactly how much labor went into its creation, and they are very impressed. Bodybuilding luminaries like Lou "The Incredible Hulk" Ferrigno, Rachel McLish, Flex Wheeler, Shawn Ray, Lenda Murray, Dorian Yates, and Lee Haney—that is to say, the best in the business—all pay homage to the impact Bruce Lee's physique had on their bodybuilding careers. Even Schwarzenegger was suitably impressed with the quality of Lee's muscularity to tell me recently: "Bruce Lee had a very—I mean a very—defined physique. He had very little body fat. I mean, he probably had one of the lowest body fat counts of any athlete around. And I think that's why he looked so believable [in his films]. There's a lot of people that do all those [martial art] moves,

and they do have the skill, but they don't look visually as believable or as impressive as Bruce Lee did. He was one of a kind." High praise indeed!

Some may find this hard to believe. After all, by North American standards, Lee was not a physically imposing man. So what would behemoths like Schwarzenegger and Ferrigno, for example, see in Lee's physique that would possibly inspire them? The answer, in a word, is *quality*. We have seldom seen—shy of a jungle cat—such a combination of excellent lines, pleasing shape, and chiseled definition on a male physique. It was both graceful and awe-inspiring. He was hypnotic in movement, and poised, even elegant, in repose. When relaxed, many bodybuilders and football players look like the farthest thing from athletes. And when they move, the bulk they've built up moves with them—but

The Art of Expressing the Human Body

nothing happens with it; it's simply a moving (and largely uncoordinated) bulk, like an enervated piece of Jell-O. Lee's physique, by way of contrast, was always tight, compact, tasteful, refined, and defined—both at rest and in motion.

One of the reasons for the difference in musculature between the typical bodybuilder and Bruce Lee was that Lee's muscles were not built simply for the purpose of show, as were many bodybuilders'. To quote his first student in the United States, Seattle's Jesse Glover, Lee was "above all else concerned with function." The impressive physique that Lee developed was a by-product, or effect, of this primary concern. Leaping eight feet in the air to kick out a light bulb (as he did in the movies *Marlowe* and *The Way of the Dragon*) or landing a punch that was initiated from over three feet away in five-hundredths of a second, were attributes of power and speed respectively, that Bruce Lee had worked long and hard in the diligent training of his body to obtain. The fact that he created an extraordinary suit of muscles as well was nice, but was never the primary objective behind his training.

Perhaps never before—or since—has such a confluence of physical attributes been cultivated to such a degree in one human being. Lee developed lightning-fast reflexes, supreme flexibility, awesome power, and feline grace and muscularity in one complete—and very lethal—package. Furthermore, his physique was balanced and symmetrical, and while not everyone admires the massive musculature of a Mr. Universe contender, most everyone I've spoken to—from Mr. Universe contenders to the average man or woman on the street—seems to admire the total package that Bruce Lee's physique represents.

The fact that he influenced so many champion bodybuilders is no small accomplishment when you consider that Lee never entered a physique contest in his life. He was never interested in becoming massively muscled. As Ted Wong, one of Lee's closest friends and most dedicated students, recalled, "Bruce trained primarily for strength and speed." Those who were fortunate enough to meet him, from Hollywood producers to his fellow martial artists, say

that Lee's muscles carried considerable impact. This is not to suggest that Lee was not interested in building an impressive physique. Taky Kimura, perhaps Lee's closest friend (and the best man at Lee's 1964 wedding), observed that his friend was never loath to remove his shirt and display the results of his labors in the gym—often just to witness the reactions of those around him. "He had the most incredible set of lats

[upper back muscles] I'd ever seen," Kimura recalls, "and his big joke was to pretend that his thumb was an air hose, which he'd then put in his mouth and pretend to inflate his lats with. He looked like a damn cobra when he did that!"

Functional Fitness and Extraordinary Strength

Dan Inosanto, another close friend of Lee's and the man he chose to assist him in teaching his martial art curriculum to students at Lee's Los Angeles school from 1967 to 1970, added that Lee was only interested in strength that could be readily converted to power. "I remember once Bruce and I were walking along the beach in Santa Monica, out by where The Dungeon [a gym originally owned by famed Muscle Beach denizen Vic Tanny] used to be, when all of a sudden, this big, huge bodybuilder came out of The Dungeon," Inosanto related. "I said to Bruce, 'Man, look at the arms on that guy!' I'll never forget Bruce's reaction. He said, 'Yeah, he's big—but is he powerful? Can he use that extra muscle efficiently?'" Power, according to Lee, was demonstrated by an individual's ability to use the strength developed in the gym quickly and efficiently for real-world purposes.

Certainly Lee's feats of power are the stuff of legend, from performing one-finger or thumbs-only push-ups, to supporting a 75-pound barbell at arm's length in front of him with elbows locked for several seconds, to sending individuals who outweighed him by as much as 100 pounds flying 15 feet through the air with one of his famous one-inch punches. The power he possessed at a bodyweight of between 127 and 135 pounds was extraordinary; Lee could send 300-pound punching bags slapping against the ceiling with a simple side kick.

Strength and its acquisition were Lee's primary concerns in his weight training. Eventually his weight work evolved to the ultimate limits of intuitive knowledge—what some in the body-

building business refer to as "instinctive" training. According to those who worked out with him from time to time, such as martial artist/actor Chuck Norris, Bruce Lee may have been, on a pound-for-pound basis, one of the strongest men in the world.

Lee's Road to Bodybuilding

Lee's studious research into human physiology and kinesiology allowed him to quickly discern a useful exercise from an unproductive one, which meant that he never wasted time in his workouts and that they were geared to produce specific results. Lee believed that the student of exercise science should aim at nothing less than physical perfection, including great strength, quickness, and skill, exuberant health, and the beauty of muscular form that distinguishes a physically perfect human being. Lee believed each day brought with it the opportunity to

The Art of Expressing the Human Body

improve ourselves physically and mentally; we could choose either to seize the moment to take a step closer to maximizing our potential and progress, or to decline the opportunity and thereby stagnate or regress.

Lee realized early on that in order for us to fulfill our physical potential, we had to approach our exercise endeavors progressively and fight against the desire to pack it all in and retire to the sofa and the television, where we could escape from our "duty" of self-actualization by partaking in its opposite—that is, shutting off our minds and allowing our muscles to atrophy. Lee wanted to learn as much about his mind and body as possible. He wanted to know what he was truly capable of, rather than settling for what he already knew he could accomplish. To this end, he viewed each training session as a learning experience, an opportunity for improvement to take himself to a new level. As a result, he had a keen eye for spotting people who were selling themselves short by either slacking off in their training or by underestimating what their true capabilities were.

Stirling Silliphant (a student of Lee's) relates an interesting story that perfectly embodies Lee's attitude toward progressive resistance in cardiovascular training, as well as his refusal to let a person—in this case Silliphant—underestimate his own physical potential:

Bruce had me up to three miles a day, really at a good pace. We'd run the three miles in twenty-one or twenty-two minutes. Just under eight minutes a mile [Note: when running on his own in 1968, Lee would get his time down to six-and-a-half minutes per mile]. So this morning he said to me "We're going to go five." I said, "Bruce, I can't go five. I'm a helluva lot older than you are, and I can't do five." He said, "When we get to three, we'll shift gears and it's only two more and you'll do it." I said "Okay, hell, I'll go for it." So we get to three, we go into the fourth mile and I'm okay for three or four minutes, and then I really begin to give out. I'm tired, my heart's pounding, I can't go any more and so I say to him, "Bruce if I run any more,"—and we're still running—"if I run any more I'm liable to have a heart attack and die." He said, "Then die." It made me so mad that I went the full five miles. Afterward I went to the shower and then I wanted to talk to him about it. I said, you know, "'Why did you say that?" He said, "Because you might as well be dead. Seriously, if you always put limits on what you can do, physical or anything else, it'll spread over into the rest of your life. It'll spread into your work, into your morality, into your entire being. There are no limits. There are plateaus, but you must not stay there, you must go beyond them. If it kills you, it kills you. A man must constantly exceed his level."

This attitude of "there are no limits" is, of course, the central thesis of Lee's art and philosophy of jeet kune do. He even placed Chinese characters around the yin-yang symbol in his jeet kune do logo that read "Using no way as way/Having no limitation as limitation." (In Cantonese, *Yee Mo Faat Wai Yao Faat/Yee Mo Haan Wai Yao Haan*). Lee once wrote a letter to American tae kwon do pioneer Jhoon Rhee, in which Lee cautioned that "Low aim is the worst crime a man has," further underscoring his view of self-imposed limitations—in exercise and in all areas of life.

Bruce Lee was persistent in his quest to express the full potential of his body. Through his research he learned the physiological fact that a stronger muscle is a bigger muscle, and that discovery led him to explore the superior health-building benefits of bodybuilding. However, it would take a violent encounter to bring home the merits of a regular and dedicated approach to "pumping iron."

The Turning Point

According to Lee's widow Linda Lee Cadwell, when the couple was living in Oakland, California, one day her husband received an ornate scroll that issued an ultimatum in bold Chinese characters: Either he stop teaching gung fu (the Cantonese pronunciation of *kung fu*) to non-Chinese students, or else agree to fight—at a designated place and time—with their top man. In Oakland's Chinatown of the early 1960s, teaching Chinese "secrets" to non-Chinese individuals was perceived as the highest form of treason among members of the martial art community.

Though Lee had many virtues, he did not suffer fools patiently. Lee decided to accept the challenge rather than bow to the dictates of racists. By his words and demeanor, Lee effectively threw the gauntlet back at the feet of his would-be challenger. Later that week, at the appointed time, a group of Chinese martial artists led by a man who was their best fighter and designated leader arrived at Lee's Oakland school. Linda, who was eight months pregnant with Brandon, the couple's first child, and Lee's student James Yimm Lee were witnesses to what happened next.

The fight began, and in a matter of seconds, Lee had the previously bold and self-righteous kung fu "expert" running for the nearest exit. After considerable leg work, Lee had thrown the man to the floor and extracted a submission from him. He then tossed the entire group off the premises. To his dismay, however, Lee discovered that he'd expended a tremendous amount of energy in the altercation. "He was surprised and disappointed at the physical condition he was in," Linda recalled later. "Although it took all of three minutes, he thought that the fight had lasted way too long and that it was his own lack of proper conditioning that made it such a lengthy set-to. He felt inordinately winded afterward."

The incident caused Lee to investigate alternative avenues of physical conditioning, and he concluded that his martial art training—by itself—was not sufficiently taxing to further strengthen his body on a progressive basis. Lee concluded that he needed to develop considerably more strength in both his muscular and cardiovascular systems if he was ever going to reach the fullest expression of his physical potential.

The Art of Expressing the Human Body

Since muscle magazines were the only existing source of health and strength-training information at the time, Lee immediately subscribed to all the bodybuilding publications he could find. He ordered courses out of the magazines and tested their claims and training theories in the laboratory that was his body, in addition to frequenting secondhand book stores to purchase books on bodybuilding and strength training, including ones written prior to the turn of the century (such as *Strength and How to Obtain It* by Eugen Sandow—originally published in 1897!).

Lee's hunger for knowledge was so great that he purchased anything he could get his hands on, from hot-off-the-press training courses, to back-listed classics in the field of exercise physiology. Once applied, this knowledge resulted in increased strength, speed, power, and endurance.

The results of Lee's comprehensive research are revealed in the chapters that follow. They address, specifically, how Lee trained to develop each and every muscle group of his body, the type of training system he found to be most effective, the training principles he incorporated, and the programs he gave to his students. Two appendixes provide information on Lee's vital statistics and his exercise machine. The material in the book is created from Lee's own writings—not from the misguided interpretations of accumulated myth that surround his legacy. At long last, readers can learn about the process that resulted in a level of muscularity that would set physique standards and be talked about for decades.

1. THE PURSUIT OF STRENGTH

Training for strength and flexibility is a must. You must use it to support your techniques. Techniques alone are no good if you don't support them with strength and flexibility.
—Bruce Lee

There is a tremendous soliloquy made by veteran Chinese character actor, Shek Kien (actually voiced by veteran Chinese character actor Keye Luke), near the end of Bruce Lee's last film, *Enter the Dragon*. It occurs when Kien's character, the evil Han, is taking John Saxon's character, Roper, on a small tour of his "museum" of feudal weaponry. As they walk, Han says:

> It is difficult to associate these horrors with the proud civilizations that created them. Sparta, Rome, the knights of Europe, the Samurai. . . all shared the lone ideal: the honor of strength, because it is strength that makes all other values possible. Nothing survives without it. Who knows what delicate wonders have died out of the world for want of the strength to survive?

Although excised from the final print, in Bruce Lee's copy of the script, Han's peripatetic continues:

> Civilization's highest ideas—justice—could not exist without strong men to enforce it. Indeed, what is civilization but simply the honor of strong men? Today, the young are taught nothing of honor. The sense of life as epic, of life as big, of life as something for which one learns to fight— this is foolish to them. To them, grandeur is irrelevant. The young no longer dream.

The Art of Expressing the Human Body

For a villain, Han makes perfect sense. That is, he makes a wonderful apology for why our species has so ardently pursued the acquisition of strength throughout the centuries.

The pursuit of strength is by no means something antiquated; it is still revered today, albeit in its many different forms: strength of character, strength of will, strength of resolve, strength in the face of adversity, strength of patience, strength of belief, and of course, physical strength. In all of these realms, there is much to learn from Bruce Lee. This book reveals the methods Lee employed to develop such legendary physical strength.

While most of his contemporaries considered training to be simply the performance of their martial art techniques, Bruce Lee's regimen involved all the components of total fitness. Apart from his daily martial art training, Lee engaged in supplemental training to improve his speed, endurance, strength, flexibility, coordination, rhythm, sensitivity, and timing. In fact, in a book published by one of his students, Dan Inosanto, the author lists no less than forty-one different types of training made use of by practitioners of Lee's art of jeet kune do.

Lee learned early on that the role strength played in the overall scheme of things was of vital importance, not only for its own sake (in building stronger muscles, tendons, and ligaments), but also because an increase in muscular strength brings with it greater mastery of striking techniques, increased speed and endurance, better-toned muscles, and improved body function. However, Lee did not regard weight training as the "open sesame" to athletic success. He recognized it for exactly what it was: an important facet of total fitness that had to be integrated into one's workout schedule along with other exercises to improve one's technique, speed, agility, and so on.

Increased Speed Through Strength Training

Lee was particularly impressed with the fact that strength training, which typically involved weight training, could increase one's speed and endurance capacities. The popular belief at the time was that weight training contributed to nothing but the development of big, "bulky" muscles. But in his readings on physiology, Lee happened upon a review of a book entitled *The Application of Measurement to Health and Physical Education* by H. H. Clarke, who was then the director of graduate studies at Springfield College. The review, which synopsized the book, stated that "Speed also depends upon strength . . . the stronger the individual, the faster he can run . . . moreover, endurance is based on strength."

These statements were not merely opinions but conclusions based on scientific experiments, such as those of Karpovich (the head of the department of physiology at Springfield College in 1951) and Pestrecov on training curves, experiments which further concluded that "strength is definitely shown to be a prerequisite for the development of endurance." Such statements led Lee to study the realm of strength with keen interest. He pored over many scientific papers and books and came away convinced that strength was a prerequisite to *all* physical activity and that it played a vital role in many of his martial art movements.

On the Value of Strength Training

Bruce Lee's belief that a martial artist must engage in training methods apart from the techniques and movements of the art he or she has been trained in was based on purely scientific grounds. For example, one study that caught Lee's eye regarding the subject of supplemental training involved the training methods of competitive swimmers. During the early 1950s American swimming coaches, particularly those at Yale University, found that the muscles used for swimming did not increase their strength enough during actual swimming training because the resistance applied to the muscles from the water was not great enough. To correct this, weight training was introduced. The coaches wisely ignored the objection that their swimmers would become muscle-bound by engaging in weight training, and quickly learned that the weight-training exercises, far from producing negative effects on their swimmers, produced huge increases in strength in their upper arms, shoulders, and back, allowing the swimmers to make great improvements in their performance. Lee immediately saw a parallel between the swimmers in the water and the "dryland" martial art training in which he was engaged where he typically performed kicks and punches in the air with no resistance. Lee noted that such movements were a form of calisthenics, which have value but are limited in their results because they lack any progressive resistance for the muscles to overcome and thus become stronger. Lee's conclusion was the same as that of the Yale swimming coaches: It was time to incorporate weight training into his workouts.

The Advantage of Resistance Exercise

Lee liked the fact that the training motions used with barbells and dumbbells were natural body motions that could be adapted to strengthen any positioning or movement of the limbs. The exercises to be performed with barbells were basically simple movements that required little if any skill or learning. Lee further found that barbell and dumbbell exercises were perfectly adaptable to all muscle groups, resulting in improvement in mechanical efficiency. Further, resistance exercises could be measured and increased by adding weight, sets, or repetitions, according to one's own innate adaptability to exercise. Another appeal was the fact that, at its most basic level, Lee's strength-training workouts required but a mere fifteen to thirty minutes to

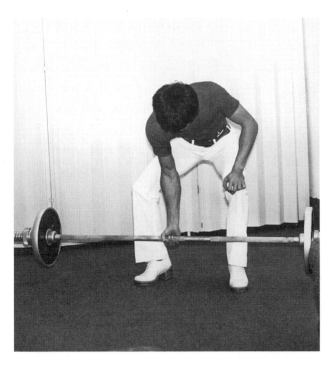 

complete, and were performed only three times a week (or, in the case of his isometrics program, a mere ninety-six seconds a day). Despite their brevity, these workouts produced outstanding results in Lee's speed, power, muscle development, and overall physical fitness far beyond anything that he was able to produce with any other form of training in a comparable length of time. In addition, Lee found that strength training was also an activity he could continue with great benefit throughout the remainder of his life.

Velocity—The Forgotten Factor in Strength Development

As well as progressing in weight and repetitions, Lee believed that velocity could also be quantifiable as a calculated progression. An increase in speed—speed of movement and speed of recovery—he reasoned, should be a planned part of the training scheme of any serious martial artist. To this end, Lee found it beneficial to occasionally ignore adding repetitions or weight, and concentrate instead on working to reduce the overall performance time of his workout. Lee would carefully time his workouts, striving to execute each repetition as quickly as possible. The recovery period between muscle groups was also timed and, if increased stamina was one of his goals during a particular workout, an effort would be made to reduce the length of his recovery periods between sets.

In attempting speed training for yourself, you'll find that you will not be able to handle quite so much weight as you would if the exercises were performed in the normal way, but the weight should be heavy enough to make the last few repetitions of the last set a distinct effort. Like Lee, you should set yourself a target time and not alter your exercise poundage or repetitions until this target is reached.

Express Your Own Unique Potential

It is important to recognize that, in terms of the results and benefits obtained from strength training, the only person with whom you can make any meaningful comparison is yourself. Owing to genetic variations among individuals (such as bone length, muscle-fiber density, neuromuscular efficiency, etc.), the results that one individual may display might well be physiologically impossible for another. However, as long as you are progressing in either sets, reps, or work performed in a given unit of time, then you know that your muscles are getting stronger as a result of your strength-training workouts.

It is always important to keep the various physical factors in their true perspective in order to fully appreciate the benefits derived from a program of strength training. Hefty golfers have been known to wonder why less powerful players can sometimes hit the ball farther; this is certainly difficult to explain, since timing and coordination are also involved as variables. However, it does provide a good example of an event where strength and power, though important, are actually of less value than other physical and mental qualities. Note that I say "less value." Some people maintain that power is of no value in such sports, but this is not altogether accurate. If the less powerful players added strength, speed, and muscular endurance, while still retaining the same degree of skill, their play would improve purely because of the increased physical efficiency. The old adage of "a stronger athlete is a better athlete" comes to mind here. In short, the development of muscle and strength cannot be carried far without the intelligent use of the strength acquired. Bruce Lee held that strength without skill is incomplete, as skill is an essential part of one's physical development.

The Role of Overload in Strength Training

Excluding physical defects and some pathological conditions, your present physical condition is not static or fixed. Your physical condition merely reflects the specific adaptation of your body to your everyday life. In other words, you are trained for whatever activity you have been practicing, and no more. Changes in the state of your physical condition are possible, however. Muscles can be strengthened through strength training. Your heart can become more efficient through endurance training, and usually the range of motion of joints can be improved by incorporating a sound flexibility program. However, if you wish to improve in any or all of these areas, then you must follow the overload principle by altering your daily work habits or by adding appropriate exercises. Whichever procedure is decided on, the overload should be gradual to permit adaptation to take place without undue strain on the body.

Excessive muscle soreness and fatigue due to overwork is unnecessary. However, it is normal to have some muscle soreness and fatigue at the start of training. In fact, muscle soreness may reflect the effectiveness of the training. As an example, consider the man who lifts a maximum of 60 pounds in his daily work. If he wishes to increase the strength of the muscles used in that movement without undue soreness, he should start training by lifting 70 or 75 pounds, not 100 or 120 pounds, even though his rate of improvement would be faster 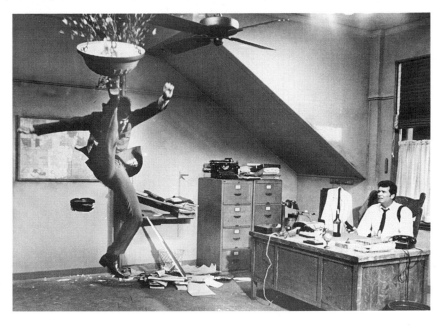 with the heavier load. If an unconditioned individual who can do a maximum of ten push-ups with extreme effort wishes to train to do more, he or she should start below his or her maximal level until some conditioning for that activity is attained. After this, the overload principle may be applied without undue stress.

Regarding the nature of overload, it should be remembered that the strength of a muscle is determined by the use made of it in carrying on your daily activities. For example, if no supplementary exercises are taken and the maximum load placed on a muscle during your daily activities does not exceed 60 pounds, then this is the strength of that muscle. The muscle strength has adapted specifically to your needs. If greater strength is desired, it will be necessary to make that muscle contract against a greater load until it has adapted to the overload. The essentials of training, therefore, are overload and adaptation.

What Is Strength Training?

What exactly is strength training? Does it mean struggling against tremendously heavy weights and seeing how much weight you can hoist overhead in a single-attempt lift? Not necessarily. Weight training is simply one aspect of strength training, which is broadly divided into four main activities:

1. Weight Lifting

Weight lifting is a sport in its own right, in which competitors attempt to lift the maximum possible weight in certain specifically defined techniques.

2. Bodybuilding

In bodybuilding, lighter weights are used in a variety of exercises and in varying sets of repetitions in order to develop the physique. The main objectives are usually to increase muscle size, remedy physical defects, or proportionately and harmoniously develop the body as a whole.

3. Weight Training

Weight training is training with light weights, again in a variety of exercises and in varying sets of repetitions, but with more specific objectives in view, such as improving your physical condition or health or for the purpose of improving your performance in activities such as martial art.

4. Isometrics

Isometrics is a mode of training without any weight. What is required is a maximal contraction of the muscles against a fixed or immovable resistance, such as a bar that has been placed through the appropriate holes in a power rack.

Your Training Record

No matter what forms of strength training you opt to incorporate into your total fitness routine, if increased strength is your goal, it is imperative to be systematic about it. Keep a note of your schedules and progressions, and ensure that you continually increase the amount of work you do. Just as you should keep a training and performance book for your martial art and daily thoughts and discoveries, so too should you record your progress with strength training. You will find it most encouraging (particularly with weight training and bodybuilding) to note the steady increase in the weights you are handling. A convenient way to do so is on a record card, which is used in many weight-lifting clubs, such as the one that Bruce Lee used while in Hong Kong (see Chapter 3). You will find it very useful for quick reference and guidance on the exact amount of work to be done during each session. Bruce Lee himself utilized both day-timer diaries and notepads to keep track of his workouts and to note his progress.

Application of Research Findings to Strength Training

During his research into strength training, Lee learned that training with submaximal loads (as little as two-thirds of maximum strength) twice weekly, and maximal loads once weekly, would result in as much strength improvement as training maximally three times per week.

Differences Between Weight Training and Isometrics

Although Bruce Lee incorporated both weight training and isometrics into his total fitness routine, by no means did he consider these two forms of strength training as being equal in principle, value, and result. Granted, both methods of exercises do build strength. But there are differences in both their purpose and results. While isometrics firms and strengthens muscles rapidly, it makes little contribution to muscular endurance. Therefore, isometrics can never constitute a complete exercise program, but must be combined with aerobics and flexibility training. Weight training, on the other hand, leads to increased muscle size, which may or may not be a desirable objective for the trainee. Since the movement involved typically takes the muscles through a full range of motion again and again (by repetitions), this can lead to enhanced flexibility and also contribute to building muscle tone and endurance in addition to strength.

Isometrics performed in the conventional manner—that is, without resistance—cannot be measured without the use of special equipment. Weight training can be measured in terms of both the exact amount of weight you lift during any given exercise and the number of repetitions you perform. More recently, with the creation of Power Factor Training, weight training can be measured in terms of the amount of work you perform over a given unit of time.

Different combinations of weights and repetitions yield different types of benefits. We can see this clearly by considering three possible weight-training programs: (1) A heavy weight used with relatively few repetitions would roughly approximate the results of isometrics: Since

there is little movement but much contraction, the accent is clearly on strength building, rather than endurance. (2) Using a moderate weight with a moderate number of repetitions puts an equal emphasis on strength and endurance. (3) A very light weight used with many repetitions would almost approach calisthenics: It will produce greatly increased endurance, but will cause little increase in strength. In other words, weight training can be adjusted from the extreme of strength building (like isometrics) to the extreme of building tone and endurance (like calisthenics). The formula is simple: More weight with less repetitions equals strength; less weight with more repetitions equals tone and endurance.

ISOMETRICS	WEIGHT TRAINING
The quickest builder of raw strength	Increases strength
Exercises can be done every day, seven days a week	Exercises should only be done every other day
Little or no equipment needed; equipment is relatively inexpensive	Complete training program requires considerable equipment or access to a gym
Requires little time, with only short rests between exercises	Can be quite time-consuming, requiring moderate rests between exercises
Can be performed in privacy of room or office, without having to change from street clothes	Must exercise where weights are located; changing into old clothes necessary since workout produces perspiration
Limited increase in muscle size	Greater increase in muscle size
Exercises a muscle in one position only	Exercises a muscle through complete range of movement
Cannot constitute a complete workout; must be combined with calisthenics	Can constitute a complete workout (if you use light weights with many repetitions)
Increase in your strength must be measured by periodically lifting weights or using special testing equipment	Can measure developed strength on a pound-by-pound basis

2. MOTIONLESS EXERCISE: THE BASIC 8 OF ISOMETRICS

As mentioned earlier, in the course of learning all he could about muscle and strength development, Bruce Lee read all the various bodybuilding magazines found on newsstands throughout the mid-1960s through the early 1970s. He studied them thoroughly, cutting through the hype and sales pitches to find subject matter that interested him or held particular relevance to his training objectives, such as gaining muscle mass, strengthening his forearms, or creating definition. When he came across such an article, he would cut the article out and save it in an appropriate folder. And in his quest for strength, the first training theory that caught his attention was the then revolutionary method of isometric or static contractions.

Bruce Lee was a firm believer in isometrics training and utilized it extensively throughout the mid- to late 1960s. Isometrics had received a great deal of press, particularly in the weight-training and bodybuilding publications coming out of York, Pennsylvania, which reported monthly on the spectacular results of competitive weight lifters who had incorporated this training technique into their programs.

What the magazines failed to mention, however, was that most of these same athletes were incorporating pills known as anabolic steroids into their programs as well. Once this was discovered, the general response was to dismiss isometrics as a fad that only worked when performed in conjunction with synthetic testosterone. This may have been a case of throwing the baby out with the bathwater, however, as a very real case for the benefit of isometrics in building strength can be made.

The most convincing defense of isometrics, and the one that won Bruce Lee over to incorporating it into his total fitness program, came from Bob Hoffman, a man who admittedly made money from propagating the system but who was also no stranger to the realm of strength training, having coached championship weight lifters from 1932 through 1954. He was named coach of the United States Olympic weight-lifting teams of 1948 and 1952, both of which won the unofficial team scoring.

Hoffman's position was, simply, that strength is the most important quality in every form of athletic or physical endeavor. Endurance (the ability to continue this strength over a long period), coordination, control, balance, and judgment of space and distance, which come from strength-building exercises, are roads to championship performance in every sport. More strength, he reasoned, and the ability to properly control that strength through the practice of one's particular sport, made it possible for the person with more strength to outdo another person.

To this end, Hoffman designed a series of eight basic exercises that were to be performed isometrically in a special device called a power rack. Many people wonder how a single exercise without movement could produce results comparable or even superior to an exercise with movement. Let's consider movements such as the weight-lifting movements of the curl and press that Bruce Lee incorporated into his barbell workouts. Only one or two seconds are required to take a curl from thigh level to chin height. The hardest part of the curl is not the start or the finish, but instead the middle of the curl, where leverage causes the greatest effort. Yet the muscles are in this position for only a fraction of a second. With isometric contraction, the muscles would be exerting full force in this position for twelve seconds, so, theoretically, one effort here could build as much strength as more than a dozen repetitions performed in the conventional fashion.

Hoffman advised that the trainee must be sure to continually and conscientiously exert all possible pressure upon the immovable bar. Since no actual movement is involved, no results are observable while doing an exercise, and easing off must be guarded against. Bruce Lee believed that 100 percent effort at all times was necessary, so he concentrated fully on generating such effort while performing each movement.

There are three basic positions in the conventional performance of isometric exercise: one about three inches above the starting position, one about three inches below the finishing position, and an intermediate position. In a full-range barbell movement, the weight resistance is only in the most difficult position for a fraction of a second, but in the practice of isometric contraction, the resistance is applied with maximum force for nine to twelve seconds in the most difficult position. That is the chief reason for the rapid gains in strength that result from the practice of isometrics, and one of the reasons Bruce Lee thought so highly of it.

In addition to using his power rack, Lee also liked working with a portable isometric training device made for him by one of his students, George Lee (no relation). This piece of apparatus allowed him to push, pull, press, and curl against an immovable object. The photograph on this page shows Lee adjusting the bar attached to a chain that, in turn, was attached to a block of wood upon which he stood, thus rendering it immovable.

Some Pointers on Performing Isometric Exercises

1. Do not do too much! One repetition in 8 different movements is plenty.
2. Conscientiously strive to put forth 100% effort in each exercise for 6 to 12 seconds.
3. You should be able to complete your isometric exercise routine in 15 to 20 minutes. Be sure not to rest too long between movements.

The Art of Expressing the Human Body

4. Always keep an accurate record of your workouts and chart your progress.

The Isometric Basic 8 Exercises

1. Press Lockout

Set the bar in the power rack at a height of about 3 inches below lockout position, arms fully extended overhead. Grasp the bar, keeping hands about shoulder-width apart, look straight ahead, tighten leg, hip, and back muscles, and push on the bar as hard as possible from 6 to 12 seconds.

2. Press Start

Set the pins about chin height. Use the same grip as in Exercise 1. Again, tighten legs, hips, and back muscles, look straight ahead, and push on the bar as hard as possible for 6 to 12 seconds.

3. Rise on Toes

Set the bar at a height where it will rest just a little above your neck and shoulders when you are standing in front of it with your back straight. Keep the knees and hips locked tight, the back straight, and the head slightly turned back. Place your hands on the bar at a comfortable position. Rise up on your toes and push on the bar as hard as possible for 6 to 12 seconds.

4. Pull

Set the bar at a height where it will be 6 or 7 inches below your waist. Be sure to use the same grip as in Exercises 1 and 2. Rise up on your toes slightly, look up slightly, bend your arms, and pull as hard as you can for 6 to 12 seconds.

5. Parallel Squat

Set the bar in the power rack at a height where it will rest on the back of your neck and shoulders when you are in a squat position with thighs parallel to the floor. Place your hands on the bar in a comfortable position and rise, pushing with the legs as hard as possible for 6 to 12 seconds.

6. Shoulder Shrug

Set the bar in the power rack at a height where it will be in your hands when your arms are fully extended downward. Grip the bar, keeping your hands about shoulder-width apart. Shrug your shoulders upward as hard as possible for 6 to 12 seconds. Keep your arms and legs fully extended at all times.

7. Dead-Weight Lift

Set the bar in the rack at a height where it will be about 2 inches below your knees when you are holding it. Keeping hands about shoulder-width apart, your head up, hips down, and back flat, push hard on the legs and pull up as hard as you can for 6 to 12 seconds.

8. Quarter Squat

Set the bar in the rack about 4 inches below the height it would be if you were standing erect, with the bar across the back of the neck and shoulders. Grip the bar with the hands in a comfortable position, and push up against it by contracting the muscles of your thighs as hard as possible for 6 to 12 seconds. Keep your head up, your back flat, and your heels on the ground.

The Frog Kick

Bruce Lee liked to perform an exercise called the frog kick after completing a session of isometric exercises. This movement served to stretch out his lower back, work his abdominals and hip flexors, and proved to be an effective cool-down exercise. Immediately after performing the quarter squat, Lee would set the bar in the highest position in the rack and then hang by his hands while drawing his knees up to his chest for a final set of 10 to 20 repetitions.

The isometric routine listed above is the same one that Bruce Lee incorporated into his own schedule. Lee would perform each exercise once a day. He believed that doing more would slow or stop his improvement. It may take you anywhere from one to two weeks to get the feel of this routine, so don't give up after a few days if you don't feel it is helping you. You should notice definite, measurable improvement within one to two months.

Lee also modified the isometric exercises he performed in order to enhance his chi sao (sticking hands) proficiency. He would place the bar through its supports at roughly the height of the lower portion of his chest. From here, Lee would step back two paces and press his forearms up against the bar as hard as he could, sustaining this maximal contraction for up to twelve seconds. This allowed him to "flow his energy" through his forearms  and helped him develop tremendous forearm power and sensitivity.

Again, Lee used all types of strength-building exercises and apparatus, including cables, compression machines, and spring-loaded devices. He firmly believed that there was not just one way to increase one's strength. Like all things pertaining to learning and self-knowledge, strength was a process of personal growth that only time and hard work could cultivate.

3. ENTER THE BARBELLS: THE BEGINNER'S BODYBUILDING ROUTINE

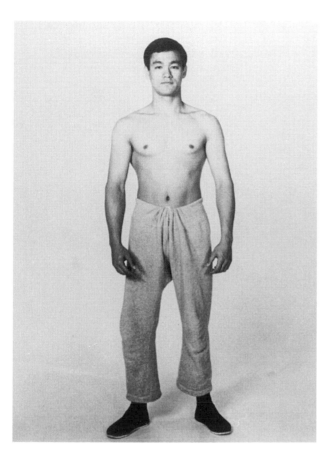 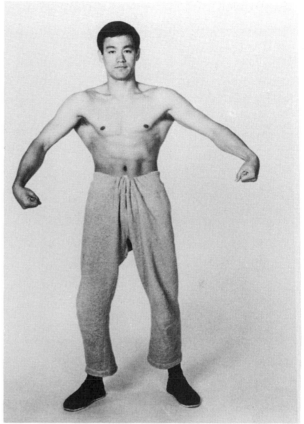

Shortly after his encounter with the Chinese martial artists in Oakland (see page 24), Bruce Lee became motivated to learn of other ways to increase his strength—not only strength of stamina or endurance, but overall muscular strength. To this end, he sought out the opinion of two trusted individuals who were not only his students, but more importantly, his friends: James Yimm Lee and Allen Joe.

Both James and Allen were experienced bodybuilders who had developed imposing physiques as a result of their commitment to "pumping iron." Allen Joe, in fact, had won numerous bodybuilding titles and had trained alongside the legendary bodybuilder Steve Reeves under the watchful eye of the renowned gym owner Ed Yarrick.

According to Allen Joe, "James Lee and I introduced Bruce to basic weight-training techniques. We used to train with basic exercises like squats, pullovers, and curls for about three sets each. Nothing really spectacular but we were just getting him started. We taught him the basic program." While on this basic program, Bruce Lee's body quickly began to get stronger and his upper torso muscles began to stretch the seams of his T-shirts. Once he experienced the results of his new training program, pumping iron became a part of Lee's life. The only record of his

weight-training routine during this period is a card he filled out at the Hak Keung Gymnasium while on a visit to Hong Kong in 1965.

In addition to consulting with his friends, Lee read voraciously and was busy testing the theories he read about and formulating his own bodybuilding routine. Lee came to realize certain fundamental truths about building up his body, which he jotted down:

> This [weight training] causes great muscle stimulation, forcing muscles to grow in both size and strength. This is why weight training is often referred to as "bodybuilding" exercise.

> Since weight training involves repetitions, a great deal of energy must be exerted. Therefore, weight training should be practiced only every other day.

However, Lee was careful to exercise caution in his weight training. He did not simply want to develop bigger muscles, which would not serve his functional purpose as a martial artist. So he also made notations to remind himself of the other physical qualities he needed to balance his bodybuilding training, such as:

> The athlete who is building muscles through weight training should be very sure to work adequately on speed and flexibility at the same time.

and

> My muscles are developed mainly from practicing martial art, which is different from training purely for big, bodybuilder-type muscles.

Lee therefore designed a simple, three-day-per-week bodybuilding program with particular emphasis on the muscle groups he would be using most frequently as a martial artist: the legs, triceps, biceps, and forearms. To Lee's delight, his program proved to be incredibly effective. How effective? In a mere 44 days (from May 27, 1965, to July 10, 1965), and after a total of only 14 workouts, Bruce Lee recorded the following gains:

1. an increase of 2½ inches on his "relaxed" chest measurement
2. an increase of ¼ inch on his neck
3. an increase of ¾ inch on both his right and left biceps
4. an increase of ¾ inch on his left forearm
5. an increase of ½ inch on his right forearm
6. an increase of ½ inch on his left and right wrists
7. an increase of 1½ inches on his left thigh
8. an increase of 1¼ inches on his right thigh
9. an increase of ⅝ inch on his left calf
10. an increase of ½ inch on his right calf
11. a decrease of ½ inch from his waist.

These are spectacular results, regardless of one's level of training experience. A beginner with no athletic background who undertook this program could expect to see dramatic results (how dramatic would depend on certain genetic predispositions), since moving from "zero" muscular output to the kind required on this program would constitute a quantum leap, physiologically speaking, to his or her body. However, when you take into account the fact that when he undertook this program, Bruce Lee was already a well-conditioned athlete used to the rigors of working out, and combine it with the fact that these results came from less than two months of training, you can begin to appreciate just how effective this program is! What follows is the specific routine Bruce Lee created to accomplish such impressive results.

1965
學生體格進度表
BODY IMPROVEMENT LIST

Name BRUCE LEE Age 24 Sex M.

肌肉部份 Parts of Muscles		五月廿七日 Date	七月十日 Date	月日 Date
頸 Neck		15¼	15½	
胸 Chest	平常 Nor.	39	41½	
	擴張 Exp.	43	44¼	
上膊 Biceps	左 L.	13	13¾	
	右 R.	13½	14¼	
前膊 Fore Arm	左 L.	11	11¾	
	右 R.	11¾	12¼	
腕 Wrist	左 L.	6¼	6¾	
	右 R.	6½	6⅛	
腰 Waist		30	29½	
大腿 Thigh	左 L.	21	22½	
	右 R.	21¼	22½	
小腿 Leg	左 L.	12¼	12⅞	
	右 R.	12½	13	
體重 Weight		140	140	
體高 Height		5'8"	5'8"	

The Routine (Emphasizing Triceps, Biceps, and Forearms)

Although each of these exercises is explained in great detail in the following chapters, the particular movements of each are briefly explained here.

1. Squat: 3 sets of 10 repetitions (weight: 95 lbs.)

Squats develop the quadriceps muscle group (at the front of the thighs), in addition to the glutes, hip flexors, hamstrings, calves, lower back, trapezius, abdominals (as stabilizers), and shoulders. The quadriceps group is the most powerful in the body and these muscles can withstand a lot of work. Not only will the exercise build great thigh size and power, but the heavy breathing that the movement causes will help pack on size and weight to the entire body. Place a barbell on your shoulders and lower yourself to a full squat position. From this position, rise to a fully standing one. Repeat for 3 sets of 10 repetitions.

2. French Press: 4 sets of 6 repetitions (weight: 64 lbs.)

The French press develops the triceps muscle at the back of the upper arms. You can either stand or sit, whichever is more comfortable. Place your hands on the shaft of a barbell, about two hand-widths apart. Raise the bar above your head, then lower it behind your neck. Be sure to keep your upper arms close to the sides of your head. Only your elbows are bent. From the lowered position, press the weight overhead by moving your forearms until your elbows are locked.

3. Incline Curl: 4 sets of 6 repetitions (weight: 35 lbs.)

Inclining the body isolates the stress of this movement to the biceps muscle on the front of your upper arms. With a dumbbell in each hand, lean back on an incline bench. Let the weights extend the arms to a natural hanging position. From there, curl the weight to your shoulders. Return to the original position and repeat until you have completed 4 sets of 6 repetitions.

4. Concentration Curl: 4 sets of 6 repetitions (weight: 35 lbs.)

The concentration curl develops your biceps muscle (at the front of your upper arms). Sit on a bench with a dumbbell in your right hand and the elbow of the arm holding the weight braced

克 強 健 力 學 院
HAK KEUNG GYMNASIUM

運動程序
Exercise List.

繳費日期

學生姓名 Name *BRUCE LEE* 性別 Sex *M* Date *MAY 27* 1965.

	運動名稱 EXERCISE	組数 SETS	磅 LBS	次数 TIMES	運動名稱 EXERCISE	
1	SQUAT	3	95	10	SQUAT	
2	FRENCH PRESS 1	4	64	6	FRENCH PRESS	TRICEPS
	INCLINE CURL	4	35	6	FRENCH PRESS	
3	FRENCH PRESS 2	4	64	6	PUSH UP	
	"CON" CURL	4	35	6	TRICEP STRETCH	
4	PUSH UP	3	70–80	10	INCLINE CURL	BICEPS
	TWO HAND CURL	3	70–80	8	"CON" CURL	
5	TRICEP STRETCH	3	3	8 (6)	TWO HAND CURL	
	DUMBELL CIRCLE	4	16	INF.	REVERSE CURL	FOREARMS
6	REVERSE CURL	4	X64	6	DUMBELL CIRCLE	
	WRIST CURL 1	4	64	INF.	WRIST CURL	
7	WRIST CURL 2	4	10	INF.	WRIST CURL	
	SIT UP	5	B.W.	12	SIT UP	
	CALF RAISE	5	B.W.	20	CALF RAISE	

此表請勿携出院外 Please do not take it away

against the inside of your right thigh. Curl the weight to your shoulder. Do this movement slowly and watch your biceps while you work. Repeat for 6 repetitions. Then transfer the weight to the opposite arm, reverse your curling position so that your left elbow is braced against the inside of your left knee, and curl the weight for 6 repetitions. Repeat this alternating process until you have performed 4 sets of 6 repetitions per arm.

5. Push-up: 3 sets of 10 repetitions (weight: 70–80 lbs. placed on the upper back)

Push-ups are excellent for the chest, shoulders, and the back of the upper arms (triceps). Place your hands approximately shoulder-width apart. Hold your body perfectly straight and exhale as you push your body up until your arms are straight. Pause. Inhale as you lower your body to the floor, allowing only your chest to touch. Your stomach should still be an inch or two off the floor when you touch with your chest, because your toes lift the body up a bit. Repeat for 3 sets of 10 repetitions.

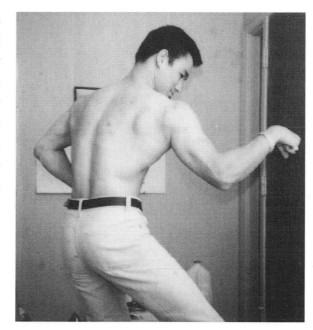

6. Two-Hand (Barbell) Curl: 3 sets of 8 repetitions (weight: 70–80 lbs.)
This is a basic barbell movement that creates a tremendous amount of size and power in the biceps. Start with your arms extended straight down. Curl the bar upward, bringing it as close as possible to your shoulders. The upper body may move very slightly. Form is a real priority here. Repeat for 3 sets of 8 repetitions.

7. Triceps Stretch: 3 sets of 6 to 8 repetitions (weight: 3 lbs.)
The triceps stretch is a single-arm version of the French press. Begin with a dumbbell held at arm's length overhead. Lower the dumbbell to the back of your neck, keeping your biceps as close to your ear as possible. (This will keep upper-arm movement to a minimum, which will rapidly increase the results.) From this position, bring the dumbbell to arm's length again. Contract the triceps vigorously as you extend the arm overhead. Lower and repeat until 3 sets of 6 to 8 repetitions have been completed.

8. Dumbbell Circle: 4 sets of as many repetitions as possible (weight: 16 lbs.)
This exercise builds strong wrists, forearms, biceps, triceps, and brachialis muscles. The dumbbells are simultaneously rotated in vertical circles in front of the body, with the wrists turned up at the bottom of the outward arc and turned down on the inner arc. Perform three sets of as many repetitions as possible (as Bruce Lee wrote, "infinity").

9. Reverse Curl (Barbell): 4 sets of 6 repetitions (weight: 64 lbs.)

The reverse curl affects the upper and outer forearm muscles, the brachialis muscles, and the biceps. Take a shoulder-width grip on a barbell, with your feet set shoulder-width apart. Stand erect, with your arms hanging down at your sides and the barbell resting across your upper thighs. Press your upper arms in against the sides of your rib cage. Without allowing your torso to move forward or backward, slowly curl the barbell upward in a semicircular arc, from your upper thighs to a point directly under your chin. Squeeze your forearms and upper-arm muscles as tightly as possible for a moment, then slowly lower the weight back along the same arc to the starting point. Repeat for 4 sets of 6 repetitions.

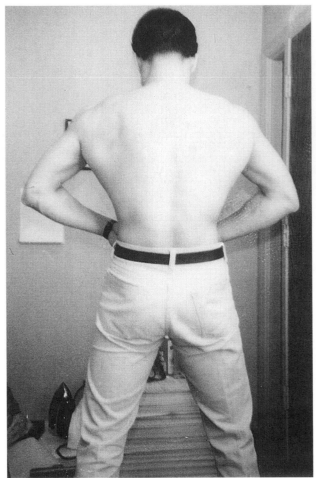

10. Wrist Curl (seated): 4 sets of as many repetitions as possible (weight: 64 lbs.)

The wrist curl targets the belly of the forearms, or the flexor muscles. With your forearms lying on your thighs, your palms up and hanging over your knees, grasp a barbell with your fingers. Slowly curl the weight into the palm of your hand, and then flex the wrist as far as possible. Lower the weight and repeat for 4 sets of as many repetitions as possible.

11. Reverse Wrist Curl (seated): 4 sets of as many repetitions as possible (weight: 10 lbs.)

The reverse wrist curl targets the top or extensor muscles of the forearms. Turn your forearms so that your palms face down. Grasp the barbell and then flex the wrist as far back as possible. As with the previous exercise, concentration on the task at hand is very important. Repeat for 4 sets of as many repetitions as possible.

12. Sit-up: 5 sets of 12 repetitions (weight: body weight only)

Sit-ups are a good workout for the entire abdominal area. With your knees bent (to prevent your thigh muscles from helping in the pull) and your hands behind your neck, raise your upper body until your head touches your knees. Repeat for 5 sets of 12 repetitions.

13. Calf Raise: 5 sets of 20 repetitions (weight: body weight only)

The calf raise adds size and power to the calf muscles of the lower leg. Stand with your toes on a block. The block should be high enough to allow for a full extension of the calf muscles. Lock your knees and flex your calves until you are up on the tips of your toes. Repeat for 5 sets of 20 repetitions.

This three-day-per-week routine served to build the foundation of muscle mass and shape that Bruce Lee later refined with the routines outlined in the chapters that follow. For a beginner, this routine is second to none, as it pays huge dividends in increased size and strength.

4. THE GENERAL (OVERALL) DEVELOPMENT ROUTINE

If you are talking about sport, that is one thing. But when you are talking about combat—as it is—well then, baby, you'd better train every part of your body.
—Bruce Lee

Not long after discovering the benefits to be attained from proper bodybuilding and strength training, Bruce Lee decided that he should balance his muscular development and strength by subjecting each muscle group of the body to progressive-resistance exercise. However, as he once told a Hong Kong interviewer, "My muscles are developed from my martial art training; it's a different type of training than is performed simply for the sake of developing big, bodybuilder-type muscles." While this is true, it is obvious that Bruce Lee considered supplemental training—including weight training—part and parcel of proper "martial art training." Nevertheless, while weight training was included in his training schedule, there is little evidence that Lee routinely performed isolation exercises such as those practiced by most competitive bodybuilders (with the exception of Zottman curls, which he did while seated at his desk reading or watching television, to develop his forearms).

In fact, when Lee devised muscle-development programs either for himself or his students, he always stressed compound exercises—that is, exercises that required two or more muscle groups to be involved in the execution. Lee's reasoning was simple: He wanted harmony among all of his muscle groups so they could generate power in concert, and would combine to accomplish a single objective, whether it be the execution of a powerful punch or kick, an efficient trapping combination, or even to dodge a blow. Because this objective was planted firmly in Lee's mind, he devised a strength-training/bodybuilding routine that would develop each of his muscle groups collectively and further serve the purpose of laying down neuromuscular pathways that would accustom the various muscle groups of his body to working together.

To this end, Lee devised the following general (overall) development routine, to be followed three days per week (Tuesday, Thursday, and Saturday), which consisted of what he

The Art of Expressing the Human Body

considered to be the best exercises for each of the body's major muscle groups. While Lee left no exact record of the weight, sets, or repetitions he employed with this particular routine, there is ample evidence in the more detailed weight-training records that he did leave, in addition to the recollections of his students, to indicate that 2 sets of between 8 and 12 repetitions was the most likely formula. The only exception was for leg training, which he believed required more repetitions (from 12 to 20).

The General (Overall) Development Routine

1. Arms

a. Clean and Press: 2 sets of 8 to 12 repetitions

The "clean and press" exercise was one of the staples of Bruce Lee's weight training routine when he lived in Bel Air. It is a tremendously effective exercise because it effectively taxes every muscle group in the body (and in particular the shoulders, biceps, and triceps). Lee found that the clean and press did such a thorough job in warming up all of his muscles that he almost always began his workout routine with it. By doing so, he not only gave his arms and shoulders a great workout, but warmed up the body parts he subsequently would be training during that particular session.

To perform the clean and press properly, your feet should be approximately shoulder-width apart, for in this position you will get a good leg drive as you pull the weight to your chest. Your insteps should be under the bar and your legs should be bent, but not bent to the extent of having the top of the thighs parallel to the ground. The back should be flat. (This does not mean vertical or horizontal, it means that the spine should be in a straight line instead of being rounded.) The hands should grasp the bar just a little wider than shoulder-width apart and the arms should be perfectly straight, as the first pull is produced by the leg and back muscles. As you lift the bar off the ground, the weight must be evenly balanced on both feet and not too far forward or backward. The movement should be a very vigorous one, with the legs and back extending quickly. Pull hard and then quickly dip a little at the knees to receive the bar at the chest. It should land in the pressing position at the top of the chest and the legs should be straightened immediately. This is all performed in one fast, continuous movement. As you straighten the legs, ease your thighs forward and lift your chest high pulling the shoulders back and down. Your chin should be pulled in for two reasons: first, if you press directly upward, as you should, you will hit your chin if it is not pulled in; second, if you tuck your chin in and lift your chest high as recommended you will give yourself an excellent, rigid base on which to work, for this action places the vertebral column in a very strong position. With the bar over the heel of the hand and the forearms in a vertical position, press the bar over your head until your arms are fully extended. Lower the bar to your chest and then back to the floor in one motion. Repeat for 2 sets of 8 to 12 repetitions.

b. Curl: 2 sets of 8 to 12 repetitions

The curl is the granddaddy of all biceps builders, but very few trainees—including some top bodybuilding champions—know how to perform the movement properly. Bruce Lee believed

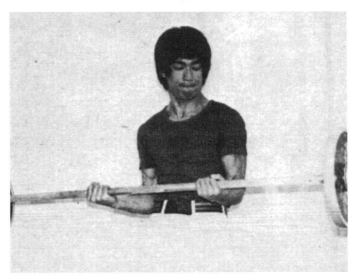

that you should grasp a barbell with a shoulder-width grip (not so close that your hands are touching one another, and not so wide that your natural range of motion is compromised), palms forward, and stand upright with your arms hanging in front of the thighs, the elbows straight. While maintaining this erect position, slowly curl the weight up to your shoulders by bending the elbows, keeping the upper arms still. Bring the bar right up to your chin and flex hard, making sure to hold this maximum contraction for a two count before slowly lowering the bar back down to the starting position. Remember to inhale as the weight is raised and to exhale as it is lowered. Repeat for 2 sets of 8 to 12 repetitions.

2. Shoulders

a. Press Behind Neck: 2 sets of 8 to 12 repetitions

The "press behind neck" was an exercise that Bruce Lee often performed in his workouts to strengthen his deltoids or shoulder muscles. This exercise can be performed either standing or seated, and Lee was known to have performed both versions: standing if working out with a barbell and seated if training on his Marcy Circuit Trainer (see Appendix B) in Hong Kong. Since Lee recorded this particular routine prior to acquiring the Marcy Unit, we'll focus here on how he performed the barbell version.

Grasping hold of a barbell with a shoulder-width grip, bring it from the floor to the shoulders in one movement so that it comes to rest at the top of your chest at the point where the sternum and collarbone meets. Keeping your torso perfectly straight, press the barbell in an arc close to your face to arm's length overhead. Then lower the barbell behind your neck until it comes to rest briefly on your trapezius muscles (at the base of your neck), and then press it to arm's length overhead. Repeat the lowering and pressing out in a continuous motion for 2 sets of 8 to 12 repetitions.

b. Upright Rowing (2 sets of 8 to 12 repetitions)

Upright rowing places particular emphasis on the trapezius and anterior deltoid muscles, but it is also beneficial for the allied upper-back muscles and the arms. Take hold of a barbell with your palms facing toward your body. With a narrow hand spacing, let your arms fully extend so that the barbell is resting across the front of your thighs. Keeping your elbows higher than the barbell throughout the movement, pull it up along the abdomen and chest to the throat or chin. The legs and body should remain straight throughout the exercise. The entire action is the pull from the "hang" position in front of the thighs to the throat. Repeat this action for 2 sets of 8 to 12 repetitions.

3. Leg

a. Squat: 2 sets of 12 to 20 repetitions

The number-one leg-training exercise in Bruce Lee's book was the barbell squat—and for good reason. Not only does the squat strengthen all the thigh muscles, but it has a very marked effect on the entire respiratory system, and a strong heart and lungs are of great importance to any athlete. Therefore, the squat builds great legs, chest, and stamina. Stand with your feet approximately shoulder-width apart and your toes pointing to the front. With a barbell supported across the shoulders behind your neck, bend your knees and lower yourself until your thighs are parallel to the ground. Immediately return to the upright position. Inhale deeply just prior to the knee bend, and exhale as you come to the upright position. Fill the lungs a couple of times before each repetition. It is important to keep your back flat, and your glutes should not in any way come up first. (At no time must the back be allowed to sag.) Keep your heels on the ground for the entire exercise. If you have difficulty keeping your heels on the ground, raise them on a block of wood. Repeat for 2 sets of 12 to 20 repetitions.

b. Breathing

Bruce Lee believed that how you breathe during the squat will impact its effectiveness. He noted that a deep breath should be taken just prior to the knee bend and held until the upright position is reached again. On regaining the upright position, several quick, deep breaths should be taken before the next repetition. The heavier the poundage used, the more breaths you should take before each repetition. Lee did not believe that you should restrict your breathing to the nose. Open your mouth and get in all the air you can.

4. Back

a. Rowing: 2 sets of 8 to 12 repetitions

According to Ted Wong and Herb Jackson, who frequently trained with Bruce Lee, one of his favorite lat (latissimus dorsi) exercises was the bent-over-barbell row. To perform this exercise, grasp the barbell as if you were going to pick it off the floor and press it overhead, but, instead of doing this, stand erect with the barbell hanging in front of your thighs. Place your feet about 8 inches apart and lean well forward at the hips, keeping the back as flat as possible. Hold this position. Pull the barbell to the lower chest by bending the arms and raising the elbows backward in an action similar to rowing a boat. The bar should be raised until it touches the lower ribs. Inhale during the raising movement and exhale as the weight is lowered. Repeat for 2 sets of 8 to 12 repetitions.

5. Chest
a. Bench Press: 2 sets of 8 to 12 repetitions

One of the core exercises in Bruce Lee's overall bodybuilding and strengthening routine was the bench press. The bench press can be performed on the floor, but it is better done on a bench so

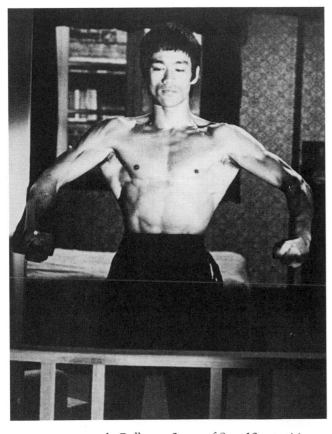

that full play is given to the arms and chest and movement is not restricted. To correctly perform the bench press exercise, lie back on a flat bench so that your shoulders are pressed firmly on it. Bring a bar to arm's length, using a fairly wide grip. Lower the bar to the chest, and then press it overhead to arm's length, ensuring that it is kept fairly high up over the chest and not allowed to come too far toward the abdomen when it is lowered. Take a deep breath as you lower the bar to the chest, and breathe out as the press to arm's length is completed. Repeat for anywhere between 6 and 30 repetitions. This is a great exercise for the entire chest, pectorals, and triceps, and some of the back muscles. It is one of the recommended basic exercises for all athletic events and sports. Note that in all the exercises performed lying on a bench, it is better to keep your feet firmly on the floor rather than on the bench, so that better balance can be maintained.

b. Pullover: 2 sets of 8 to 12 repetitions

The bent-arm pullover is one of the most effective exercises for the tie-in of back and chest muscles. To perform this exercise properly, lie back on a flat bench and take hold of a barbell. Hold the bar at arm's length over your chest, bending your elbows slightly. From this position, lower your arms overhead, keeping your elbows slightly bent, until you feel a full stretch in the latissimus dorsi muscle of your back. At this point return the bar to the starting position over your chest. It is recommended that you inhale as the bar is lowered to the full stretch position and then exhale as it is raised over the chest. Repeat for 2 sets of 8 to 12 repetitions.

The Art of Expressing the Human Body

5. THE 20-MINUTE STRENGTH AND SHAPE ROUTINE

Above all, never cheat on any exercise; use the amount of weight that you can handle without undue strain.
—Bruce Lee

Continuing on with his research into human muscle physiology and his own body's response to exercise, Lee gradually refined the general development routine outlined in Chapter 4. True to his philosophy of jeet kune do, Lee began a shedding process, discarding those exercises he felt to be unnecessary in order to get the utmost out of the minimum—Lee's definition of "simplicity." Lee cut back on the weights and the extra protein drinks until his weight stabilized at a chiseled 136 pounds.

In time, Bruce Lee settled on a new program, which he retained, essentially unchanged, for the rest of his life. Gone was the heavy emphasis he had placed on arm training in his first barbell routine. However, he realized that he was onto something with the employment of heavy compound exercises. The program still fit his three-day-per-week schedule, which Lee felt met his needs perfectly, but as he was now appearing more frequently in films, the program was additionally geared to provide a more balanced development and shape to his muscles. Also, since the new program used compound movements exclusively (which meant much heavier weights were employed and therefore much more energy required to move them), it became even more crucial to have adequate recovery time or rest days between training sessions. As Lee noted: "Since weight training involves repetitions, a great deal of energy must be exerted. Therefore, weight training should be practiced only every other day."

The every-other-day schedule that Lee devised saw him working out with weights on Tuesdays, Thursdays, and Saturdays, with Mondays, Wednesdays, Fridays, and Sundays off to allow for the oft-neglected aspect of recovery and growth. Because weight training demands a great deal of energy, recovery time or days off must be taken between workouts to allow the body to recover fully from and compensate for the exercise sessions.

Lee further coordinated his bodybuilding workouts so that they fell on days when he wasn't otherwised engaged in either endurance or strenuous martial art training. And one of the benefits of his new program—apart from the obvious results it achieved—was the fact that it took only twenty minutes to perform!

Lee incorporated three core tenets of total fitness into his bodybuilding routine: stretching for flexibility, weight training for strength, and cardiovascular activity for his heart and respiratory system. In other words, he was the original cross-trainer. This twenty-minute routine served to build and to maintain the physique Lee displayed in his films *The Big Boss* (released in North America as *Fists of Fury*), *Fist of Fury* (released in North America as *The Chinese Connection*), and *The Way of the Dragon* (released in North America as *Return of the Dragon*).

The 20-Minute Strength and Shape Routine

1. Clean and Press: 2 sets of 8 repetitions

Begin this movement by taking a shoulder-width grip on an Olympic barbell. Bending your knees, squat in front of the resistance and, with a quick snap of your arms and a thrust of your legs, clean the barbell to your chest and stand upright. After a brief pause, thrust the barbell to arm's length overhead, pausing briefly, and then lower it back to the top of your chest. After another brief pause, lower the bar back to the floor. With absolutely no rest, you should then initiate your second repetition, and keep going in such a fashion until you have completed 8 repetitions. To take full advantage of the cardiorespiratory benefits, take only a short rest and then perform your second—and final—set.

2. Squat: 2 sets of 12 repetitions

This staple of bodybuilding was the cornerstone of Lee's barbell training. He had clipped more than 20 articles pertaining to the squat, and he practiced many variations of it. In this routine, however, he performed the squat in the standard fashion. Resting a barbell across your shoulders, place your feet approximately shoulder-width apart. Making sure that you are properly balanced, slowly lower yourself to a full squat position. With no pause at the bottom position, use the strength of your hips, glutes, hamstrings, calves, and quadriceps to rise to the starting position, where you will commence repetition number 2, and so on, until you have completed 12 repetitions. Once again, take only a short rest before performing your second set.

3. Barbell Pullover: 2 sets of 8 repetitions

Although there is no written record indicating that Bruce Lee super-setted barbell squats with barbell pullovers, there's ample circumstantial evidence and eye-witness testimony to suggest that this was the case. For one thing, the magazine articles that he read at the time suggested this coupling of exercises quite frequently, and second, it satisfied Lee's desire to get the most out of a given amount of training time by performing two exercises back to back in the time it would take most people to perform one exercise. Squats were considered a great overall muscle builder (and still are), whereas pullovers were held to be a "rib-box expander" or breathing exercise. Consequently, the practice in the late 1960s and early 1970s was to incorporate pullovers as a "finishing" movement for squats. To perform this exercise correctly, you should lie down on a flat bench and take a shoulder-width grip on a barbell, which you should then press out to full extension above your chest. From this position, lower the barbell behind your head—making sure to keep a slight bend in your elbows so as not to strain the tendons in your elbows—until the bar touches the floor ever so slightly and provides a comfortable stretch in your lats. From this fully extended position, slowly reverse the motion by contracting your lats, pecs, and the long head of your triceps. Repeat this for 8 repetitions and then, after a brief rest, perform a second set.

4. Bench Press: 2 sets of 6 repetitions

Bruce Lee was able to develop an incredible chest musculature. Interestingly, his personal records indicate that the only direct barbell movement he performed for his chest during this period was the good, old-fashioned bench press. To perform this exercise, lie back on a flat bench and take a shoulder-width grip on an Olympic barbell, and press the weight up and off the support pins to arm's length above your chest. From this locked-out position, lower the barbell to your chest, and exhale as you press it back up to the fully locked-out position. Repeat this movement for 6 repetitions and re-rack the barbell. Then, after a short rest, perform a second—and final—set of bench presses.

5. Good Morning: 2 sets of 8 repetitions

A word of caution about this exercise: Bruce Lee performed it to strengthen his lower back, but one day in early 1970, he loaded up a barbell with 135 pounds (his approximate body weight at the time) and—without a warmup—proceeded to complete 8 repetitions. On the last repetition he felt a twinge in his lower back and an accompanying "pop." He later discovered that he'd damaged the fourth sacral nerve in his lower back. As a result, he experienced intense back pain for the rest of his life. That's not to say that this exercise is without merit—just make sure that you perform an adequate warm-up before you begin. Lee would later tell his friend and student Dan Inosanto that "you don't need any weight at all for this exercise, simply use the bar by itself." If you wish to strengthen your lower back, resistance must be provided on a progressive basis, which means weights must be employed—but so, too, must caution.

Begin by placing a barbell across your shoulders and position your feet shoulder-width apart. Bend at the waist, keeping your hands on the barbell at all times. Keep bending until your back is at a 90-degree angle to your hips, and then return to the upright position. Repeat for 8 repetitions. Rest briefly, and then perform a second set.

6. Barbell Curl: 2 sets of 8 repetitions

The barbell curl directly stresses the biceps of the upper arm. It was responsible for developing Lee's impressive upper arms—not to mention his incredible pulling (lop sao) power, which he

used to good effect in almost all of his sparring sessions. To perform this movement properly, take a shoulder-width grip on an Olympic barbell with your palms facing forward. Keeping a slight bend in your knees for stabilization, contract your biceps and curl the barbell up until it is level with your upper pecs. Pause briefly in the fully contracted position, and then slowly lower the barbell back to the starting position, and repeat the procedure until you have performed 8 repetitions. After a brief rest, perform a second—and final—set of barbell curls.

Going Beyond "Routine"

Bruce Lee didn't just train with the above-listed exercises, but also incorporated other forms of weight training into his martial art workouts.

The Art of Expressing the Human Body

According to Inosanto's recollection:

> Bruce would sometimes shadowbox with small weights in his hands, and he did a drill in which he punched for 12 series in a row—100 punches per series—using a pyramid system of 1-, 2-, 3-, 5-, 7-, and 10-pound weights—and then he would reverse the pyramid and go back down: 10, 7, 5, 3, 2, 1, and finally 0 weight. He had me do this drill with him and—man!—what a burn you got in your delts and arms!

When Lee wasn't training with weights in his martial art workouts or during one of his thrice-weekly whole-body sessions, he could be found curling a 35-pound dumbbell that he kept in the office of his Bel Air home. Linda Lee Cadwell, who was herself an early student of her husband's, recalls: "He was always using that dumbbell, primarily to strengthen his forearms." Lee's interest in supplemental forearm training (see Chapter 10) harkened back to his days of training in the Wing Chun system of gung fu. As Linda explains,

> There is so much forearm work required in, say, the practice of chi sao [sticking hand] training in Wing Chun, or in doing routines on the wooden dummy. And all the trapping that Bruce emphasized at that point in time further emphasized the need to develop strong forearms. But fortunately, Bruce had the unique ability to do several things at once. It wasn't at all unusual for me to find him watching a boxing match on TV while simultaneously performing a full side split, reading a book in one hand, and pumping a dumbbell in the other.

The 20-minute strength and shape workout, and the ancillary weight training drills he incorporated into his martial art workouts, further increased Lee's muscularity. Never satisfied to rest on his laurels, however, Lee wanted to improve his conditioning even more. He decided to create an exercise routine that would incorporate the benefits of strength training while also enhancing his already excellent cardiovascular system.

6. THE SEQUENCE (CIRCUIT) TRAINING ROUTINE FOR TOTAL FITNESS

One of Lee's favorite strength training and bodybuilding magazines was *Ironman*, which during Lee's heyday was owned by Peary and Mabel Rader. The Raders were constantly featuring cutting-edge training information and shied away from the commercial hype that prevailed among competing publications. Many intriguing training principles were being propagated in the magazines of the time, such as Giant Sets, Flushing, and Rest/Pause. However, Lee was becoming more and more interested in researching the effects of a then radically new weight training system he had read about in *Ironman*: Peripheral Heart Action.

The Peripheral Heart Action (PHA) System

The PHA system had been set up to diametrically oppose the more popular flushing or pumping systems of that time. In the late 1960s, the leading exponent of the PHA system was a young bodybuilder named Bob Gajda, who explained through a series of articles in *Ironman* (which Lee clipped and saved) that PHA placed its main emphasis on "continuous circulation of the blood." From Gajda's writings (which, in turn, were based on the empirical research of physiology pioneer Dr. Arthur Steinhause), Lee reasoned that if he could keep his circulation at elevated levels throughout the course of his workout, it would tremendously benefit his muscle strength, endurance, and, if the exercises were performed over a full range of motion, flexibility—in other words, the three pillars of total fitness.

The thrust of Gajda's articles was that one should not congest the blood in one area or one muscle group throughout the course of a workout, but rather keep it moving in and out of several muscle groups—at all times—during the workout. Exercise systems like PHA were actually forerunners of what is now commonly called circuit training. A *circuit* is defined as one complete performance of a group of movements (usually five or six different exercises), each of which targets a different body part. The underlying idea of such training is never to exercise the same muscle group twice in succession, but rather to move on—immediately—to another muscle or body part. As explained by Gajda in one of the articles saved by Lee:

> *If you, for instance, performed two or more sets of curls in succession you would be doing the pump or flushing system. On the sequence system you would do a set of curls, then perhaps go to a set of calf raises or abdominal work or back work. In other words, do not exercise the same muscle two sets in succession. Do not even use what is called the supersets in which you alternate between the biceps and the triceps for several sets. This will bring about a congestion of the whole arm. Go to some other body part. Then on to another body part. The object being that in the PHA system, the exercises are spread over the entire body.*

In the PHA system there is tremendous muscle stimulation and uninterrupted blood flow over the entire body, because the entire body is exercised during each workout. And because there is no rest between exercises, the accelerated flow of blood is maintained, and thus you can delay the onset of fatigue for extended periods of time.

Always ahead of his time, Lee saw much merit in the concept of circuit training, not so much for the purposes for which it was then being promoted—that is, building massive muscles, but as a very effective means of consolidating his cardiovascular, flexibility, and strength-training workouts into one routine. To this end, Lee created his own program, which hit on these three touchstones of total fitness while still adhering to the guidelines or general principles of PHA.

Bruce Lee's Sequence Training Routine (for Total Fitness)

Bruce Lee performed his sequence training six days a week, alternating between two programs. He also included running on a daily basis to boost his cardiovascular system further.

Sequence 1a (Monday, Wednesday, Friday)
   1. Rope Jumping (1 minute)
Skip rope in a vigorous fashion for 1 minute. Move immediately to the next exercise.

2. Forward Bend (1 minute)

From a standing position, with your legs perfectly straight and close together, bend over at the waist and try to touch your head to your shins. Hold this position for the duration of the set. Move immediately to the next exercise.

3. Cat Stretch (1 minute)

The cat stretch was one of two exercises popularized by a man named Gama, the most famous wrestler in India. Lee read two articles about Gama and how he employed these exercises to build his legendary strength for wrestling, and Lee quickly incorporated them into his own routine. The cat stretch is also known as a *dand*, and is really just a push-up—with variations.

Get down on all fours, supporting the body on your hands and feet, keeping your hips and shoulders parallel to each other in a straight line. In the North American version of the exercise, you hold this straight line while bending the arms until your chest touches the floor, then straighten. In India, you raise the buttocks as high as you can and then slouch down on your thighs. Now, bending the arms, push the body forward with your legs until your chest grazes the floor, then straighten your arms. Raise your buttocks. Repeat. This is the basic Indian dand. Move immediately to the next exercise.

4. Jumping Jack (1 minute)

The jumping jack is also known as the stride jump. To begin, stand perfectly straight with your feet together and your arms straight down at your sides, with your hands touching your hips. In one motion, jump up slightly, allowing your legs to spread out (knees slightly bent to help absorb the impact safely) until they are 6 inches beyond shoulder-width apart; simultaneously raise your arms (which should be held straight) upward until your hands meet overhead. As soon as your hands touch, the movement should be reversed so that your hands and feet return to the starting position. Repeat for as many repetitions as you can within 60 seconds. Then move immediately to the next exercise.

5. Squat (1 minute)

The free-hand or body-weight squat is the second exercise that Lee picked up from the training methods of the Indian wrestler Gama. In India it is called the *baithak* and is simply the deep-knee bend—hands on hips, bend legs, squat, raise body, squat, stand, squat, and so on. Do this sequence for one minute. Move immediately to the next exercise.

The dand and baithak built up Gama's chest to 56 inches in circumference, his arms to 17 inches, and his thighs to 30 inches. The secret lies in the way Gama performed these two movements. According to an article that Lee saved about Gama's training methods, boys of 12, 13, and 14 in India will do 1,000 baithaks and 500 dands every day, while professional wrestlers such as Gama would get up at 3:00 AM to do baithaks—deep-knee bends. Gama would perform 4,000 repetitions of the baithak in the morning, have breakfast, perform his dands—2,000 of them in the afternoon—take a walk or run 4 miles, and finish up his day by wrestling 3 or 4 hours without rest.

6. High Kick (1 minute)

If you saw Bruce Lee's warm-up sequence before he fought Chuck Norris in the film *The Way of the Dragon,* you'll remember this particular exercise. With the kicking leg locked perfectly straight, Lee would swing it up in front of himself as high as it would go (in Lee's case, his thigh would actually slap against his chest) and allow it to return to the starting position. He would repeat the movement several times—as many as he could fit in a 60-second time span. You are allowed to keep a slight bend in the knee of the supporting leg throughout the movement. Upon completion, switch legs and repeat the exercise. Move immediately to the next exercise.

Sequence 1b (Monday, Wednesday, Friday)
Forearm/Waist Emphasis
1. Waist Twisting (1 minute)
Standing erect, take a wooden staff or broomstick (even an empty barbell will suffice) and place it across your shoulders. Place your feet shoulder-width apart, and twist your upper torso as far as you can to the right and then as far as you can to the left. Repeat for as many repetitions as you can per side in 1 minute. Move immediately to the next exercise.
2. Palm-Up Curl (1 minute)
Sitting down on a flat bench, take hold of a moderately weighted barbell with your palms facing upward. Place the backs of your wrists over your knees. The knuckles of your hands should be facing the floor. Now contract the flexor muscles of the belly of your forearms until your knuckles are facing the ceiling (or at least are pointing toward the wall in front of you). Lower the barbell to the starting position and repeat for as many repetitions as you can in 1 minute. Move immediately to the next exercise.
3. Roman Chair (1 minute)
The Roman chair is a version of the sit-up that allows your torso to extend down below the level of your hips. You need a special Roman chair exercise apparatus (as Bruce Lee had) for this but you can also make do with a flat bench and something (such as a barbell) under which you can anchor your feet. With your feet securely under either a barbell or the padded bar on a Roman chair unit, place your hands either on your chest or behind your head. From a position of sitting up straight, lower your torso down until your head almost touches the floor and then return to the full-erect or starting position. Repeat for as many repetitions as you can manage in 1 minute. Move immediately to the next exercise.

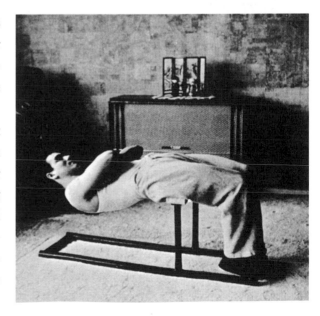

4. Knee Drawing (1 minute)

This exercise can be performed either lying on your back on the floor or on a special knee-up/leg-raise unit. If you are lying on your back on the floor, place your hands, palms down, upon the floor just underneath your buttocks. Now with your legs perfectly straight, lift your feet three to four inches off the floor. In one smooth motion, bend your knees and draw your thighs in to your abdominal area and then return to the legs-straight position, still with your feet three to four inches off the floor. Repeat for as many repetitions as possible in one minute. Move immediately to the next exercise.

5. Side Bending (1 minute)

Stand with your feet shoulder-width apart and both hands at your sides, holding a light dumbbell in either your right or left hand. Making sure to keep both knees locked, bend your torso directly to the side on which the dumbbell is held until the weight is level with your knee joint. Then bring your body back to the erect or starting position, inclining your trunk slightly past the perpendicular on the other side. During the movement, the elbow of the lifting arm and the knees must be kept straight. Repeat for as many repetitions as you can in 30 seconds. Then switch the dumbbell to the other hand and again repeat for as many repetitions as you can in 30 seconds on that side. Move immediately to the next exercise.

6. Palm-Down Curl (1 minute)

Sitting down on the same flat bench on which you performed the palm-up curl, take hold of a light barbell with an overhand or palm-down grip. Place the underside of your wrists over your knees and relax your hands so that your knuckles are facing the floor. Now contract the muscles on the tops of your forearms until the backs of your hands have been drawn up as far as they can go—without once allowing the bottoms of your forearms to leave the tops of your thighs. Return to the starting position and repeat for as many repetitions as you can complete in 1 minute.

Sequence 2a (Tuesday, Thursday, Saturday)

1. Groin Stretch (1 minute)

Sitting down on the floor, draw your knees back and place the soles of your feet together. Place your hands on your feet and your elbows on the insides of your knees, and gently push your knees down toward the floor as low as they can comfortably go while keeping your feet together and your elbows touching the insides of your knees. Do not apply more than a gentle pressure with your elbows. Hold for 60 seconds and then move immediately to the next exercise.

2. Side Leg Raise (1 minute)

Standing erect, lock your right leg straight and lift it up laterally as high as it can go. Keeping

The Art of Expressing the Human Body

the raise under full muscular control, hold this position for a full 30 seconds. Lower the leg and repeat the movement with the left leg, holding the fully raised position for 30 seconds before lowering. Move immediately to the next exercise.

3. Jumping Squat (1 minute)

From a standing position with your feet shoulder-width apart, lower yourself into a full squat position and then explode upward in a jump, landing in the standing position. Repeat for as many repetitions as possible in 60 seconds. Move immediately to the next exercise.

4. Shoulder Circling (1 minute)

This is another warm-up exercise that Bruce Lee performed during his Collesium calisthenics prior to fighting Chuck Norris in *The Way of the Dragon*. Standing erect with your feet shoulder-width apart and your arms at your sides, begin rotating your shoulders from front to back in little circles, drawing the shoulders up high, pulling them back, lowering them and raising them as high as they will go. Repeat for as many repetitions as you can complete in 30 seconds, then switch the direction of the rotation from back to front for another 30 seconds. Move immediately to the next exercise.

5. Alternate Splits (1 minute)

Standing with your feet shoulder-width apart and your arms at your sides, simultaneously draw your right leg forward and the left leg back (with only a slight bend in the knees) into a semi-split position. At the same time, raise the left arm forward to shoulder height and the right arm back behind the body. From this position, exchange positions by advancing the left leg and right arm forward and the right leg and left arm backward. Continue on in this alternating splits fashion for as many repetitions as you can manage in one minute. Move immediately to the next exercise.

6. Leg Stretch (A, B) (2 minutes)

You will need a chair or low horizontal stretching bar for this movement. Place the heel of your right foot onto the back of a chair or stretching bar. (This should be high enough so that your foot is well above your waist.) (A) Face the stretching bar or chair front with your right leg locked straight and your toes facing upward. Hold this position for 30 seconds. (B) Rotate your right foot into a side kick position so that the inside of your right ankle is resting on the chair back or stretching bar, and rotate your hips to the left. Hold this position for 30 seconds. Switch legs and repeat the exercises. Move immediately to the next exercise.

Sequence 2b (Tuesday, Thursday, Saturday)

1. Leg Raise (1 minute)

Lying on a flat bench or on your back on the floor, place your hands either on the upright support bars of the flat bench or under your buttocks on the floor. With your knees locked straight, lift your heels 3 to 4 inches from the ground. Keeping your knees locked and ankles touching each other, lift your legs up until they are at a 90-degree angle to your torso, then lower them back to the starting position of 3 to 4 inches off the floor. Repeat for as many repetitions as you can perform in 60 seconds. Move immediately to the next exercise.

2. Reverse Curl (1 minute)

Grab hold of either a standard barbell or an E-Z curl bar with an overhand grip, so that your palms are facing down toward the floor. Standing erect, with your feet shoulder-width apart and your elbows pinned to your sides, contract the brachialis muscles of the upper arm and curl the barbell up from the starting position in front of your thighs to your shoulders. Pause briefly at the fully contracted position, then lower the barbell back to the starting position. Repeat for as many repetitions as you can perform in 60 seconds. Move immediately to the next exercise.

3. Sit-Up Twist (1 minute)

Lying on your back, with your feet secured (either under a barbell or, if you are using an abdominal board, under the strap attached to its end), bend your knees until your heels almost come in contact with your buttocks. Place your hands behind your head with your fingers interlaced. Now curl your trunk up toward your knees trying to touch your left knee with your right elbow. Return to the starting position and curl your trunk back up toward your knees, this time trying to touch your right knee with your left elbow. Return to the starting position and repeat this procedure for as many repetitions as you can manage in 60 seconds. Move immediately to the next exercise.

4. Leverage Bar Twist (1 minute)

With your right hand, take hold of the empty end of a leverage bar (a dumbbell that has barbell plates affixed to only one end). Kneel down on one knee, placing the hand with the leverage bar in it over the higher knee, with palm facing down. Rotating the bar clockwise, twist it as far to the opposite side as it will go and then return it to the starting position. Perform as many repetitions as you can for 15 seconds. Next, rotate your wrist with the leverage bar in it so that the back of your forearm is now resting over the higher knee and rotate the bar counterclockwise, again twisting it as far as it will go in the opposite direction and return it again to the starting position. Repeat for as many repetitions as you can perform in 15 seconds. Then switch hands and repeat both movements for as many repetitions as possible in 15-second intervals per movement. Move immediately to the next exercise.

5. Alternate Leg Raise (1 minute)

Lying on your back on the floor, place the palms of your hands flat on the floor beneath your buttocks. Keeping both legs locked straight, lift both of your heels 3 to 4 inches off the floor. From this starting position, raise one leg up approximately 12 inches, and then return it to the starting position. As it is being returned to the starting position, begin to lift the other leg up approximately 12 inches. Continue to raise both legs in an alternating fashion for as many repetitions as you can complete in 1 minute. Move immediately to the next exercise.

6. Wrist-Roller (1 minute)

This last exercise was one of Bruce Lee's favorites because of the tremendous workout it provides the forearms. A wrist-roller (a thick-handled bar with one end of a small piece of cord attached to it and the other end of the cord attached to a light weight), is a very effective forearm developer. To maximize its benefits, hold the bar, firmly grasped, directly out in front of you. Then, with the knuckles up, revolve the bar by rolling your wrists until the cord is rolled up completely around the bar. When winding up, turn the top of the bar away from you; do not bend your elbows or the effects of the exercise will be divided between your forearms, biceps, and shoulders. After winding up the weight, loosen the grip and unwind the cord. Rewind the cord by turning the top of the bar in your hands toward you. Be sure to hold your arms straight throughout the exercise and try at all times to hold the bar horizontally. Every time you wind the bar, move your hand through as large an arc as possible; and perform the winding steadily. Use a weight light enough to allow you to wind the cord 4 times, doing the winding 2 times either way in 1 minute.

The results of training on this modified PHA routine were exactly what Bruce Lee had envisioned: He increased his muscular endurance, improved his overall conditioning, and further strengthened his entire body.

7. THE CIRCUIT TRAINING ROUTINE FOR INCREASED MUSCULARITY

Certainly any Bruce Lee fan knows that Lee's physique looked its most defined (or, to use the bodybuilding nomenclature, "ripped") during the movie *Enter the Dragon*. Not that his muscles were any bigger or more shapely, but the level of definition they had acquired by the time Lee had lensed this film was absolutely astounding.

Even bodybuilding magnate Joe Weider, the man responsible for bringing Arnold Schwarzenegger to this country and someone who has "seen them all" in terms of muscle development, told me recently that he had "never seen a level of muscular definition to equal that of Bruce Lee in the photographs I've seen of him in *Enter the Dragon*." This is not to suggest that Lee had a poor physique prior to this film—but there unquestionably had been a marked difference in his muscular definition. He had amped his muscularity somehow—but what was the contributing factor? Certainly he was very physically active during this period of his life; choreographing take after take of fight scenes, running up to two miles a day, perfecting his martial art techniques, and performing the bodybuilding routines outlined in the previous chapters. All of these activities contributed to creating the physique Lee displayed in the films *The Big Boss*, *Fist of Fury*, and *The Way of the Dragon*. But why did Lee's physique look leaner and more defined, with each muscle group standing out in bold relief, in his last film, *Enter the Dragon*? The sole contributing factor (remember Lee's diet and aerobic and activity levels had not changed) was his acquisition in December 1972, and subsequent implementation into his daily training, of a multi-exercise weight-training machine called the Marcy Circuit Trainer.

The Art of Expressing the Human Body

This unit, serial number 2175, was manufactured in Glendale, California, and shipped to Lee on the ocean freighter *Lexa Maersk,* and arrived in Hong Kong's Victoria Harbor on December 25, 1972. It arrived in one pallet and one crate, and cleared local customs for transportation to his home on January 6, 1973.

A Trip to Hong Kong

Fortunately, preceding the machine's arrival into Hong Kong by several days were two of Lee's favorite students and close friends, Ted Wong and Herb Jackson, the latter being an extremely talented welder and craftsman and the man who would in fact sign for the machine at Hong Kong Harbor, be responsible for its transport to Lee's house, and ultimately assemble it.

Both Jackson and Wong had loaded up their suitcases with exercise equipment for Lee to train with prior to their trip to Hong Kong, for Lee had lamented the fact that he'd left all of his training apparatus behind in California when he moved. The two men arrived just as *The Way of the Dragon* was premiering in Hong Kong. Lee told them, "Guys, you've arrived at just the right time! I've finished some preliminary shooting for *The Game of Death* [a film in which two more

of Lee's students, Kareem Abdul-Jabbar and Dan Inosanto, had shot sequences during the two months preceding Jackson and Wong's arrival] and now I've got some time off before my next film." This next film, as it turned out, was *Enter the Dragon.*

Jackson and Wong were able to do some light training with Lee while in Hong Kong, but because of Lee's new and demanding schedule, it was very sporadic, consisting of a few runs, stretches, and light technique training. Lee was delighted that Jackson was available to assemble his new machine for him, which Jackson did in early January 1973, a week or so after Wong had to return home to Los Angeles to resume his work. Lee relied on Jackson for many things throughout the time the two men had known each other: Jackson had assembled the Lee family's washer and dryer, cut down rotten trees on their property, manufactured novel training equipment according to Lee's exacting specifications, and even drove Lee's wife Linda to the hospital to deliver their second child, Shannon, while Lee was employed as a fight choreographer for a film shot in Tennessee.

Lee was Jackson's martial art instructor, his guidance counselor, and, most importantly, his friend. The two of them frequently shared dinner, conversation, and life experiences. Jackson was also pivotal in the acquisition of the Marcy Circuit Trainer; he set up Lee's transaction with Walter Marcian, the owner/president of the Marcy Gymnasium Equipment Company, on November 7, 1972. Jackson, now in his mid-seventies, smiles when he recalls the purchase:

> You see, Walter Marcian was my uncle, and one day I drove Bruce out to visit the Marcy plant in Glendale, California. I was hoping to get Bruce a discount because I was the owner's nephew, and Walter agreed. I said to him, "You know, my friend over there is the world's top martial artist—but he doesn't have much money, so I'd really appreciate it if you could give him a discount." I looked over at Bruce, who just rolled his eyes skyward—you see, Bruce was a master haggler, and he thought my approach was pretty amateurish. Nevertheless, it worked. My uncle gave him the same discount that he normally only gave universities—15 percent.

Lee liked what he saw in the Marcy unit and plunked down a deposit for $500 with no regrets. After all, the machine had every feature he knew he would require—and suited his very exacting standards. The stations (of which there were nine) were developed, not by bodybuilders—that is to say, not by people with an eye toward the development of muscles solely for cosmetic purposes—but by kinesiologists and exercise physiologists for the express purpose of training each muscle group for a functional purpose. Yes, the machine, being a progressive resistance device, developed Lee's muscles, but more importantly, to use his own phraseology, the machine allowed him to "express" his total fitness potential to its ultimate limits.

The Marcy Circuit Trainer boasted the following nine stations, or circuits:
- a bench press
- a lat pull-down
- two high pulleys
- two low pulleys
- an isometric rack
- a knee-up or leg-raise station
- a shoulder press
- a chin-up bar
- a leg-press/leg-thrust station

The leg-press/leg-thrust station had a particular appeal; it was in many respects the forerunner to today's Nordic Trak. Two tracks came out from the base of the machine, each containing a foot stirrup of sorts that resembled the starting blocks you see most sprinters employ at the beginning of a race. These blocks were connected to twin weight stacks that ranged in weight from 10 to 220 pounds each.

According to the literature that arrived with the machine, the object was to spend 30 seconds at each station, performing as many repetitions as possible in that time. Then, with absolutely no rest, in order to take advantage of your elevated heart rate, you would proceed from station to station until you had run through all nine.

By the time that production on *Enter the Dragon* was rolling, Lee had incorporated his new muscle machine into his daily training. He told a reporter in June 1973: "My minimum daily training is two hours; this includes running three miles, special weight training, kicking, and hitting the light and heavy bags."

The "special weight training" was where the Marcy machine came in. According to Bob Wall, the California-based businessman and 1970 world heavyweight karate champion who had a supporting role in Lee's *Enter the Dragon*, "When I saw him train during the filming of *Enter the Dragon*, Bruce was really into cable work where he'd pull this way and then the other way, curl that way—he was into angles, and he'd never do the exact same angle. He was always doing different angles and trying a different way. He did a lot of cable triceps extensions and things like that."

Another individual who appeared in *Enter the Dragon* and who saw Lee train on the machine was Yang-tze (or Bolo Yeung, as he has since become known in this country). According to Bolo, "Bruce's house had a Marcy gym in it—just off the kitchen. Bruce liked bodybuilding movements. He worked out every day. Standing presses, pulldowns—the works."

Oxygen—The Fire Within

When you eat food, it is stored as fuel in the form of fat and/or converted to protein, the fat is reserved for use as energy and the protein utilized in rebuilding and increasing the body's muscular tissues. What is needed to oxidize or burn body fat to produce energy is oxygen. Thus, the more oxygen your body metabolizes during training, the faster and more completely fat will be burned from your body.

There must be a natural, involuntary demand (not a deliberate or voluntary one) for the lungs to aerobate (i.e., to take in continuous quantities of air). This natural demand is caused by prolonged vigorous exercise or rapid motion.

Therefore, fat will not be burned away successfully unless a steady, continuous demand is made on the respiratory system. As more oxygen is carried by the bloodstream in continuous quantities to the remotest areas where fat abides, more cutaneous fat is burned, allowing muscle definition to become visible.

What Makes a Circuit?

A circuit consists of 8 to 12 stations. Each station represents one exercise. At each station you perform a specific exercise, with a specific weight resistance, for a specific number of repetitions that you must do in a time-space of 30 to (a maximum of) 60 seconds. With no rest between stations, you go from exercise to exercise (station to station) until you complete the entire circuit.

Clocking the Circuits

You should record the time it requires you to go through a complete circuit. When you are capable of doing all the repeated circuits in less time than the initial clocking, increase the resistance used in each exercise and set a new target time for yourself. Thus, the total circuit workout becomes a game. You are competing with yourself, and while building muscle and endurance you are adding fun and variety to your workouts.

How to Estimate the Amount of Resistance You Should Handle

If you are eager to try Lee's circuit training workout but are puzzled by how much weight to use, follow this arbitrary rule: Take about one-half the weight you would normally use in a single-attempt lift. For example, if you can do a single-rep bench press with 400 pounds, you should use 200 pounds for your repetitions in a circuit training workout, doing from 30 to 60 seconds worth of repetitions. To make the set progressively more difficult you can also:

1. Increase the resistance used.
2. Increase the total time for the set.
3. Increase the speed of the repetitions (to get more reps).

However, form must not be sacrificed for speed. Do not exceed 30 reps on any one exercise. The concept of circuit training is to increase endurance by aerobic respiration rather than to simply increase strength. However, it can be adapted for strength by decreasing the repetitions but at a continuing fast pace.

The Three Variables of Circuit Training

Lee's method of circuit training has three variables:

1. load (weight resistance)
2. repetitions (sets and reps)
3. time (duration of the circuit or circuits and the tempo or speed of the repetitions employed).

The Art of Expressing the Human Body

Other forms of training, such as Olympic weightlifting, are based on only two variables:

1. load (working with limit poundages)
2. repetitions (low reps and single-limit lifts).

Singular forms of training, such as interval running, make use of two variables:

1. repetitions (fast)
2. time-space (alternating intervals of running/walking or sprinting/slow running).

All three main body functions are affected by this circuit training, and time is the paramount factor. Movements and pace are increased. Progressively greater demands on the respiratory system are comparable to the muscle-growth process caused by increasing the workload, hence building strength and endurance and increasing respiratory capacity.

Thus, the advantage of circuit training for those interested in refining their physique is that while obtaining the aerobic effect of endurance training, you are also performing exercises with weights, which continue to define your muscles and give them added tone, hardness, and separation (referred to in bodybuilding nomenclature as "muscle density" or "quality")—all the while maintaining your ideal muscle size and increasing your endurance capacity for even heavier training!

Who Should Take up Circuit Training—and Why?

Anyone can benefit from Bruce Lee's circuit training program. The program will increase the efficiency of any athlete in any sport, and is of particular value for those seeking to create a highly defined physique. However, aerobic circuit training should not be thought of as just running (which is how most martial artists would define it). Martial artists since Lee's time have understood the value of running for building lung and heart power, but they also realize that they do not wish to break down their doggedly acquired muscle size and development. In short, martial artists do not want to look like runners! That is why Lee's method of circuit training is important

to martial artists: By adding circuit training to a basic bodybuilding and martial art program (albeit with fewer exercises), respiratory function, heart function, power and endurance reserves, and muscle density are all increased.

Acutaneous and subcutaneous fat is oxidized, shape and symmetry are better sculpted, and the loss of fat removes incalculable burdens from the heart while the capacity for muscular endurance is optimally increased. Those who need to get in shape fast can do more circuits in each workout, while those already in good shape should limit their training to about 20 minutes. However, these suggested norms do not include time for post-workout running or martial art training.

How to Get the Most out of Your Circuit Training

If you are heavy, circuit training should be emphasized first in your workout. If you are in good shape, place it at the end of your regular cardiovascular or martial art workout, making sure that your first energy is used to perfect your technique. Then you can apply your remaining energy to circuit training.

Some Pointers for Circuit Training

1. Wear casual or "sweat" clothes, since the purpose of circuit training is to force you to sweat and thus make greater demands on the respiratory system for deeper breathing.
2. Do not rest between stations (exercises). Go from one to another quickly, but be sure to do each exercise with perfect form.
3. Concentrate on speeding up the circuit cycle—in other words, speed your repetitions. Don't pause unnecessarily. Make a determined effort to complete each circuit faster than the previous one.
4. Breathe through your mouth, and breathe as much as you can. Try to inhale as much oxygen as possible while on this circuit workout.
5. After you have become familiar with circuit training and have established a training rhythm, begin to add a few pounds of resistance to each exercise every 2 weeks.
6. Limit each exercise to a maximum of 60 seconds.
7. A complete circuit workout should take at least 8 to 12 minutes. Try to complete at least one circuit, depending on what you want to achieve.

The following is the suggested routine (along with a brief description of the exercises to be performed) that came with Lee's Marcy Circuit Trainer and that he followed for a period of time in 1973.

Bruce Lee's Circuit Training Routine

1. Overhand Pull-Up

Flex your biceps to the point where your chin touches the top of the bar. Lower and repeat for as many repetitions as you can perform in 30 seconds. Move immediately to the next exercise.

2. Seated Leg Press

Sit down in the leg-press seat and place your feet on the uprights. Lean your upper body forward and, using your legs, press yourself away from the machine (push with power). Perform 8 to 12 repetitions in 30 seconds. Move immediately to the next exercise.

3. Bilateral Alternate Hip/Knee Extension (Standing Leg Thrust)

Place shoulders on the vertical pads of the standing leg-thrust station and your feet in the track stirrups. Extend one leg back. Keep your back straight on each leg thrust, alternating legs in a definite rhythm for as many repetitions as possible in 30 seconds. Move immediately to next exercise.

4. Shoulder Press

Grasp the shoulder-press bar and thrust it to full extension overhead. Do not permit your lower back to flex inward. Lower and repeat for 8 to 12 reps in 30 seconds. Move immediately to next exercise.

5. Standing Calf Raise on Shoulder-Press Unit

Adjust the bar on the shoulder-press unit to its highest position. Place a small bench directly underneath the bar and, taking hold of the handles of the bar in each hand, step onto the bench, with your toes facing forward. Flex your ankles as high as possible on each repetition, performing as many repetitions as possible in 10 seconds. Then immediately position your feet so that your toes face outward, and again perform as many repetitions as possible in 10 seconds, then immediately reposition your feet so that your toes face inward and perform a final set of as many reps as possible in 10 seconds. Move immediately to the next exercise.

6. Alternating Cable Curl

Take hold of the cable handles (one in each hand) and alternate curling the handles up to your chin—utilizing biceps strength only. Do not use your lower back. Perform 8 to 12 repetitions for each arm in 30 seconds. Move immediately to the next exercise.

7. Standing Unilateral Horizontal Arm Adduction

Take hold of one of the cable handles and, standing sideways from the machine with your arm fully extended, pull the handle across your chest to full arm adduction. Return the resistance and repeat for the maximum number of repetitions you can perform in 30 seconds. Switch arms and repeat. Move immediately to the next exercise.

8. Bench Press

Lay down on a flat bench and take hold of the bench press bar. Thrust the bar to full extension, keeping your back in contact with the bench at all times. Perform 8 to 12 repetitions in 30 seconds. Move immediately to the next exercise.

9. Regular Deadlift (Squat) on Block, Using Bench Press

Raise the shoulder-press bar to its lowest position and place a small bench underneath it. Stand on the bench. From a deep squat, hold the bar in your hands, your hips and knees flexed, face forward, and buttocks low. Using only the strength of your legs, stand up straight. Return to full-squat position and repeat as many reps as you can in 30 seconds. Move immediately to the next exercise.

10. Kneeling Pull-Down Behind Neck

Kneel beneath the lat pull-down bar and hold it with a wide overhand grip. Pull the bar down behind your neck, pause, and return to the start (i.e., fully stretched) position. Repeat for the maximum number of repetitions you can perform in 30 seconds. Move immediately to the next exercise.

11. Triceps Push-Down

From a standing position, take an overhand grip on the lat pull-down bar. Keeping your thumbs close to your chest, push the bar down until your arms are fully extended. Return the bar to the starting position and repeat for the maximum number of repetitions you can perform in 30 seconds. Move immediately to the next exercise.

12. Cardiovascular Efficiency Activity

Run a short course (outdoors) with enough vigor to be sufficiently winded at the finish. Use short, controlled strides if running downhill, lengthen your stride if you're running on a level surface, and decrease your stride if you are running on an incline. Run as far and as fast as you can in 1½ minutes. Move immediately to the next exercise.

13. Standing Wrist-Roller

Take hold of a wrist-roller bar with a weight attached to the end of it. Hold the roller and weight horizontally out from your shoulders: Wind the weight up with flexions of your forearm and unwind it with extensions. Wind it once, taking no more than 1 minute to complete it, each way. Move immediately to the next exercise.

14. Neck Flexion/Extension

Attach a neck harness weighted with a small weight to your head. Assume a support-hip and knee-flexed position and flex your neck fully, then extend your neck fully. Rotate your neck clockwise, then counterclockwise. Perform 8 to 12 repetitions in each position of extension, flexion, and rotation in 1 minute.

Although this was just one of Bruce Lee's training routines, it ranks among the most effective ever devised for muscle condition and definition and for the well-balanced total fitness that serves a "real-world" purpose.

8. THE *ENTER THE DRAGON* ROUTINE FOR MARTIAL ARTISTS

Once Lee had grown accustomed to the previous circuit-training program, he devised a strength-training workout that he felt was geared more toward his needs as a constantly evolving martial artist.

The muscle groups Lee decided he wanted to emphasize with his strength training were the upper and lower back, the thigh and hip flexors, the calves, the brachialis muscle of the upper arm, the brachioradialis muscle of the forearm, and the shoulders. He also hooked up the low-pulley attachment of his Marcy Circuit Trainer to a special padded strap that he then fastened to his ankle in order to practice the initiation of three kicks: the front kick, the hook kick, and the side kick. This not only allowed Lee to strengthen the muscles involved in the execution of these martial art techniques, but also to focus on the all-too-often neglected aspect of balance during the performance of a kick, and the ability of his muscles to recover to a balanced position immediately after launching it (as well as during its execution). Additionally, working with this strap and pulley against resistance, Lee was effectively strengthening the stabilizer muscles of the lower limbs, thus ensuring that the muscles required for balance would be strengthened and his agility and recovery ability improved.

While this workout focused primarily on several stations on the Marcy Circuit Trainer, Lee incorporated some conventional free-weight exercise equipment into it as well. Lee wrote out this particular routine within the pages of his choreography notes for *Enter the Dragon*, so it is safe to assume that he used it, probably in conjunction with the circuit training routine outlined in Chapter 7, throughout the production of the film and, indeed, for the remainder of his life. In fact, during Lee's last visit to Los Angeles in May and June 1973, he dropped by to see some of his students, including Richard Bustillo, who recalled:

> *The last time I saw Bruce was two months before he died, and I asked him, "Are you working out every day still?" And Bruce jumped to his feet and said, "Oh yeah, check this!" He flexed his quadriceps and a muscle that inserted right into the hip joint [the tensor fascia latae] just popped out. "Hit that!" he said. So I did—Jesus! It was just like hitting a piece of wood! Man, it was*

hard! I said, "What's that muscle for?" And he said, "This is for the inverted kick—that's the muscle that pops it out there." He told me that he had been doing special weight training to develop that.

That "special weight training," particularly the low-pulley kicking exercises, constitutes the routine that follows.

A. The Back

1. Kettlebell Rows (25, 50, 75, and 100 lbs.)

A kettlebell is a form of dumbbell with a handle (much like you would find on a suitcase) that is connected to a dumbbell bar with weights on either end. The kettlebell allows you to perform your dumbbell exercises without any undue wrist strain, and also to increase the effective range

of motion in most conventional dumbbell exercises. As with most rowing movements, one-arm dumbbell rows—performed either with or without the kettlebell attachment—place direct stress on the latissimus dorsi, trapezius, rear deltoids, biceps, brachialis, and forearm flexor muscles, and secondary stress on the remaining muscles of the back. To perform this exercise, place a moderately weighted kettlebell on the floor next to a flat bench. Grasping the weight in your left hand, place your right hand on the bench to brace your torso in a position parallel with the floor (a position you should retain for the duration of your set). Place your right foot forward and left foot to the rear, straighten your arm, and raise the kettlebell 1 or 2 inches from the floor. Keeping your elbow back, slowly pull the kettlebell upward until its inner plates touch the side of your torso. In this position, rotate your left shoulder upward. Reverse the movement and then return the kettlebell slowly to the starting position. Repeat for 8 to 12 repetitions, then reverse your body position, transfer the kettlebell to your right hand, and repeat the exercise for an equal number of repetitions. Then, increase the weight by picking up the next-heaviest kettlebell in the sequence and repeat the exercise.

2. Deadlifts

This is one of the best movements for building terrific back-muscle mass and overall body power. Direct stress is placed on the spinal erectors, buttocks, quadriceps, forearm flexors, and trapezius muscles. Secondary stress is placed on virtually every other muscle group in the body, but particularly the remaining muscles of the back and hamstrings. To

perform this movement, load up a barbell and place it on the floor. Set your feet about shoulder-width apart, with your toes pointing straight ahead and shins touching the bar. Bend over and take a shoulder-width overgrip on the bar. Keep your arms straight throughout the movement. Flatten your back and dip your hips to assume the correct pulling position, in which your shoulders are above the level of your hips and your hips above the level of your knees. Slowly lift the barbell from the floor to a position across your upper thighs first by straightening your legs and then extending your torso so that you are standing erect with your arms straight down at your sides and the bar now resting across the front of your upper thighs. Reverse the movement to slowly return the barbell back along the same arc to the floor. Repeat the movement for 8 to 12 repetitions.

3. Hyperextensions on the Back Machine

This exercise places direct stress on the hamstrings, glutes, and spinal erectors. Minimal secondary stress is placed on the other muscles of the back. To perform this movement, stand in the middle of a hyperextension bench facing the large pad. Lean forward and place your hips on the pad, allowing your heels to come to rest beneath the smaller pads behind you. Keep your legs straight for the entire set. Place your hands behind your head and neck. Allow your torso to hang directly downward from your hips. Use your lower back, glutes, and hamstring strength to raise your torso upward in a sort

of reverse sit-up, until your torso is above an imaginary line parallel with the floor. Return slowly to the starting point and repeat for 8 to 12 repetitions. Incidentally, if you do not have a hyperextension bench, you can still perform this movement with the assistance of a training partner. Simply lie with your legs across a high exercise bench or a strong table. Your partner can restrain your legs by pushing down on your ankles, allowing you to do the exercise. For added resistance, hold a loose barbell plate (or two) behind your head and neck as you do the movement.

B. The Thighs

1. Standing Leg-Thrust Machine

This exercise strengthens and assists the hip-extension efforts of the hamstrings group and the gluteus maximus. It brings into play the fixation work of the iliocostalis lumborum and quadratus lumborum. With the body weight forward, the extension of the knee backward results from the combined pulling action on the joint by the hamstrings and the gastrocnemius. Note that the starting position must be forward of the vertical line of the trunk and hips. Standing next to the thrust station, place one foot on the stirrup in one of the two tracks on the leg thrust station. After settling in so that you are perfectly balanced, take hold of one of the two vertical uprights at the front of the station and thrust your right leg behind you (simulating a rear kicking motion) forcefully. Repeat for 12 to 20 repetitions and then switch legs.

2. Leg Extensions

This exercise can either be performed on a proper leg-extension machine, or by attaching a leather strap to one or both of the base pulleys, putting your feet through the straps, and then sitting down on a flat bench and extending your legs. In either case, make it a point to keep your upper body vertical—do not allow forward or backward trunk movement to occur. Fully extend your lower legs and lower the resistance back to the starting position under full muscular control. Perform the maximum 3 to 4 sets of 12 to 15 repetitions.

3. Seated Leg-Thrust Machine

These seated leg extensions serve to stabilize the movement of the hips and place the rectus femoris in a rather poor mechanical position. This requires that the greatest extension work be done by the quadriceps: the vastus group (externus, internus, and intermedius). The upper body must be kept vertical and slightly forward. To begin, place a padded seat on the leg-thrust machine and sit down, placing your feet on the foot pedals. Sit in the seat, with your torso erect, and grasp the sides of the seat at the sides of your hips to keep your body in the seat as you do the exercise. Extend your legs to push yourself away from the pedals as far as possible, and then return under control to the starting position, making sure that the weight stacks just touch each other, then repeat the movement for 4 sets of 12 to 20 repetitions.

C. The Calves

1. Calf Raises

The calf raise is one of the best exercises for developing power in the calf muscles and other leg extensors. It also strengthens the tendons surrounding the all-important ankle joint. The calf raise is performed by standing with the toes a few inches apart, supported on a block of wood (or two thick books or two bricks—anything suitable for raising the toes 3 or 4 inches on a steady base). The heels should be lowered so that the feet are well dorsi-flexed. A barbell should be supported across your shoulders and behind your neck, or you should be holding onto the bench press handles of the Marcy Bench Press station. Raise and lower your heels at a steady rate, rising as high as possible on the toes so that there is a full range of movement at the ankles. For the first month, use just your body weight; do 3 sets of 8 repetitions then increase gradually to 3 sets of 10 repetitions. After one month, add resistance to the exercise.

D. Cable Machine (Hand)

1. Reverse Curl

Performing reverse curls with a cable and floor pulley provides constant tension to the muscle group being trained (in this case the brachialis muscle of the upper arm). In truth, the palms-down grip places the biceps at their greatest mechanical disadvantage. All variations of reverse curls place primary stress on the upper/outer forearm muscles, biceps, and brachialis muscles, and secondary stress on the forearm flexors, assisted by the pronator teres and quadratus. To perform this movement, take hold of the two handles that are attached to the floor pulleys of the Marcy Circuit Trainer, one in each hand. Set your feet a comfortable distance apart and 6 to 8 inches back from the pulley, and stand erect with your arms running straight down from your shoulders directly toward the pulley. Press your upper arms against the sides of your torso in this position, and keep them motionless throughout your set, making sure to keep your wrists straight. Without allowing your torso to move forward or backward, slowly curl the pulley handle in your right hand upward in a semicircular arc from the starting point to a position directly beneath your chin. Tense your upper arm and forearm muscles as tightly as possible in this position for a moment, then, as you begin to return the handle back along the same arc to the starting position, begin to curl the left handle up toward your chin. Continue in alternating fashion until you have completed between 8 and 12 repetitions. Repeat for 3 to 4 sets.

E. Cable Machine (Leg)

1. Lifting the knee and forcefully extending it to front kick
2. Lifting the knee and forcefully extending it to hook kick
3. Lifting the knee and forcefully extending it to side kick

This exercise involves a forceful and vigorous lifting effort of the hip and thigh. A leather ankle strap is attached to the low base pulley on the Marcy machine (or a lower wall pulley S hook). Fasten the strap around your right ankle. Ideally, you should be standing with your support (i.e., nonkicking) leg on a block of wood (which allows you to swing your leg freely without bumping your foot on the floor) about 2½ to 3 feet back from the pulley, facing away from the weight stack. Grasp a sturdy upright or two to restrain your upper body as you do the movement. Allow the weight at the end of the cable to pull your right foot to the rear as far toward the pulley as comfortably possible. Hold both legs relatively straight as you get ready to begin.

Using only the strength of your hip flexors and quadriceps, move your foot forward in a semicircular arc from the starting point to as high a position in front of your body as possible. This movement should involve a real snap: First the thigh is raised, then the lower leg extended to execute a front kick. Lowering your leg back to the starting position, swing your thigh up while simultaneously extending your lower leg into a hook (or roundhouse) kick. Lowering your leg back to the starting position again, position yourself to throw a side kick. Lower your kicking leg back to the starting position and repeat for 8 to 10 repetitions per kick. Place the strap on the opposite ankle and repeat for the opposite leg.

F. The Shoulders

1. Shoulder Press

This exercise, like the standing barbell press, strongly affects the anterior and medial deltoids, the triceps, and the upper-back muscles that impart rotational force on the scapulae. To perform this movement correctly, place a stool between the handles of the shoulder press station of the Marcy Circuit Trainer machine. Sit on the stool facing toward the weight stack, locking your legs around the uprights of the stool to secure your body in position (alternatively, you can face away from the weight stack as you do the movement). Overgrip the handles attached to the lever arm of the press station. Slowly extend your arms to push the handles to straight arms' length overhead. Pause briefly and then slowly return your hands to the starting point and repeat for 10 to 12 repetitions. Perform 3 to 4 sets.

It must be emphasized that this program was just one of many that Bruce Lee experimented with in an attempt to extend the upper limits of his physical potential. To this end, he

The Art of Expressing the Human Body

refused to accept anything—from an exercise routine to training apparatus—that he felt had outlived its productiveness. Such a belief was in keeping with Lee's personal philosophy of jeet kune do, which he described as "Using no way as way; having no limitation as limitation." Lee therefore refused to limit himself to only one routine or one way of working out. He instead employed many different routines and exercises, which effectively served his training and body-building purposes, and prevented his body from becoming accustomed to a prolonged training stress. The constant variety he infused into his workouts not only staved off the possibility of motivational boredom, but also kept his muscles adapting to new and constantly changing training stimuli.

9. SPECIALIZATION: ABDOMINALS

My strength comes from the abdomen. It's the center of gravity and the source of real power.
—Bruce Lee

Of all Bruce Lee's highly developed body parts, perhaps the most visually striking were the muscles of his abdomen. His waist was wasp-thin, with perfectly layered abdominals as well as highly defined serratus and intercostal muscles. Lee was justifiably proud of his abdominal development, for it represented almost a lifetime of sacrifice and denial at the dinner table and tremendous dedication in the gym. As with anything that held his interest, Lee thoroughly researched anything that pertained to the training of the abdomen.

In addition to books on bodybuilding, physiology, and anatomy, Lee kept a separate folder filled with articles from different muscle magazines detailing the principles and routines that the various bodybuilding champions employed in developing their own award-winning abdominals. Lee, in keeping with his philosophy of jeet kune do, conducted research, absorbed what was useful for his interests, discarded the material he considered irrelevant, and came up with a series of exercises and a method of employing them that was essentially his own.

Lee narrowed the field to five major exercises, three of which he would usually perform for his abdomen on any given day (only occasionally would he perform all five, depending on his energy level). Descriptions of these five exercises follow.

The 5 Basic Abdominal Exercises

1. The Sit-Up

Lee's version of the sit-up targeted his upper abdominals and intercostal muscles. He believed that in order to get the most out of any abdominal exercise, fairly high repetitions (15 to 20 reps per set) had to be performed. To perform sit-ups as Lee did, you will require a special slant or abdominal board. Lie down

on the board, securing your feet under a special strap, bend your knees slightly, and then roll your torso upward until your chest is pressed firmly against your knees. Hold this fully contracted position for 1 or 2 seconds and then lower your torso slowly back to the starting position. Lee would also hold his hands behind his neck and twist as his elbow came up, touching his left elbow to his right knee and on the next repetition his right elbow to the left knee. This twisting, Lee believed, increased the effectiveness of the ordinary sit-up.

2. Leg Raises

Lee liked the effect that leg raises had on developing his lower abdominals. Lie back on a flat bench and grasp hold of the uprights (the bars used to support the barbell). Raise your legs about 18 inches past parallel, and then lower them, under control, back to the starting position. (By using the flat bench, Lee's legs were elevated well off the floor from the start, which meant that whenever he lowered them he could obtain a greater range of motion from the movement.) Repeat the exercise for as many repetitions as possible. Lee also performed this movement when hanging from a chin-up bar, locking his legs straight and then lifting his straightened legs up to a 90-degree angle from his torso before lowering them back to the starting position. In addition, Lee would sometimes hold his legs in the raised position on the last repetition and crisscross them back and forth.

3. The Twist

Although this movement can be performed either seated or standing, Lee preferred the latter, believing it was easier to achieve a full range of motion. Lee incorporated the twist into his routine to target his oblique muscles (which reside on either side of your waist—the "love handle" region) and to develop a firm, tight waistline. To perform this movement, stand upright, with your legs straight and feet shoulder-width apart. Holding a stick or light bar across the back of your shoulders, bend forward from the waist as far as is comfortable. From this position, turn from the waist (not allowing your hips to move at all) and try to touch the left end of the bar to your right foot. Then immediately straighten up and repeat the movement, this time trying to touch the right end of the bar to your left foot. Lee determined that 50 repetitions of this movement were the minimum one should perform.

4. Frog Kicks

This is the same exercise described in Chapter 2. The frog kick was said to be the brainchild of Dr. John Ziegler, who worked at the York Barbell Club in York, Pennsylvania, during the 1960s, had stated "Frog kicks stretch and shape the waistline and at the same time help to remove the excess inches deposited around the lower abdomen". Their performance is simple—just hang from a chinning bar and raise your knees up to touch your chest. Repeat for between 15 and 20 repetitions. It's easy, but effective, and is said to work wonders for a bad back.

5. Side Bends

Like the standing twist, the side bend targets the oblique muscles. Stand with your feet wide apart, both hands at your sides, and a dumbbell grasped in one hand only. Making sure to keep both of your knees locked straight, bend your torso directly to the side on which the dumbbell is held until the weight is level with your knee joint. Then slowly bring your body back to the erect position, inclining your trunk slightly past the perpendicular on the other side. During the movement, both the elbow of the lifting arm and the knees should be kept straight. After

The Art of Expressing the Human Body

performing 2 to 4 sets of 15 to 20 repetitions on one side, shift the dumbbell to the other hand and repeat the movement. Lee also made it a point to exhale as he inclined his body to the side and inhale as he regained the erect position.

Reducing and Conditioning the Abdominal Area

Lee believed that the type of food you eat ultimately governs the thickness and density of the outer tissue covering your abdominals, and once you work off this fatty tissue through a combination of a reduced-calorie diet and sufficient aerobic or endurance activity, you can simply continue with a daily exercise program and a proper diet. Lee trained his abdominals daily, which maintained his healthy abdominal wall and extremely trim (at its lowest, 26 inches!) waistline. Lee always ate the right foods, especially those high in protein. He believed that one should keep starches, sweets, and fats to a minimum—after all, why add to the problem while working on it? Occasionally, while training his abdominals or engaging in aerobic activity such as cycling, Lee would wear a neopryne heat belt around his waist. This built up heat in the area he was targeting and helped sweat out much water, resulting in a slimmer appearance.

Abdominal Training Tips and Pointers

1. Work fast, but concentrate.
2. When you can't do any more full repetitions, continue with short range "burns" to give greater muscle development and separation.
3. At the end of each workout, a session of abdominal tensing (i.e., static contractions) will help.
4. Never do any more sets and repetitions on abdominal work than you would on any other muscle you wish to develop. Abdominal work does not reduce—only nutrition and a workout with a minimum of rest between sets can reduce.

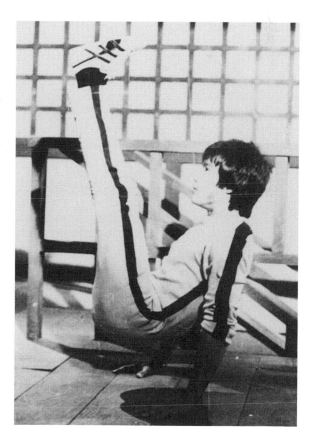

Bruce Lee cautioned students about the mistaken notion of using abdominal exercise as a means to remove fat. It simply cannot do this. Abdominal work will only build muscle. To reduce fat deposits, you must pay strict attention to your nutritional habits and the pace of your workouts.

Lee's Notes and Thoughts on Abdominal Training

> The abdominal and waist region coordinate all parts of the body and act as the center or generator. Therefore, you can promote the ability to control the body's action and master your will more easily.

I haven't been doing the rest of the exercises, but I'm still keeping up with the stomach exercises.

Exercise the abs daily and with patience. Results will soon come.

The proper way of doing sit-ups isn't just to go up and down, but to curl yourself up; to curl your back up, like rolling up a roll of paper.

Bruce Lee's Abdominal Routines

Stomach Exercises

1. Waist twist—4 sets of 70
2. Sit-up twist—4 sets of 20
3. Leg raises—4 sets of 20
4. Leaning twist—4 sets of 50
5. Frog kick—4 sets of as many as possible

Stomach/Waist Exercises (2 sets)

1. Roman chair sit-up
2. Leg raises
3. Side bends

Running

1. Sit-up—4 sets of 20
2 Leg raises—4 sets of 20
3. Side bends—4 sets of 15 to 20

The Art of Expressing the Human Body

10. SPECIALIZATION: FOREARMS

Never cheat on any exercise; use the amount of weight that you can handle without undue strain.
—Bruce Lee

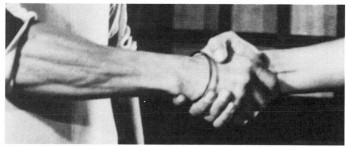

Bruce Lee was a strong believer in forearm training to improve gripping and punching power. "He was a forearm fanatic," recalls Linda Lee Cadwell, laughing. "If ever anyone came out with a new forearm course, Bruce would have to get it."

Lee even commissioned an old friend of his from San Francisco, George Lee (no relation), to build several forearm training devices to which Bruce could add weight for additional resistance. "He used to send me all these designs for exercise equipment," says George Lee, "and I'd build them according to his specs." Bob Wall remembers that Lee's devotion to forearm training certainly paid great dividends in terms of his power and muscularity. "Bruce had the biggest forearms proportionate to anybody's body that I've ever seen," says Wall. "I mean, his forearms were huge! He had incredibly powerful wrists and fingers—his arms were just extraordinary."

Lee was able to beat all opponents in wrist-wrestling, a contest where the two combatant's arms are fully extended with the aim of twisting the opponent's wrist in a counterclockwise direction to win. Lee not only exercised at wrist-wrestling, but according to Herb Jackson, a family friend of the Lee's and another man who used to construct equipment for Bruce, "he wanted to be world champion at it."

"If you ever grabbed hold of Bruce's forearm, it was like grabbing hold of a baseball bat," says Taky Kimura, one of Lee's closest friends and a man who has continued to teach Lee's art in private classes in Seattle, Washington. Lee was so obsessed with strengthening his forearms that he used to train them every day. "He said that the forearm muscle was very, very dense, so you had to pump that muscle every day to make it stronger," recalls Dan Inosanto.

Like the rest of his body, Lee's forearms possessed considerable power, which resulted in devastating punching techniques. (In the photograph below, note the development of the extensor digitorum of his right forearm!) This chapter details Lee's favorite forearm exercises and his instructions on how to perform them.

Forearm Exercises

Wrist-Roller

One of Bruce Lee's favorite forearm training devices was the simple wrist-roller. The wrist-roller, a thick-handled bar with one end of a small piece of cord attached to it and the other end of the cord attached to a light weight of several pounds, is a very effective forearm developer. To maximize its benefits, hold the bar, firmly grasped, directly out in front of you. Then, with the knuckles up, revolve the bar by rolling your wrists until the cord is rolled up completely around the bar. When winding up, turn the top of the bar away from you; do not bend the elbows or the effects of the exercise will be spoiled and much effort will be wasted. Unwind the cord by turning the top of the bar toward you in your hands. When winding either way, be sure to observe the following rules for best results:

1. Hold the arms straight throughout the exercise. Try at all times to hold the bar in a horizontal position. Each time you wind the bar, move your hand through as large an arc as possible.

The wrists will reverse their position each time you wind the bar. Perform the winding steadily. Use a weight light enough to allow you to wind the cord four times, then wind two times either way.

2. Gradually increase the weight used in the exercise. The weight must be limited because of the tiring effects it produces. Since the wrists and forearms tire during this exercise, the tendency will be to twist the bar only a little at a time. However, you should twist the bar as much as possible for the fullest benefit.

An alternative method of performing the wrist-roller is to stand in a raised position on a high box or chair and let the arms hang in front of the body. Grasp the bar as just described and perform the exercise in the same manner. This method will not tire the arms as quickly as when you hold your arms directly in front of you (the muscles are affected somewhat differently). It is less difficult to perform but still effective. Perform the exercise using the standard method then follow with this method. You may also alternate during various exercise periods. The wrist-roller is an excellent exercise for the forearms and wrists and must be included in your training program. It has been used for years by many outstanding strongmen.

Fingertip Push-up

Fingertip push-ups are excellent for developing and strengthening the fingers. Assume the same position that you would if you were about to perform a series of push-ups on the floor, except you should support the weight of your body on the fingers. At first it may be necessary to use all the fingers to support the body, but as they strengthen, use one finger less—it will result in great development and strength. Lee was able to perform this exercise using only the index finger and thumb—of one hand!

Reverse Curl

The reverse curl strengthens the extensor muscles on the backs of the forearms. Grasping a barbell with an overhand grip, stand erect so that the barbell is resting in front of the thighs, at arm's length. Keeping the upper arms motionless, bend the elbows and raise the barbell until the forearms are horizontal to the floor. Pause for 2 seconds and then continue the movement until the bar touches the chest. Lower the barbell at the same speed as during the upward movement, observing the pause when the forearms are horizontal to the floor. Inhale as the weight is raised; exhale as it is lowered.

Cable Reverse Curl (Marcy Circuit Trainer)

Performing reverse curls using a cable and floor pulley provides constant tension to the muscle group being trained (in this case the brachialis muscle of the upper arm) from beginning to end.

In truth, the palms-down grip represents the position of the biceps's greatest mechanical disadvantage. All variations of reverse curls place primary stress on the upper and outer forearm muscles, biceps, and brachialis muscles, and secondary stress is on the forearm flexors, assisted by the pronator teres and quadratus.

To perform this movement, take hold of the two handles attached to the floor pulleys of the Marcy Circuit Trainer, one in each hand. Set your feet a comfortable distance apart and 6 to 8 inches back from the pulley, and stand erect, with your arms running straight down from your shoulders directly toward the pulley. Press your upper arms against the sides of your torso in this position, and keep them motionless like this throughout your set, being sure to keep your wrists straight. Without allowing your torso to move forward or backward, slowly curl the pulley handle in your right hand upward in a semicircular arc from the starting point to a position directly under your chin. Tense your upper-arm and forearm muscles as tightly as possible in this position for a moment, then, as you begin to return the handle back along the same arc to the starting position, begin to curl the left handle up toward your chin. Continue, in alternating fashion, until you have completed between 8 and 12 repetitions.

Gripping Machine

This unique forearm-training apparatus was built specifically for Bruce Lee by his friend and student, George Lee. Bruce Lee actually designed the machine on paper according to his own exacting standards, and had George Lee (who was a masterful metal worker) construct it. The device was kept in Bruce's office in Bel Air, so that he could train the gripping or flexor muscles of his forearms whenever he had a spare moment. The machine featured an upper bar that was fixed in position, and a lower handle that could be pulled up to come in contact with the upper bar. Attached to the lower handle were several barbell plates (totalling, in some cases, in excess of 100 pounds!) that provided the resistance Lee required to overload his forearms on a progressive basis.

The object of this exercise is to open and close your hand into a fist, with every movement of your hand subjected to intense muscular overload. Lee performed 8 to 20 repetitions of forearm gripping with the tops of his hands facing forward, and then 8 to 20 repetitions of forearm gripping with the tops of his hands facing backward.

The Art of Expressing the Human Body

Zottman Curl

According to Linda Lee Cadwell, Lee practiced Zottman curls constantly, usually while he was in his office reading a book. Lee kept a dumbbell in his office, and whenever the mood would strike him, he'd pick it up and perform Zottman curls to strengthen his forearms. To execute this exercise properly, stand with your feet shoulder-width apart, holding a dumbbell in each hand in the "hang" position (you can also perform this exercise using only one dumbbell and alternating it after each set). Curl the dumbbell in the left hand to the left shoulder, keeping the upper arm still but permitting the dumbbell to pass toward the right side of the body during the movement. When the elbow is fully bent, rotate the hand so that the palm is downward; then lower the dumbbell to the starting position, at the same time taking the dumbbell away from the body as far to the left as possible (without altering the position of the left upper arm). When the left hand has been rotated and the weight is being lowered, the dumbbell in the right hand should be curled (across the body) to the right shoulder. The dumbbell in the left hand will be starting again on the upward movement as the right hand is rotated and the (right) dumbbell is lowered. Each dumbbell makes a circular movement, which should be performed smoothly and rhythmically.

Barbell Wrist Curl (Seated)

The barbell wrist curl targets the flexor muscles on the underside of the forearm. Take a look at Bruce Lee's forearm in the picture shown here, a scene from the film *The Game of Death*, in which he is spinning the nunchaku. This shows just how impressive the gripping, or flexor, muscles can become. Note the thickness of the belly of Lee's flexor muscles, such as the flexor carpi ulnaris, palmaris longus, flexor carpi radialis, flexor digitorum superficialis, and flexor digitorum profundus.

To begin this exercise, take hold of a barbell with your palms forward and your hands spaced shoulder-width apart. Sit on a chair or stool and rest your forearms along your thighs so that your hands project 2 or 3 inches in front of the knees. Maintaining this position of the forearms, extend the wrists, lowering the barbell as far as possible, then flex the wrists, raising the barbell by forearm strength only. Return to the original position and repeat. The barbell should be grasped tightly, and only the hands should move in this exercise.

Reverse Wrist Curl (Seated)

The reverse wrist curl is often neglected, but it can add bulk and strength to the many muscles on the top of the forearm. Take hold of a lightweight barbell with your palms facing downward toward the floor. The hands should be spaced a little closer together than shoulder-width. Sit on a chair or a stool and rest your forearms along your thighs so that the hands project 2 or 3 inches in front of the knees. Maintaining this position of the forearms, extend the wrists, lowering the barbell as far as possible, then contract the flexor muscles, raising the barbell by forearm strength only. Return to the original position and repeat. As with the previous exercise, the barbell should be grasped tightly, and only your hands should move in this exercise.

The Leverage Bar

A leverage bar can be almost anything. Grab an empty exercise bar a little off center and you've got a leverage bar. Bruce Lee used to use the leverage bar quite frequently: He would flex his wrist upward for a series of repetitions, then switch his grip and flex his wrist backward for a series of repetitions. Then he would rotate the bar clockwise and counterclockwise to work every fiber group in his forearms. Certainly there could be no arguing with the results he achieved!

Lifting Weights with Different Fingers

This type of exercise, in which often only one finger is used, is a superb way of building a tenacious grip. The great German strongman, Herman Gorner, often lifted weights with different fingers as a means of strengthening his digits so they could hold the massive weights his back was capable of hoisting in the deadlift. There are many, many different ways of performing this type of strengthening exercise: chinning, lifting barbells and dumbbells, and so on.

The Isometric Squeeze

The beauty of this exercise is that you simply need something to grab (such as a pair of spring-loaded grippers or a tennis ball) and a little determination. Try to sustain the squeeze for 10 to 15 seconds. The only drawback to this exercise is that it's not too interesting, since you can't

measure your progress. You can, however, if you have access to a dynamometer. Though a bathroom scale can also be used, a dynamometer is superior because the needle stops at the highest mark registered during the squeeze.

The "Dos" and "Don'ts" of Forearm Training

- Do a complete extension and contraction.
- Do all exercises at a reasonable speed to keep the muscles warm.
- Don't cheat on any of the exercises.
- Don't allow the weight to roll down the fingers—keep fingers closed and maintain a good grip on the bar at all times.

Tips, Pointers, and Additional Programs

Any movement that involves both a fairly complete contraction and extension of the wrist and resistance will benefit the strength, size, and shape of the forearms. In beginning a forearm-specialization program, which should be done approximately three times a week, choose one exercise for the inner forearm and one for the outer forearm. Begin with your exercise for the inner forearm and perform 3 sets of 10 repetitions. After a brief rest, commence the exercise you have chosen for the outer forearm and perform 3 sets of 10 repetitions. Add a set for each muscle group every week until you have 6 sets for each group. If the weights become light as you progress, add a few pounds from time to time, until it becomes an effort to do the last few repetitions of each set.

The Power Program

The power program starts with whatever weight you can handle for 5 sets of 15 repetitions. Each week try to add 5 pounds to the exercises and keep the reps at 15.

The Muscularity Program

The muscularity program uses more repetitions than added weight, and can be used to give variety to the

power program. Start with 6 sets of 20 reps and add 5 reps each week. In one month, you will be up to 40 reps per set.

The Size Program

If your forearms are small and obtaining size is important to you, spend more time on the inner forearm after you have finished your initial training period. Until you have obtained the girth you feel is right for you, pick two exercises for the inner forearm and perform 4 sets for each exercise for a total of 8 sets. You can experiment on the weight and repetitions as you go along for the sake of deviation.

The Need for Variety

It is advisable to change the exercises (i.e., wrist curl, gripping machine, wrist-roller, etc.) as you go along. The variety will work the muscle groups at different angles and give you a better overall development.

Use Thick-Handled Dumbbells and Barbells

Since thick-handled dumbbells and barbells can be difficult to find, simply wrap a thick piece of foam rubber or tape around a bar where it is to be gripped. This way, any desired thickness can easily be achieved. After a few workouts with these thick bars, you will quickly begin to fill out your shirtsleeves.

Bruce Lee's Writings on Forearm Training and Equipment

Do the exercises with complete extension and contraction by maintaining a good grip on the bar at all times. For better results, thicken the bar by wrapping something around it; above all, never cheat on any exercise; use the amount of weight that you can handle without undue strain.

Carry sponge gripper and use daily as much as possible.

[To George Lee] By the way, the grip-machine you made for me is darn good, and it helps me in my training very much.

[To George Lee] I must thank you once more for the grip machine (not to mention the dip bar, the name plate, and others). When you make something it's always professional. . . . My gripping power and forearms have improved—thanks for your wrist-roller.

Bruce Lee's Forearm/Grip Training Routines

Forearm Exercises
1. Underhand wrist curl—4 sets of 17
2. Overhand wrist curl—4 sets of 12
3. Leverage bar curl (A)—4 sets of 15
4. Leverage bar curl (B)—4 sets of 15
5. Reverse curl—4 sets of 6
6. Wrist-roller—4 complete windings
7. Leverage bar twist—3 sets of 10

Grip Training (every chance—daily)
1. Gripping machine—5 sets of 5
2. Pinch gripping—5 sets of 5
3. Claw gripping—5 sets of 5

Finger Lifts
1. All five (left and right)

Wrist Training
1. Barbell rotation—5 sets of 5
2. Leverage bar—3 sets of 10
3. Extended leverage bar—3 sets of 5

Forearm Training
1. Reverse curl—3 sets of 10
2. Palm-up wrist curl—3 sets of 12
3. Palm-down wrist curl—3 sets of 12

4. Wrist-roller—wind up and down once

(*Note:* Carry sponge gripper and use daily as often as possible)

1. Reverse curl—3 sets of 10
2. Flexor wrist curl (B or D)—3 sets of 10
3. Extensor wrist curl (B or D)—3 sets of 10
4. Wrist-roller—as much as you can

(*Note:* B = barbell; D = dumbbell)

Forearm Grip and Wrist Exercises

1. Finger—finger lift
2. Grip—pinch grip, claw grip, gripping machine
3. Forearm—palm up, palm down, reverse curl
4. Wrist—leverage bar, barbell rotation

11. BRUCE LEE'S TOP 7 EXERCISES FOR THE NECK AND SHOULDERS

We should not neglect the training of our neck muscles.
—Bruce Lee

Anyone who saw Bruce Lee's phenomenal shoulder-blade rotation sequence in the movie *The Way of the Dragon* came away amazed at how a person could elicit such dramatic development and control over their muscles. Lee's deltoids and neck muscles were dense and defined—largely the result of many hours of martial art training, such as hitting the heavy bag, the top-and-bottom bag, and the speed bag, practicing chi sao and, of course, more conventional exercises. The only time Lee ever spoke publicly about the importance of neck training was during an interview he gave to Hong Kong's TV-B television station in 1972:

> *We should not neglect the training of our neck muscles.*
> *This kind of training is very important in sports. In the*

training of neck muscles, an athlete may use the "neck press" method and "neck lift" method. In these methods, you tie a weight to your neck and lift it up with your neck, then move to the left and right. As time goes by, your neck muscles will become stronger and more powerful. It also strengthens your alimentary canal and bronchial nerve.

Later in the interview Lee elaborated on some of the reasons one should strive to develop a strong neck in his or her training:

If a man has a strong neck, he probably is a man of power. This training will also strengthen the tissues of your head. A man with a strong neck will not be knocked out easily. An athlete is like this. A boxer should also be trained in this way so that he will not be beaten down easily. A martial artist should do more neck muscle training so that he can have a strong neck.

With this in mind, here are the neck and shoulder exercises that Bruce Lee held to be the most effective:

1. The Wrestler's Bridge
One of the fundamental exercises Bruce Lee found effective for strengthening and developing the neck was the wrestler's bridge. To perform this movement properly, lie down with your back on the floor and a cushion or mattress under your shoulders. Draw your feet up close to your buttocks. With the assistance of your hands, arch your back so that your legs

The Art of Expressing the Human Body

and the crown of your head (which should rest on the cushion or mattress)—and not your shoulders—are supporting your body weight. Maintaining this position, grasp hold of a light barbell with a shoulder-width grip, pull it over your face to your chest, then press it to arm's length. Holding the weight in this position, lower your shoulders by neck strength alone until they almost touch the floor. Then, by neck strength, lever them up again until the resistance is once again borne by the crown of the head. (It may be necessary to perform this movement without weights during the first 2 weeks of training.) This exercise is effective for building a strong, muscular neck. Lee recommended that you start out by performing 8 to 10 repetitions with a suggested starting weight of 15 pounds.

2. Upright Row

The upright row places particular emphasis upon the trapezius and anterior deltoid muscles, but is also beneficial for the allied upper-back muscles and the arms. With your palms facing toward your body, take hold of a barbell. Using a narrow hand-spacing, let your arms fully extend so the barbell is resting across the front of your thighs. Keeping your elbows higher than the barbell throughout the movement, pull the barbell along the abdomen and chest to the throat or chin. The legs and body should remain straight throughout the exercise. The entire action is the pull from the "hang" position in front of the thighs to the throat. Repeat for 8 to 12 repetitions.

3. Standing Barbell (Military) Press

With your hands at shoulder-width, grasp hold of a barbell and raise it to your shoulders. Then raise (or "press") the bar over your head until your arms are fully extended. Repeat for 8 to 12 repetitions. This exercise is great for developing the shoulders, some of the muscles of the upper back, and the extensor muscles (the triceps) of the upper arms.

4. Clean and Press

To perform the clean and press properly, your feet should be approximately shoulder-width apart; in this position you will get a good leg drive as you pull the weight to your chest. The insteps should be directly under the bar and the legs should be well bent, but not bent to the extent of having the tops of the thighs parallel to the ground. The back should be flat. This does not mean vertical or horizontal, it means that the spine should be straight instead of rounded. The hands should grasp the bar just a little wider than shoulder-width apart and the arms should be perfectly straight, since the first pull is produced by the leg and back muscles. As you lift the bar off the ground, keep your weight evenly balanced on both feet and not too far for-

ward or backward. The movement should be a vigorous one, with the legs and back extending quickly. Pull hard and then quickly dip a little at the knees to receive the bar at the chest. It should land in the pressing position at the top of the chest and the legs should be straightened immediately. This is all performed in one fast, continuous movement. As you straighten the legs, ease your thighs forward and lift your chest high, pulling the shoulders back and down. With the bar over the heel of the hand and the forearms in a vertical position, you are then ready to press on (see military press, above). Repeat for 8 to 12 repetitions.

5. Press Behind Neck

A variation of the military press Lee used from time to time was the press behind neck. This exercise is performed identically to the military press, with the exception that when the barbell is cleaned to the chest, it is then pressed

upward and back behind the head so that it comes to rest across the back of the neck. Maintaining the erect position of the trunk, the movement is simply a press of the barbell to arm's length overhead, then lowering at the same speed to the starting position behind the neck. It is important to keep your trunk vertical during this exercise. Make it a point to inhale during the pressing movement and exhale as the weight is lowered. Repeat for 8 to 12 repetitions.

6. Seated Shoulder Press (Marcy Machine)

Like the standing barbell press, the seated shoulder press affects the anterior and medial deltoids, the triceps, and the upper-back muscles that impart rotational force on the scapulae. To perform this movement correctly, place a stool between the handles of the shoulder press station of the Marcy Circuit Trainer machine. Sit on the stool facing toward the weight stack, locking your legs around the uprights of the stool to secure your body in position. (Alternatively, you can face away from the weight stack as you do the movement.) Take an overgrip on the handles attached to the lever arm of the press station. Slowly extend your arms to push the handles to straight arm's length overhead. Pause briefly, then slowly return your hands to the starting point and repeat for 8 to 12 repetitions.

7. Dumbbell Lateral Raise Standing

The lateral raise is an effective isolation movement for the lateral head of the deltoid or shoulder muscles. It can be performed either sitting or standing, although Lee's preference was to perform it from a standing position. To get the maximum benefit from this exercise, stand erect with the feet slightly apart and the dumbbells held in the "hang" position in front of your thighs.

Keeping your arms straight—and without leaning backward from the waist—raise the dumbbells sideward, with your knuckles facing upward, until your hands are level with the shoulders. Pause for 2 seconds, at the same time turning the dumbbells so that your palms face upward. Now raise the dumbbells—with your arms still straight—until they are overhead. Resume the starting position by reversing the movement, again observing the pause at shoulder level. Inhale as the weights are raised; exhale as they are lowered. Repeat for 8 to 12 repetitions.

12. BRUCE LEE'S TOP 10 EXERCISES FOR THE CHEST

Bruce Lee didn't want to build a big, bodybuilder type of chest for the simple reason that it wasn't practical in his line of work. In fact, he considered an overdeveloped chest to be an obstacle that could prevent an individual from covering up properly if a blow should suddenly be shot at one's midsection. But Lee certainly recognized the importance of a strong chest. He realized that even to move your hand across your midline to block a strike requires a contraction of the pectorals, or chest muscles. The pectorals are involved in any type of punching movement, such as uppercuts, hooks, and crosses, for their primary function is to draw the arm from an outstretched position toward the centerline of the body.

Lee narrowed down the field of chest exercises to several variations of the bench press as well as a couple of isolation movements. The instructions that follow were created by Lee for his student Dan Inosanto, and show Lee's knowledge of the regions of the chest that were affected by specific chest exercises.

1. The Bench Press

To perform the bench press exercise correctly, lie back on a flat bench so that your shoulders are pressed firmly on it. Bring a barbell to arm's length, using a wide grip. Lower the barbell to the chest, then press it overhead to arm's length, ensuring that it is kept fairly high up over the chest and not allowed to come too far toward the abdomen when lowered. Take a deep breath as you lower the barbell to the chest, and exhale as the press to arm's length is completed. Repeat for anywhere from 6 to 12 repetitions.

2. Marcy Machine Bench Press

This exercise can be performed on a flat, incline, or decline bench, and as such is similar to the same exercise done with a barbell. Marcy machine bench presses work the entire pectoral muscle mass, while it is believed (though not yet verified) in the bodybuilding community that incline presses work the upper pecs and decline presses stress the lower and outer sections of the pectoral complex. All three variations place intense stress on the anterior-medial deltoid heads, the triceps, and upper-back muscles. Since Bruce Lee used a flat bench when performing his machine presses, this is the movement we will focus on.

Slide a short bench between the handles of the bench press station of the Marcy Circuit Trainer machine. The bench should be positioned so that your shoulder joints are directly beneath the pressing handles when you are lying on the bench. Reach up to take an overgrip on the handles, positioning your hands in about the middle of the handles. Straighten your arms to raise the pressing handles to straight arm's length, directly above your shoulders. Be sure to keep your elbows back as you do the movement, slowly bending your arms and lowering the weight downward until your hands are resting at shoulder level. Without bouncing the weights in the stack, slowly press the handles up until your arms are straight again. Repeat for 6 to 12 repetitions.

3. Decline Press

The decline press exercise should be in the repertoire of every bodybuilder, for no exercise is as effective for carving a sharp outline under the pectorals as this one. To perform this movement, you will need a special bench that declines and that has roller pads for your feet to hook under for additional support. Remove the barbell at arm's length from the supports and hold it above the chest until you achieve a feeling of control and balance. Then slowly lower the barbell to the lower chest. A brief pause is observed before the barbell is pressed back, smoothly, to the starting position. Repeat for 6 to 12 repetitions.

4. Incline Press

The incline press can be performed with a barbell or dumbbells, and is a key exercise for acquiring that high, wide, flaring-into-deltoids look that Bruce Lee had. A special incline bench is required with supports to hold the weight. Lie back on the incline bench and take a shoulder-width grip on the barbell. Extend your arms fully, thereby lifting the barbell from its supports. Pause briefly in this fully extended position to ensure proper balance. Once balance has been obtained, slowly and deliberately lower the barbell to your upper chest. Pause briefly in this position and then press it back to the starting position. Repeat for 8 to 12 repetitions.

5. Close-Grip Bench Press

The close-grip bench press is performed with your hands closer together. The performance, apart from the hand spacing, is exactly the same as the bench press. This exercise has a terrific thickening effect on the pectorals, pumping them up tremendously. However, when the hands are touching, the triceps are affected more than the pecs. Repeat for 6 to 12 repetitions.

6. Dumbbell Press

Another variation of the barbell bench press is the two-hands dumbbell press. A far greater stretch is afforded when the bench press is performed with dumbbells instead of the barbell. The elbows can descend further, thereby increasing the effective range of motion through which the muscle can be contracted. Repeat for 8 to 12 repetitions.

7. Bent-Arm Pullover

To perform this exercise properly, lie back on a flat bench and take hold of a barbell. The bar is held at straight arm's length over the chest, with a slight bend in the elbows. From this position, the arms are lowered overhead (keeping the elbows bent slightly), until a full stretch is felt in the latissimus dorsi muscle of the back. At this point the bar is returned to the starting position over the chest. It is recommended that you inhale as the bar is lowered to the full stretch position and exhale as it is raised over the chest. Repeat for 8 to 12 repetitions.

8. Decline Pullover

The decline angle of this variation of the pullover causes a sharp delineation around and under the pectorals—more so, according to an authority such as Joe Weider, than any other form of chest work. The performance of the decline pullover is the same as the bent-arm pullover, with the exception of the bench on which it is performed. Repeat for 8 to 12 repetitions.

9. Dumbbell Flies

This is the primary isolation movement for the chest. Lie back on a flat bench, holding a pair of dumbbells at arm's length over your chest. Draw your feet up close to the buttocks by bending your knees. Keeping a slight bend in the elbows, slowly lower the dumbbells until a mild stretch is felt across the pectorals. From this position, lift the weights back up to the starting position by moving them in a wide arc to the top (the movement is performed as if you were hugging a big tree), using the strength of pectoral contraction alone—don't turn the movement into a pressing exercise. Repeat for 8 to 12 repetitions.

10. Unilateral Cable Crossover

Lee used cable work for his physique quite extensively once he received his Marcy Circuit Trainer in Hong Kong. The cables, or pulleys, allowed him to stretch his pectorals more efficiently, since there was effective resistance from the start of the movement to the end, applying constant tension to his muscles for the duration of the set. Take hold of two overhead pulley handles, grasping one in each hand and bending forward slightly. Extend your arms out to either side. Drawing your hands toward one another, allow them to cross over in front of you, continuing to pull until you feel your pectorals contract fully. Hold this position for a moment before releasing the tension and letting your arms be pulled back to the starting position. Lee used the cables frequently, for he realized that they allowed him to strengthen the primary muscles necessary to throw all varieties of powerful punches, in addition to sharply defining the pectorals. Repeat for 6 to 12 repetitions.

The Art of Expressing the Human Body

13. BRUCE LEE'S TOP 11 EXERCISES FOR THE BACK

The first and only time I ever heard an entire audience gasp at the sight of one man's physique was when I was sixteen years old. I was sitting in a crowded movie theater watching a shirtless Bruce Lee engage in a series of early morning warm-up exercises in *The Way of the Dragon.* During this sequence, which took place on the balcony of an apartment building, Lee switched from an isometric hand-pressing exercise to a full-blown lat spread—and in that instant—went from an athletic-looking martial artist to Superman! The audience suddenly and collectively gasped at the transformation, and that image of Lee remains vivid in my mind to this day.

Lee had the most pronounced lat (technically, the latissimus dorsi muscles of the upper back) development or "V-shape" ever to grace a movie screen. Undoubtedly, this was partly genetic; Bruce was naturally broad-shouldered with comparatively smaller hips, which resulted in a natural tapering effect. Nevertheless, to develop and maintain his lats required disciplined training. Here are the exercises Lee used to develop his lats and all other muscles of his back:

Upper-Back Exercises

1. Rowing Motion (Bent-Over-Barbell Row)
To perform this exercise, grasp the barbell as if you were going to pick it off the floor and press it overhead, but instead stand erect with it hanging in front of your thighs. Place your feet about 8 inches apart and lean well forward at the hips, keeping the back as flat as possible. Hold this position. Pull the barbell to the lower chest by bending

the arms and raising the elbows backward in an action similar to rowing a boat. The bar should be raised until it touches the lower ribs. Inhale during the raising movement and exhale as the weight is lowered.

2. One-Arm Low-Pulley Row

This exercise is excellent for developing the latissimus dorsi muscle, although some experts believe that the stress is more strongly felt on the lower or insertion area of this muscle group. This exercise also stresses the rear deltoids, the biceps, the brachialis, and forearm flexor muscles. To perform this movement properly you first need to attach a handle to the end of a cable running through a floor pulley. Grasp the handle in your right hand and step back 2½ to 3 feet from the low pulley. Extend your right leg toward the pulley and bend it at about a 30-degree angle. Extend your left leg away from the pulley and keep it relatively straight. Rest your right hand on your right knee and extend your left arm toward the pulley. Starting with your palm facing the floor, slowly pull your hand in to touch the side of your waist, simultaneously rotating your hand so your palm is facing upward at the end of the movement. Reverse the movement and slowly return the handle to the starting point. Repeat for 8 to 12 repetitions, then transfer the handle to your left hand and repeat the exercise. Be sure to do an equal number of sets and repetitions with each arm.

3. One-Arm Dumb-bell (Kettlebell) Row

A kettlebell is a form of dumbbell with a handle (much like you would find on a suitcase) that is connected to a dumbbell bar with weights on either end. The kettlebell allows you to perform dumbbell exercises without undue wrist strain, and also to increase the effective range of motion in most conventional dumbbell exercises.

The Art of Expressing the Human Body

As with most rowing movements, one-arm dumbbell rows—performed either with or without the kettlebell attachment—place direct stress on the latissimus dorsi, trapezius, rear deltoid, biceps, brachialis, and forearm flexor muscles, and secondary stress on the remaining muscles of the back. To perform this exercise, place a moderately weighted kettlebell on the floor next to a flat bench. Grasping the weight in your left hand, place your right hand on the bench to brace your torso in a position parallel with the floor (a position you should retain for the duration of your set). Place your right foot forward and left foot to the rear, straighten your arm, and raise the kettlebell 1 or 2 inches from the floor. Keeping your elbow back, slowly pull the kettlebell upward until its inner plates touch the side of your torso. In this position, rotate your left shoulder upward and then return the kettlebell slowly to the starting position. Repeat for 8 to 12 repetitions, then reverse your body position, transfer the kettlebell to your right hand, and repeat the exercise for an equal number of repetitions.

4. Punching with Weights

Bruce Lee used to do various punching drills while holding light dumbbells. According to Lee, this technique not only developed the proper "snap" in his punches, but effectively stressed the latissimus dorsi muscles. Stand with your back straight and bring a pair of dumbbells to your chest. Place your right foot forward, at the same time striking out with your left arm. Repeat with the left foot forward and stretch the right arm outward. This, of course, is simply one way to perform the exercise; you could also punch repeatedly for up to 100 repetitions in whatever stance you would typically adopt. (See Dan Inosanto's comments on page 49.)

5. Behind-Neck Pull-Down

This was an exercise that Lee performed routinely once he had his Marcy Circuit Trainer assembled in January 1973. The movement requires an overhead pulley and a cambered bar, which will allow you to obtain a greater range of motion. The behind-neck pull-down affects the latissimus dorsi in all of its relationships. It develops strength, such as in the holding power of the

arm extensors, adductors, and inward rotators. The posterior deltoid and teres major act with the latissimus dorsi in the downward pull, as does the pectoralis major, medial head of the biceps, the coracobrachialis, teres minor, and infraspinatus. At the start, the upper portion of the trapezius and the levator scapulae are involved. Near the end of the pull, the rhomboids and mid- and lower trapezius are associated.

To perform this movement, kneel down in front of the lat machine, take a wide overhand grasp on the bar, and allow it to pull your arms up to a fully stretched position above your head. From this position, slowly pull the bar down and behind your neck, making sure that you face forward the entire time. Pause at the bottom of the movement in the fully contracted position for a second or two, then slowly let the bar return your arms to the fully extended position. According to the instructions that came with Lee's Marcy Circuit Trainer, you should perform the maximum number of repetitions you can within a 30-second period.

6. Chin-up (Overhand)

One of Lee's favorite back-building exercises that did not require any special pulleys or other weight-training apparatus was the chin-up. Lee performed this exercise for years and would alternate between chinning to a position behind his neck, where the bar would touch the base of his neck, or to his front, where his chin would actually go over the bar. According to George Lee, his old friend and workout partner in Oakland, Bruce Lee could do other variations of this exercise: "Bruce was exceptionally strong. I vividly remember seeing him perform 50 one-arm chin-ups one day in Oakland. It was incredible! Other times I saw him knock off 50 wide-grip [overhand] chin-ups and 50 dips as well!" Obviously such maneuvers require exceptional strength, but like all athletes, Lee built up to this level of strength gradually, over many years. The standard chin-up was the one back exercise that Lee performed most consistently, however.

He would typically perform this movement with his hands facing forward, using an overgrip on the bar, his knuckles uppermost and his hands slightly wider than shoulder-width apart. Keeping his heels well back and with no forward body movements or jerking, he would pull himself up high until his chest touched the bar, and then lower himself back to the starting position. If you can do 3 sets of 8 or 10 repetitions in this exercise, you are doing very well. Resistance can be increased (should the movement become easy) simply by adding weight around your waist or in the crook behind your bent knees.

7. Chinning to the Back of the Neck

A variation of the chin-up that Lee also performed was the chin to the back of the neck. This movement is slightly more advanced than the chin-up. Instead of pulling to the chest, pull until the back of the neck touches the bar. Both versions are wonderful exercises for the whole back, particularly for the latissimus muscles. Repeat for 8 to 12 repetitions.

Lower-Back Exercises

8. Good Morning

Although Bruce Lee seriously injured his back while performing this movement (see Chapter 5), the accident occurred more as a result of an improper warm-up than of the mechanics of the movement itself. Still, before attempting this exercise it would be wise to heed Lee's retrospective thoughts on how he injured his back and the lessons he drew from the accident.

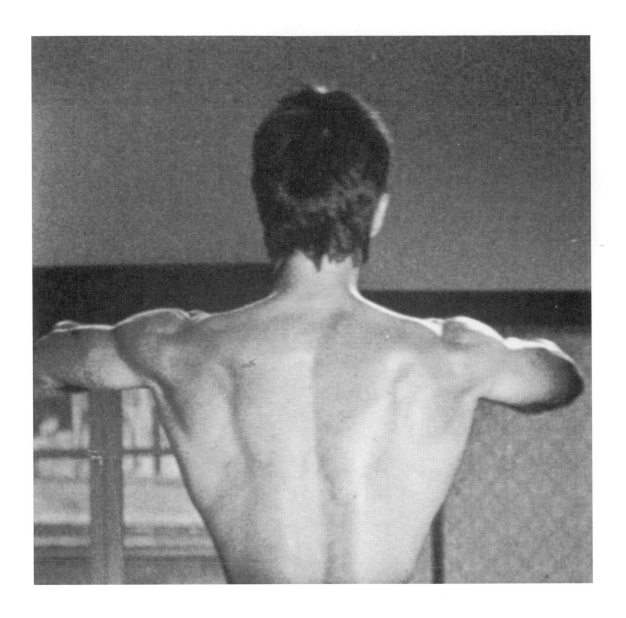

Doing weighted good mornings was stupid of me. All you need is just the bar itself.

Prior to his injury, the good morning movement had been a staple in Bruce Lee's thrice-weekly weight training programs. To perform the movement safely, warm up adequately with a lighter weight than you will be using for the exercise. Once your back (lumbar) muscles are thoroughly warmed up, you can—if you choose—add a little bit of weight to tax the muscles of your lower back. To begin, stand with your legs shoulder-width apart, holding a barbell behind your neck, across your shoulders. Bend your trunk forward, keeping your head looking forward so that the bar does not roll off your neck onto the floor. Try to bend your torso until it is at a 90-degree angle to your legs. Return to the upright position and repeat for 8 repetitions. Exhale as you lower your trunk; inhale as you come up. This is a great exercise for the lower back, and is particularly good for posture since it stretches the hamstrings (i.e., the long tendons at the back

The Art of Expressing the Human Body

of the thighs). A suggested starting weight might be 20 pounds—at the time of Lee's accident he had worked his way up to 135 pounds (his body weight at the time).

9. Hyperextension

The hyperextension places direct stress on the hamstrings, glutes, and spinal erectors. Minimal secondary stress is placed on the other muscles of the back. Lie down on a hyperextension bench so that your hips are against the large pad. Lean forward allowing your heels to come to rest beneath the smaller pads

behind you. Keep your legs straight for the entire set. Place your hands behind your head and neck. Allow your torso to hang directly down beneath your hips. Use your lower back, glutes, and hamstring strength to raise your torso upward in a sort of reverse sit-up, until your torso is above an imaginary line parallel with the floor. Return slowly to the starting point and repeat for 8 to 12 repetitions. If you do not have a hyperextension bench, you can still perform this movement with the assistance of a training partner. Simply lie with your legs across a high exercise bench or a strong table. Your partner can restrain your legs by pushing down on your ankles. For added resistance, hold a loose barbell plate or two behind your head and neck as you do the movement. Repeat for 8 to 12 repetitions.

10. Deadlift

This is one of the best movements for building back-muscle mass and overall body power. Direct stress is placed on the spinal erectors, buttocks, quadriceps, forearm flexors, and trapezius muscles. Secondary stress is placed on virtually every other muscle group in the body, but particularly the remaining muscles of the back and hamstrings. To perform this movement, load up a barbell and set it down on the floor. Set your feet about shoulder-width apart, toes pointing straight ahead and shins touching the bar. Bend over and take a shoulder-width over-grip on the bar. Keep your arms straight throughout the movement. Flatten your back and dip your hips to assume the correct pulling position—your shoulders should be above the level of your hips and your hips above the level of your knees. Slowly lift the barbell from the floor to a position resting across your upper thighs by first straightening your legs and then extending your torso, so that you are standing erect with your arms straight down at your sides and the bar is resting across the front of your upper thighs. Reverse the movement to slowly return the barbell back along the same arc to the floor. Repeat the movement for 8 to 12 repetitions.

11. Stiff-Legged Deadlift

Bruce Lee used the stiff-legged deadlift throughout 1969. He felt it was an effective way to strengthen the lower back for techniques involving throwing (such as those found in judo, wrestling, and jujitsu). To perform this movement, take a firm, overhand grip on a barbell, then raise the barbell until it is hanging in front of the thighs. Keeping the arms and legs straight, bend forward until the barbell almost touches the floor. Return to the erect position without pausing, bringing the shoulders well back. Repeat for 8 to 12 repetitions. This is a general exercise involving nearly all the muscles of the back. Inhale as the weight is raised; exhale as it is lowered.

14. BRUCE LEE'S TOP 11 EXERCISES FOR THE ARMS

As we have seen, Bruce Lee's arms were extremely muscular. Every time he gestured or threw a technique at an opponent, the fibers of his muscles would ripple and undulate throughout his arms. His biceps were peaked and dense, while his triceps (particularly their lateral heads) were exceptionally striated. Lee didn't train his arms for show; their appearance was simply the by-product of the training he engaged in to develop functional strength. Lee divided his research of arm training into two categories, one for biceps and the other for triceps. This chapter presents exercises he found to be the most effective for developing the muscles in both categories.

Exercises for the Biceps

1. Chin-up (Palms Up)

Although long considered a back-building exercise, chin-ups are also a biceps exercise. To fully stimulate the biceps, the palms should be turned in toward you when you perform the exercise and your grip should be relatively close. Jump up and take a narrow undergrip on a chinning bar (there should be only 6 to 8 inches of space showing between your hands). Fully straighten your arms. You can either hold your legs relatively straight, or bend and cross them. Slowly pull yourself up to the bar by bending your arms. At the top point, your chin should be above the bar. Hold this peak contracted position for a moment, then lower yourself back to the starting point.

2. Standing Barbell Curl

Using a shoulder-width grip, with your palms facing forward, grasp a barbell and stand upright with your arms hanging in front of the thighs, keeping the elbows straight. While maintaining this erect position, slowly curl the weight up to your shoulders by bending the elbows, keeping the upper arms still. Bring the bar right up to your chin and flex hard, making sure to hold this maximum contraction for a two-count before slowly lowering the bar back down to the starting position.

3. Concentration Curl

Many people believe that a more intense contraction of the biceps is possible when you use dumbbells, and this is certainly the case when you perform one-arm dumbbell concentration curls. Lee used to perform this movement at his home—usually in his office—where he kept a 35-pound dumbbell handy. Whenever he thought of it, he'd do multiple sets of various repetitions to shock his biceps into additional growth and strength. To perform this movement, bend forward from the waist until your trunk is nearly parallel with the ground, then pick up a dumbbell. Keeping the body in the forward-bend position, curl the dumbbell in the usual manner, making it a point to twist your palm in toward the shoulder at the top of the movement. Hold the contraction for a two-count, then lower the dumbbell slowly back to the starting position. This exercise is exceptionally difficult but worth it—some excellent arms have been credited to this movement.

4. Standing Cable Curl (Marcy Machine)

Once Lee had the Marcy Circuit Trainer set up in his home in Kowloon Tong, Hong Kong, one of his favorite exercises became standing cable curls. The advantage of using a floor pulley for this exercise is that the resistance applied to the biceps is constant (i.e., non-changing) throughout the entire movement, whereas with a

The Art of Expressing the Human Body

dumbbell or barbell, the effective resistance applied to the biceps will change—often dramatically—owing to changes in leverage (going from zero at the beginning of the movement to zero again at the very top, where the barbell falls in to the shoulders). This movement stresses the biceps primarily, and the brachialis and forearm flexors secondarily. After attaching two handles to the ends of two cables that run through the two floor pulleys on the Marcy Circuit Trainer, Lee would stand up straight and let his arms hang down at his sides. His feet would be shoulder-width apart, approximately 1 to 1½ feet back from the pulley station. He would press his upper arms against the sides of his torso and keep them motionless in this position for the entire set, without moving his upper body as he did the exercise. Using biceps strength only, he would curl the pulley handle in his right hand upward in a semicircular arc, from the front of his thighs to a point beneath his chin. The left arm would be motionless at his side until he began to lower his right arm back to the starting position, at which point he would curl his left hand upward. Lee continued curling the handles in seesaw fashion until he completed between 8 and 12 repetitions per arm.

5. Dumbbell Circle

In addition to the biceps, dumbbell circles work the forearms and also the wrists, triceps, and brachialis. The dumbbells are alternately rotated in full, flat circles in front of the body, with the wrists turned up at the bottom on the outward arc and turned downward on the inner arc. Not much weight is required to see impressive results with this exercise. If at the end of your workout you really want to pump up your arms, knock off 3 sets of as many repetitions as you can.

6. Upright Rows

This movement has long been considered one of the best deltoid and brachialis exercises. But it is also an effective biceps exercise. Use a grip (leaving about 6 or 8 inches between the hands), stand erect and pull up steadily and strongly until the center of the bar touches the chin. Pause briefly in this fully contracted position and then return the bar to the starting position. Repeat for 8 to 12 repetitions.

Exercises for the Triceps

The triceps, as its name suggests, is a three-part muscle on the back of the upper arm. If you want larger arms, this muscle group must be given priority.

7. Triceps Push-Down (Pulley)

The triceps push-down stresses the entire triceps muscle (particularly the outer or lateral head of the triceps). To perform this exercise, grasp a lat pull-down bar that runs through the high pulley of the machine. (Alternately, you can use a handle in which the ends are angled downward, or one consisting of two parallel strands of rope.) Use an overgrip on the handle, with your index fingers no more than 3 to 4 inches apart. Stand erect with your feet about 6 inches back from the push-down station, bend your arms fully, and press your upper arms against the sides of your torso. Keeping your upper arms and body motionless, slowly straighten your arms until your triceps muscles are fully contracted. Slowly return the bar back to the starting position and repeat for between 8 to 12 repetitions.

8. Push-up

The old-fashioned push-up, apart from being a wonderful chest developer, is also a prime exercise for the triceps. Many variations of push-ups can be performed, depending on your level of development and strength. They can be performed with your feet on the floor, with your feet elevated on the seat of a chair, or while in the handstand position with your heels against a wall for balance. Be sure to touch your chest to the floor at the start of each repetition and to lock your arms out completely upon completion of each repetition.

9. French Press

A barbell is satisfactory for this exercise, which targets the triceps muscles in isolation. You can either stand or sit, whichever is more comfortable. Place your hands on the shaft of a barbell, about two hand-widths apart. Raise the bar above your head, then lower it behind your neck. Be sure to keep your upper arms close to the sides of your head. Only your elbows are bent. From the lowered position, press the weight overhead by moving your forearms until your elbows are locked. Repeat for 6 to 8 repetitions. Lee would also perform this movement on his Marcy Circuit Trainer, using the base pulley on the machine.

10. Triceps Raise (Barbell Kick-Back)

From a standing position, with a barbell held behind you so that it touches the back of your

thighs, keep your arms stiff and raise the barbell upward, at the same time inclining the torso forward until it reaches a position parallel to the floor. Raise the bar just as far as it will go, and then give a little extra lift at the end to fully contract the inner head of the triceps. Repeat for 6 to 8 repetitions.

11. Dumbbell Kick-Back

The dumbbell kick-back is a very productive and more isolated form of triceps exercise, but many people find the position a bit uncomfortable. Grasping a dumbbell firmly in each hand, bend your body forward. Maintaining the bent-over position, keep your arms bent and lift backward and upward as far as possible. From here, straighten your arms with a "kick-back" action. The finished position does not need to be held for any length of time, but you should try to make it a really fierce contraction so that you will most certainly feel your triceps "burn." Repeat for 6 to 8 repetitions.

15. BRUCE LEE'S TOP 11 EXERCISES FOR THE LEGS AND CALVES

Develop your legs to their utmost strength and flexibility.
—Bruce Lee

If Bruce Lee's abdominals were his most impressive body part, then certainly his legs were the most functional. Lee took leg training seriously and he trained his own legs daily in one way or another. The legs, according to Lee, were the delivery system and one of the most important sources from which all meaningful power is derived. In punching, for example, the initial impetus for the generation of maximum impact power comes from the raised heel of the rear leg. In kicking, full power can only be obtained by the proper alignment of the legs, hips, and torso. The landing and kicking legs must reach their intended destinations (the ground and the target, respectively) simultaneously in order to achieve maximum power on impact.

Lee noted that the weak link in most martial artists' armor was the lower extremities:

In combat, the knees and shins are the weakest parts that lack adequate protection. Once they are hurt, a martial artist will not be able to fight. So it is important to strengthen the training of our knees and to avoid any attack to those parts.

The Art of Expressing the Human Body

To develop his legs to their absolute limits of strength and flexibility, Lee analyzed all types of training and finally settled on the following exercises.

Leg-Training Exercises

1. Squat

Stand with your feet approximately shoulder-width apart and your toes pointing to the front. With a barbell supported across the shoulders behind your neck, bend your knees and lower yourself until your thighs are parallel to the ground. Immediately return to the upright position. Inhale deeply just prior to the knee bend, and exhale as you come to the upright. Fill the lungs a couple of times before each repetition. The back must be kept flat and your glutes should never come up first. On no account must the back be allowed to sag. The heels must remain on the ground at all times.

2. Jumping Squat

From time to time Lee varied the squat by doing the jumping squat. While this is a ballistic movement and therefore has the potential to cause injury, it is nevertheless a very effective variation of the squat. Put a barbell across your shoulders and lower yourself into a full squat position as in the standard squat. At this point, however, you should rise very quickly and jump slightly. Lee found this exercise useful for giving his kicking muscles a quicker "snap."

3. Breathing Squat

To really stimulate his metabolism and to stimulate additional muscle growth in his legs, Lee incorporated a variation of the squat known as the breathing squat. After first warming up your knees and back with a few light squats, put the barbell on a rack and load it up. (Lee noted that if you could find a barbell with a little bend in it, it would ride easier on your shoulders.) Put padding

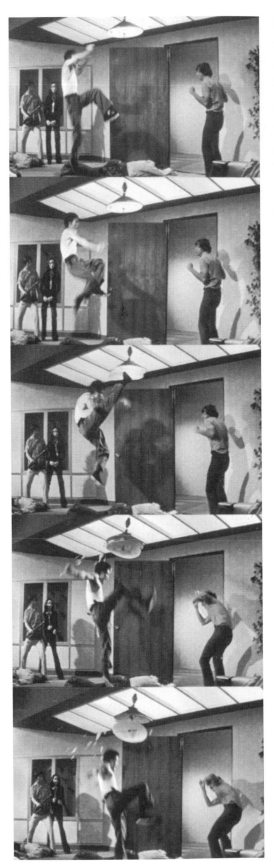

across your shoulders or wrap it around the bar and step under the bar. Straighten up. Back up 2 or 3 steps. Don't back up any further than you have to in order to face the rack when you're squatting. Keep your head up and your back as flat as possible. Fix your gaze on an imaginary spot on the wall just above head height. This will help keep your back flat.

Take three deep breaths, bringing all the air you can into your lungs. Hold the third breath and squat to a position where your thighs are parallel with the ground, then bounce back up as hard and fast as possible. Don't stay in the low position. Exhale with force when you're almost erect. Take three more deep breaths. Hold the third breath and squat. Keep this up for 20 repetitions. You should work hard enough so that squat 15 feels like your limit; then force yourself to continue to twenty. When you finish the set you should be wiped right out. This is the hardest work you'll ever do, but it's an absolute must for success.

4. The Jefferson Lift (Straddle Squat)

Another leg exercise Lee used from time to time was the Jefferson lift, or straddle squat. Straddle a heavy barbell with the right foot advanced and the feet about 24 inches apart. Using a grip slightly wider than shoulder-width, grasp the barbell with your right hand in front of the body and left hand to the rear. Keep your trunk erect and bend at the hips and knees. Stand up with the weight, keeping the arms locked at the elbows, straighten the knees and hips, and hold the trunk in the upright position. Maintaining the erect position of the trunk, bend the knees to lower the body about 4 inches, restraightening them without a pause. During this leg movement only the knees must be bent; any forward leaning of the trunk will negate the value of the exercise. The

The Art of Expressing the Human Body

movement should be performed rhythmically and fairly quickly. The straddle squat is especially valuable for developing the muscles of the thighs and buttocks. It is important to hold the spine erect and keep the knees bent so as to lower the body only about 4 inches. Very heavy weights can soon be handled in this exercise. Perform 8 to 10 repetitions in each of the two alternative hand and foot placings. (Suggested starting weight: 90 lbs.)

5. Leg Extension

Lee performed this exercise (which requires a special leg-extension machine) whenever he had a workout at Paramount Studios (where he trained personal clients such as film director Roman Polanski) or the Golden Harvest film studios in Hong Kong. To perform this exercise, sit on a leg extension machine, with the backs of your knees against the edge of the padded surface (toward the lever arm of the apparatus). Hook your toes and insteps under the lower set of roller pads (if there are two sets). To steady your upper body during your set, grasp either the handles provided at the sides, near your hips, or the edge of the padded surface of the machine. Moving only your knees, straighten your legs

under the resistance provided by the machine. Hold the top, fully contracted position of the movement (legs straight) briefly and then lower your feet back to the starting point. Repeat the movement for 12 to 20 repetitions.

6. Marcy Circuit Trainer Standing Back Thrusts

This exercise adds to the hip extension efforts of the hamstring group and the gluteus maximus. It brings into play the fixation work of the iliocostalis lumborum and quadratus lumborum. With the body weight forward, the extension of the knee backward results from the combined pulling action on the joint by the hamstrings and the gastrocnemius. The starting position must be forward of the vertical line of the trunk and hips. Standing next to the thrust station, place one foot upon the stirrup in one of the two tracks on the leg thrust station. After settling in so that you are perfectly balanced, and taking hold of one of the two vertical uprights at the front of the station, thrust your right leg behind you (simulating a rear-kicking motion) forcefully. Repeat for 12 to 20 repetitions and then switch legs.

7. Marcy Circuit Trainer Seated Leg Presses

These seated leg presses stabilize the movement of the hips and place the greatest emphasis upon the quadriceps; the vastus group (externus, internus, and intermedius). The upper body must be kept vertical and slightly forward. Place the little bench upon the leg-thrust machine and sit down, placing your feet on the foot pedals. Sit in the seat with your torso erect, and grasp the sides of the seat at the sides of your hips to keep your body in the seat as you do the exercise.

The Art of Expressing the Human Body

Extend your legs to push yourself as far as possible away from the pedals, and then return under control to the starting position, making sure that the weight stacks just touch each other. Repeat the movement for 12 to 20 repetitions.

8. Forceful Unilateral Hip and Knee Flexions (Front Kick, Hook Kick, Side Kick)

This exercise involves a powerful, forceful, and vigorous lifting effort of the hip and thigh. A leather ankle strap is attached to the low base pulley on the Marcy machine or a lower wall pulley S-hook. Fasten the strap around your right ankle. Ideally, you should be standing with your support (i.e., nonkicking) leg on a block of wood (which allows you to swing your leg freely without bumping your foot on the floor), about 2½ to 3 feet back from the pulley, facing away from the weight stack. Grasp a sturdy upright or two to restrain your upper body as you do the movement. Allow the weight at the end of the cable to pull your right foot to the rear as far toward the pulley as comfortably possible. Hold both legs relatively straight as you get ready to begin. Using only the strength of your hip flexors and quadriceps, move your foot forward in a semicircular arc from the starting point to as high a position in front of your body as possible. This movement should involve a real snap to it; first the thigh is raised, then the lower leg extended to execute a front kick. Lowering your leg back to the starting position, swing your thigh up while simultaneously extending your lower leg into a hook kick (a.k.a. a roundhouse kick). Lowering your leg back to the starting position again, this time position yourself to throw a side kick. Then lower your kicking leg back to the starting position and repeat for 8 to 10 repetitions per kick. Place the strap on the opposite ankle and repeat for the opposite leg. You can also work each kick for individual sets of 8 to 10 repetitions before moving on to the next set of kicks.

Exercises for the Calves

Bruce Lee believed that the calves were a "high-rep" muscle, meaning that you really had to work them on a daily basis with plenty of repetitions in order to achieve results.

1. Heel Raise

The object of the heel raise is to achieve a springy takeoff. The actual mechanics of the "heel, ball, toe" roll on the takeoff board depend mainly on a forcible extension of the foot from a well-flexed position. The stronger the muscles concerned with this foot extension, the more effective the action. This exercise

is one of the best for developing power in the calf muscles and other leg extensors. It also strengthens the tendons surrounding the all-important ankle joint. The heel raise is performed by standing with the toes a few inches apart, supported on a block of wood, two thick books, or two bricks (anything suitable for raising the toes 3 or 4 inches on a steady base). Lower the heels so that the feet are dorsi-flexed. A barbell should be supported across the shoulders behind the neck. Raise and lower the heels at a steady pace, rising as high as possible on the toes so that there is a full range of movement at the ankles. To start off, use the weight of an empty bar-bell, and for the first month, do 3 sets of 8 repetitions. Then increase gradually to 3 sets of 10 repetitions. Then add 10 pounds to the bar and start again.

2. Variations on the Heel Raise

Lee made it a point to lift his heels as high as he could and then hold the contraction for a second or two before lowering his heels back to the ground. The effort to achieve height is most important. The problem with the heel raise is that the effort is not made directly upward: Some bodybuilders lean slightly forward but even this little bit has a detrimental effect. As soon as you lean forward the weight pulls the body onto the toes and the heel raise then has little effect on the calf muscles. Lee believed that heel raises done with the toes pointed straight forward will have a slightly different muscular effect than those done with toes outward or inward. He per-formed some sets with his toes pointed in, others with his toes pointed out, and some with his toes pointing directly to the front. Repetitions should be in the 10 to 20 range.

3. Seated Calf Raise

Lee felt that the seated calf raise also had value. It is performed in a seated position, with a weight held so that it rests on the knees directly over the insteps. This does take some work off the gastrocnemius, the main lower leg muscle, but gives more work to the underlying muscles, which also contribute to leg size and shape. A block of wood is placed under the balls of the feet so that the heels are positioned lower than the toes. Press up onto the balls of your feet so that your heels are now higher than your toes. Hold this position for a distinct pause and then lower your heels to a position lower than your toes. Repeat for 10 to 20 repetitions.

Leg Training Methods Employed by Bruce Lee
Strength

1. Running
2. Calisthenics (step by bench, alternate splits[1])
3. Cycling[2]
4. Weight training (squat, extension table)

The Heavy and Light System

One principle that Bruce Lee found particularly useful in training his legs was the heavy and light system. Because of the density of fibers found in the lower limbs, most leg muscles respond best to higher repetitions. In Lee's case, repetitions of 12 or more proved to be very effective. With the heavy and light system, you would perform a set of, say, 15 repetitions and then add weight and perform a second set of 10 or 12 repetitions. With added weight for a third set you would probably manage only 8 repetitions, and so on. If you are employing more than one exercise, however, 10 to 12 repetitions for each should suffice.

[1] The term *alternate splits* does not refer to stretching. Instead, the alternate splits that Bruce Lee referred to consisted of alternating your legs in a forward/backward motion while standing. Keeping your knees almost perfectly straight, you would push your right foot out in front of you, and your left leg behind you. Lee also incorporated his arms into the movement by having his right arm move forward in synchronization with his left leg, and his left arm moving forward in synchronization with his right leg.
[2] The type of cycling that Lee engaged in most frequently was performed on a stationary bicycle. However, any type of cycling can be employed to benefit the legs.

16. THE TAO OF FLEXIBILITY

One of the most important components of any martial artist's training regimen is flexibility. Bruce Lee was forever coming up with new methods that helped to make him even more limber, and he always made sure he was thoroughly warmed up before commencing his martial art training. Lee's friend and student Herb Jackson recalls that the only "routine" he ever saw Bruce Lee engage in was his stretching program:

> *The only routines he did steady were the stretching routines he'd go through before a workout, before he'd start fighting or training. One stretching exercise that he did that I never saw anyone else do was one where you'd sit on the floor with a partner, your backs to one another, and he'd push back on my shoulders with his shoulders so that in the finished position my head would be down almost to the floor. This way you'd get more flexibility in the legs. We'd take turns and see how far forward we could go. It was a hamstring stretch.*

The Art of Expressing the Human Body

Even while Lee was busy dubbing dialogue for a film, it was not uncommon to see him with one foot propped up on the back of a studio chair, while he bent forward to keep his hamstrings supple and flexible. In his office at home he had a specially crafted stretching post that could be elevated to a desired level by raising a bar and then inserting two pins to stabilize it. This device allowed Lee to stretch even while watching television or reading a book in his office. Indeed, flexibility was the equal of aerobics in Bruce Lee's training program.

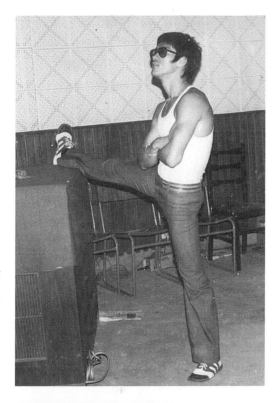

It might seem silly to need to argue the case for flexibility, especially to martial artists. After all, the general public's perception of martial art practitioners is largely one of supremely flexible athletes leaping into the air and delivering spectacular aerial kicks to dispatch adversaries. However, apart from jeet kune do, karate, savate, and certain northern styles of gung fu, flexibility training is not a staple in most martial art curricula.

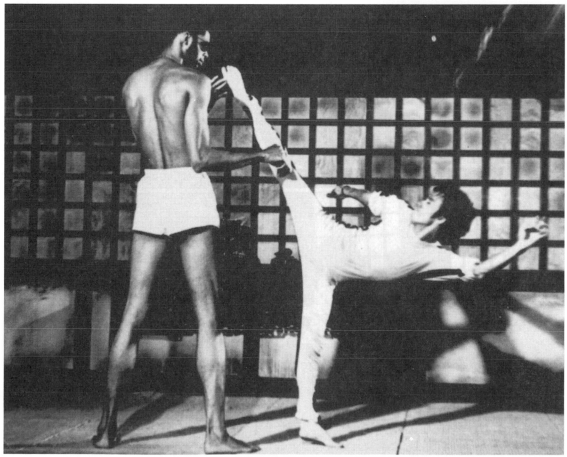

Lee realized that flexibility depends on the joints and the elasticity and firmness of the ligaments, as well as on the condition of the cartilage, which covers the ends of the bones and acts as a buffer to reduce friction. A devoted student of anatomy and physiology, Lee was well aware that the amount of movement available to a given body part depends on the nature of the joint to which it is affixed. A ball-and-socket joint, such as in the shoulder or hip, permits much greater freedom of action than the hinge joint of the elbow or knee. The sliding joint of the ankle is mostly limited to forward and backward movement, while the thumb, with its saddle joint, can be moved freely either forward and backward or sideways.

The results Lee obtained from his flexibility program are obvious whenever one views footage or photographs depicting his battle against NBA superstar Kareem Abdul-Jabbar. In some of these photographs, Lee—who stood only five feet, seven-and-a-half inches tall—kicks Jabbar (who is over seven feet tall) squarely on the chin! Such a feat requires virtually a full side split—performed from a vertical position! These photos taken on the set of *The Game of Death,* and Lee's own incredible stretching and warm-up sequence from *The Way of the Dragon* (just before he steps into the historic Roman Coliseum to engage in a chesslike battle with Chuck Norris), reveal a suppleness of limb that would make an Olympic gymnast envious.

Lee was a strong advocate of flexibility training as far back as 1963, when he devoted several pages of his self-published book *Chinese Gung Fu—The Philosophical Art of Self Defense* to the necessity of keeping limber (and cited several exercises necessary to accomplish this). Even then his knowledge of proper exercise protocol regarding flexibility training proved to be lightyears ahead of that of many of his contemporaries.

Why You Should Stretch

Here are the five most important reasons why a sound flexibility program should form a part of your exercise routine:

1. Stretching improves health and fitness. When combined with proper strength-training methods and aerobic cardiovascular workouts such as running, stretching provides the final one-third of the triumvirate necessary for total fitness.

2. Stretching reduces the risk of injuries. Most everyday injuries and athletic injuries are caused either by trauma (e.g., a fall, a car accident, or impact with another individual) or by overextending a joint, muscle, or connective tissue, which results in muscle pulls, sprains, and strains. Martial artists who follow regular and progressive stretching programs suffer at least 50 percent fewer overextension injuries than those who don't.

3. Stretching is a good warm-up/cool-down for other types of training sessions. In addition, a pre-martial art–session stretching program improves neuromuscular coordination. And when performed immediately after your workout, stretching will prevent soreness and promote faster physiological recovery.

4. Stretching improves athletic performance. A more flexible martial artist is a better martial artist, and a more flexible athlete is a better athlete. Could you, for example, conceive of a gymnast with tight muscles? Any athlete who's more flexible than another automatically has both a physiological and psychological edge.

5. When done correctly, stretching is enjoyable. Have you ever awakened in the morning and, still in bed, slowly stretched your entire body? It felt great, didn't it? In fact, just such a program ("The Wake-Up Routine," page 235) based on a series of static holds (i.e., tensing of a muscle group in its fully stretched or fully contracted position) can be performed before you get out of bed in the morning! It's a great way to prepare your body to face the day ahead.

When to Stretch

Anyone interested in improving his or her flexibility should stretch every day for at least 10 to 15 minutes. If you can manage it, stretching three to four times per week will gradually improve your joint and muscle flexibility, and daily stretching will increase your flexibility even more dramatically. Just to keep his edge, Bruce Lee used to stretch first thing in the morning and then at various times throughout the remainder of the day,

The best time for most martial artists to stretch is just prior to their martial art training—and it should not be a haphazard affair. Before engaging in an activity, many men and women do quick little stretches that are over so fast they could not possibly have warmed up their tendons and ligaments, let alone enhanced their flexibility. You've no doubt seen a runner briefly stretch his or her calves before setting off for a run, or a basketball player quickly stretch his hamstrings before going into a game, but such abbreviated stretching does very little for those looking to improve their flexibility.

For a stretching program to be truly effective as a warm-up, it should last for 10 to 15 minutes and should include flexibility exercises for every part of the body. The same flexibility workout also acts as an excellent cool-down following a strenuous martial art or weight-training workout. You'll truly be amazed at how quickly you can recuperate if you unwind with 10 to 15 minutes of stretching after a workout.

For most of us, the ideal time to stretch is in the evening, an hour or two before bedtime (perhaps even while watching television, as Bruce Lee did). This will help to relieve some of the tension you've built up during the day. It may also give you a sensation some have termed the *stretcher's high,* which is somewhat akin to the endorphin rush associated with the more commonly known runner's high or the "pump" a bodybuilder experiences. In any event, after a particularly effective evening flexibility workout, you will find yourself pleasantly relaxed and should have no problems getting to sleep.

Don't Get Ballistic!

Many martial artists stretch too hard or bounce into a stretch, losing much of the value of the exercise in the process. Correctly applied, stretching is a gentle exercise, and unless you pursue it gently, you will lose most of the benefits it can provide.

Because it's very easy to injure yourself by overextending the range of motion of a joint or a muscle, biology has provided your body with two protective mechanisms. Both are specialized types of neurons (nerve endings). One type senses when a muscle is overstretched and indicates this fact by feeding pain signals back to the brain. The second type of neuron is part of a protective mechanism called the "stretch reflex." When a stretch is sensed to be progressing too quickly, the mind reflexively begins to contract the stretched muscle, which then proceeds to act as a shock absorber, slowing and then halting the stretch before the muscle can be injured. This is somewhat akin to the way your thigh muscles flex to absorb the shock of landing when you jump off a bench or other object onto the floor.

When you stretch a muscle group ballistically (that is, in a bouncing, jerky manner), the stretch reflex is activated and neurons serving the muscle group in question send signals to the brain to actually stop the stretch. So while it may seem that bouncing would intensify a stretch and perhaps bring faster results, such ballistic stretching actually has the opposite effect.

Because of the stretch reflex, the stretched muscles actually shorten, preventing you from reaching a fully stretched position.

To fully stretch a muscle (or joint), you must slowly ease into the stretch in order to prevent the activation of the stretch reflex. In other words, simply take your time easing into the stretch: Take 30 to 40 seconds and move slowly into a stretch to the point where you just begin to feel slight discomfort in the stretched muscle. This is the maximum point to which you should stretch. Should you attempt to stretch beyond this sensory-pain periphery, you can actually begin to pull tiny muscle fibers apart, injuring the muscles.

Now you have enough physiological information to understand the requisites of the perfect stretch. Regardless of the stretching exercises you choose, be sure to take 30 to 40 seconds to ease into each stretch. Then, once you encounter the pain periphery, back off slightly until the pain disappears. Once you've reached this stretching zone, hold the stretch in that position for 20 to 30 seconds, and over time, try to work up to 1 or 2 minutes. Make it a point to breathe shallowly, although with normal rhythm, when holding a stretched position. And finally, relax the stretch and either repeat it a minute later or move on to another stretching movement.

To receive the maximum benefit from your flexibility program, you must discover your personal stretching zone. It's only while holding a stretch in this zone that you will derive the greatest benefit from a stretching program.

Progression in Stretching

When you undertake a stretching program—regardless of your present physical condition—you should try to begin very slowly, as the danger always exists of injuring muscles and becoming very sore if you push too hard.

Beginners' Concerns

Beginners should back away from the pain periphery during their first stretching efforts and hold each stretch for only 20 seconds. They should also do only one repetition of a stretch for each muscle group. From this starting point, they should slowly add to the duration of each stretch (until they are able to sustain it for one full minute) and the severity of each stretch (until they are able to hold it in the upper range of the stretching zone, close to the pain edge).

Once you reach this point, you can either add repetitions to a stretch (i.e., you can begin a second repetition by holding it for only 20 seconds, and then gradually work it up to 60) or add another stretching movement for the same body part (again, beginning with a duration of only 20 seconds). Based on conversations I've had with Bruce Lee's students, Lee worked up to holding his stretches for between 30 seconds and 1 minute.

Flexibility Exercises

Lee's knowledge of exercise science was constantly expanding, and nowhere was this more evident than in his pursuit of flexibility exercises. Every year (some have said every workout) Lee would add a dozen or so new stretches that would enhance the flexibility of his body in different angles, thereby improving his overall flexibility. Here are some of the flexibility exercises that Lee found particularly effective.

The Hamstring Stretch

Emphasis: Hamstring muscles at the back of your thighs.

Starting Position: In the basic hamstring stretch, you lock your legs and extend your arms overhead, clasping your hands.

Stretched Position: Keeping your legs straight, bend over and touch your hands to your feet. As you become more and more advanced, you will actually be able to touch your torso to your thighs in this position.

Variations: There are three variations of this exercise. In the first, the legs are spread and you bend over and grasp your legs individually with your arms. In the second, you bend slightly to the side and grasp the ankle of one leg with both hands, gently pulling your torso

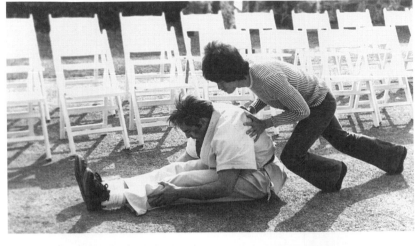

downward. In the third version, begin in a standing position and then bend over at the waist until your chin is flush against your shins.

Hamstring Stretch (with a Partner)

Emphasis: The hamstring muscles at the back of your thighs.

Starting Position: With both legs held straight, stand on one foot and extend the other foot to be held by a partner or to rest on the top of a table or other fairly high, flat surface. Herb Jackson designed a stretching

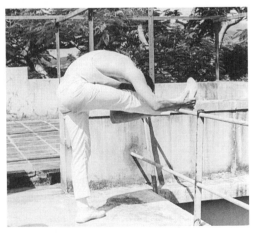

stand on which Lee would place his foot and stretch—even while reading a book. In this exercise, your torso should be relatively upright and your arms extended forward.

Stretched Position: Bend forward slowly and try to press your torso to your thigh. Both legs should remain straight throughout the movement.

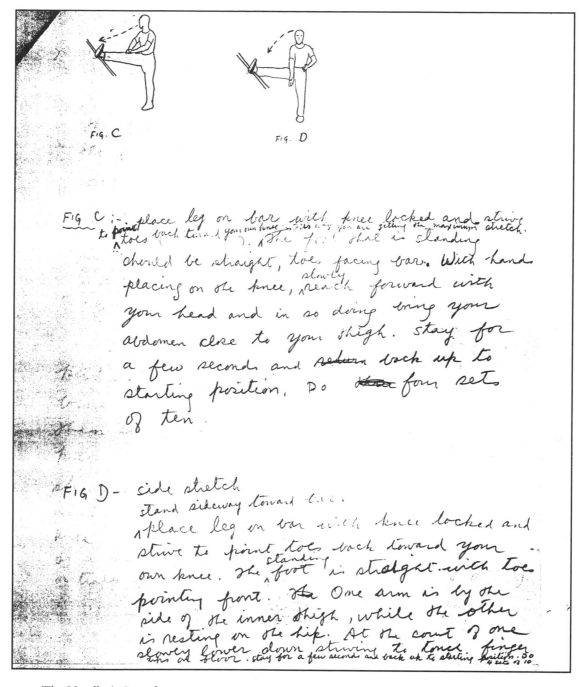

FIG C :- place leg on bar with knee locked and strive
to point toes back toward your own knee (this way you are getting the maximum stretch). The foot that is standing should be straight, toe facing bar. With hand placing on the knee, slowly reach forward with your head and in so doing bring your abdomen close to your thigh. stay for a few seconds and return back up to starting position. Do four sets of ten.

FIG D - side stretch
stand sideway toward bar.
place leg on bar with knee locked and strive to point toes back toward your own knee. The standing foot is straight with toe pointing front. One arm is by the side of the inner thigh, while the other is resting on the hip. At the count of one slowly lower down striving to touch finger tips on floor. stay for a few seconds and back up to starting position. Do 4 sets of 10

The Hurdler's Stretch

Emphasis: The hamstrings and groin muscles.

Starting Position: Sit on the floor and extend your right leg forward, locking it straight throughout the movement. Your left leg should be bent at a 90-degree angle to your right leg and lay flat against the floor behind your body. Your torso should be upright and your arms extended directly forward and parallel to the floor.

Stretched Position: Bend forward slowly over your right leg and grasp your ankle. Gently pull your torso down until it touches your right thigh. After stretching with your right leg forward, do an equal amount of stretching with your left leg forward.

Variation: This stretching exercise can be done with one leg extended directly forward and the other held straight and extended to the side at a 90-degree angle. In another variation Lee used he placed the sole of his left foot on the inside of his right thigh.

Seated Groin Stretch

Emphasis: All muscles of the groin and inner thighs.

Starting Position: Sit down on the floor and bend your legs as completely as possible (ideally, your heels should be right up against your pelvic structure); position your knees close together. Grasp your knees with your hands. Be sure to keep your torso erect throughout the movement.

Stretched Position: Use your hands to push your knees apart slowly until they are as close to the floor as possible.

Standing Hip Stretch

Emphasis: The hip and buttock muscles.

Starting Position: Stand erect. Balancing on your right foot and with your right leg held straight throughout the movement, bend your left leg and raise your knee up until you can grasp it with your hands.

Stretched Position: Pull up on your knee gently until you have reached the maximum range of motion for your hip and buttock muscles. Do an equal amount of stretching for both legs.

The Art of Expressing the Human Body

The Standing Pulley Stretch

Since equipment is required to perform this movement, some set-up explanation is needed. Attach one or two pulleys to the ceiling (if you are using two pulleys, they should be about 5 feet apart) and pass a thin, strong rope through them so that both ends reach the floor. Next, fix the ends so they can be conveniently attached to the feet.

Emphasis: Useful for limbering up and stretching the groin, hip, and hamstring muscles. It can also be used to help train the leg muscles to kick properly.

Starting Position: Attach one foot to one end of the rope and pull the other end with both hands.

Stretched Position: Continue stretching the leg up, either forward or sideward, using your arms to pull the rope gently when necessary to increase the stretch.

Variation: You can pull the rope with one hand to practice correct kicking form.

Lunging Stretch

Emphasis: The muscles of the hips, buttocks, and front thighs.

Starting Position: Stand erect, hands on hips.

Stretched Position: Step forward with either leg, and bend it fully while keeping the other leg straight. Hold this position for the required length of time and then repeat the movement for the other leg.

Variation: Lunging stretches can also be done by stepping to the side instead of directly forward, which will stretch the inner thigh muscles much more directly.

Thigh Stretch

Emphasis: The quadriceps muscles (on the front of your thighs).

Starting Position: Stand erect, balancing on your left foot with your left leg held straight. Reach behind you and grasp your right ankle with your right hand.

Stretched Position: Pull gently upward on your ankle to stretch your thigh muscles.

Variation: This movement can also be done kneeling, leaning backward, and bracing your upper body with your arms. In this variation you can increase the intensity of the stretch by merely bending your arms a little, but be careful not to overdo it.

Calf Stretch

Emphasis: Stretches and tones all of the muscles at the back of your lower legs.

Starting Position: Face a partner or a wall, and place your hands on the partner's shoulders or against the wall at shoulder height. Move your feet backward until your right leg, torso, and arms make a straight line. Your left leg should be bent.

Stretched Position: Gently press your heel down to the floor. If you can comfortably place your heel flat, put your foot back another 4 to 6 inches to intensify the stretch. Be sure to do an equal amount of stretching for each calf.

Lower Back, Partner Stretch

Emphasis: The muscles of the lower back.

Starting Position: Sit down and face your partner. Spread your legs apart and press the soles of your partner's feet against your calves. Lean inward and firmly grasp hands with your partner.

Stretched Position: One partner either pulls strongly with his or her arms or leans backward to pull the other partner forward, gently stretching all of the muscles of the upper and lower back. After one partner has been fully stretched, switch roles.

The Side Stretch

Emphasis: Stretches the muscles of the sides.

Starting Position: Stand erect with your head upright, knees straight, feet together, and arms at your sides.

Stretched Position: Raise and fully extend your right arm, keeping your knees straight and bending as far as possible to the left, at the same time keeping your right arm straight and behind your head as far as possible. Perform this exercise several times, bending alternately to the left and right.

The Art of Expressing the Human Body

The Back Bend

Emphasis: The spine and front thigh muscles.

Starting Position: Stand erect with your head upright, knees straight, feet together, and arms stretched above and close to the head.

Stretched Position: Keeping your weight on your left foot, place your right foot forward, with the heel on the ground. Keep both knees straight and bend backward—from the waist—as far as possible. Return to upright position and close your right foot to your left foot, keeping your arms stretched above your head. Perform this exercise several times, with your left and right foot alternately placed forward.

Front and Back Bend

Emphasis: The spine, the back muscles, and the tendons of the legs.

Starting Position: Stand erect with your head upright, knees straight, feet together, and arms stretched above your head.

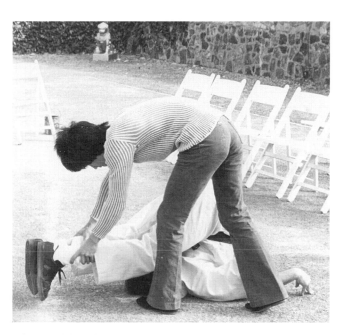

Stretched Position: Keep your knees straight and raise both arms so that they are above your head, then bend your body forward from the waist until your head touches your knees, then pass the arms back until your shoulders and arms are at a 90-degree angle behind your torso. Return to an upright position, keeping your knees straight, and bend your body backward from the waist as far as possible, then return to upright position again. Repeat several times.

Flexibility Training for Specific Body Parts

For Wrist Flexibility

Bend your elbows until the forearms are parallel to the floor, then bring your hands to the front of the body until they are almost touching each other. Keeping your forearms parallel to the floor, rotate your wrists until the palms of your hands are facing your body. Now shake the wrists lightly, then with increasing vigor. Execute the movement loosely and lazily. Work for an up-and-down movement of the wrists. This should markedly increase their flexibility—a vital factor for achieving maximum power in throwing a ball of any kind, or in finishing a golf or batting swing.

To Limber up the Shoulder Muscles

Keeping your head erect, shrug your shoulders in an exaggerated fashion, as if trying to touch your ears with your shoulders. By raising the elbows (allowing the forearms to dangle), the shoulders will go much higher. Keep your knees slightly bent while executing this upward move-ment of the shoulders—this is important for the correct execution of the next movement. Allow your head and shoulders to droop downward until your arms are fully extended and your fore-arms are between your bent knees. At the same time, let your entire body, including the head, sag loosely, or "flop." The torso and legs move as though you were sitting down in a chair—never bend over from the waist. At the lowest point of this movement, your arms should dangle loosely, full-length, but the fingertips should not touch the floor. Return to erect position. This sagging exercise is excellent for a thorough loosening of your shoulder muscles. Also, it affects a definite release of tension.

Neck Exercise

It's important when loosening your muscles to take the tension out of the neck. Revolve the head slowly in a circular motion, first to the left, and then to the right.

The Art of Expressing the Human Body

17. "REAL-WORLD POWER": THE CARDIO CONNECTION

You think a fight is one blow? One kick? Until you can put combinations together without even thinking, until you learn how to keep moving, and to endure, hire a bodyguard or lead a less aggressive life.
—Bruce Lee

This quote of Bruce Lee's was heard by millions of Americans during the summer of 1971. Lee said it during his primetime appearance on the premiere episode of "Longstreet," a television series that featured a blind private detective played by James Franciscus. The show—and Lee's characterization of Li tsung, Longstreet's jeet kune do instructor—proved so popular that, as was the case with the "Green Hornet" series five years earlier, he soon had more fan mail than the star of the series.

I mention this not to be nostalgic, but to illustrate the emphasis Lee placed on endurance or, as it is more popularly referred to these days, aerobic exercise. Although the "Longstreet" script was written by Stirling Silliphant, Lee's annotations, written in his own hand within the margins of his copy of the first draft, reveal that he made numerous changes that were later incorporated into the final episode, including the quotation above stressing the need to be mobile for prolonged periods of time—that is, to have endurance.

I remember Bruce and Linda's son Brandon once telling me that he considered aerobic or cardiovascular training to be "real-world power," because cardiovascular fitness comes in handy far more frequently in our day-to-day encounters than does lifting heavy objects (i.e., strength training). As Brandon explained it, "If you try and do a three-minute round of the Thai pads, I don't care how big your muscles are, if you don't have a real good cardiovascular system, you're going to be dead in about forty-five seconds and I'm still going to be going."

How true this is! I recall that, after speaking with Brandon, I attempted to do a three-minute round on the focus pads and felt afterward like I was going to be coughing up stuff my body actually needed. The reason? I was unable to endure.

Ironically, although the wonders of endurance training are often preached to martial art students, very few of our current martial art instructors employ cardiovascular exercise as part of their own curriculum. There are exceptions, of course, but by and large, endurance exercises such as running have taken a back seat to form or kata practice and deadly technique training. This is unfortunate, for technique is useless if you lack the requisite endurance to carry it out. It's no secret that running was Bruce Lee's preferred source of endurance exercise. He ran every day that he could, rain or shine, to maintain his fighting edge. (His fine physique and good health were by-products of his cardio commitment.) In fact, Lee believed that the tools or natural (i.e., unarmed) weapons available to the martial artist were universal—that is, two hands and two feet. However, it was how finely tuned your "machine" was that allowed you the opportunity to deploy these weapons effectively. To quote Lee directly:

Unless there are human beings with three arms and four legs, unless we have another group of beings on earth that are structurally different from us, there can be no different style of fighting.

The Art of Expressing the Human Body

Why is that? Because we have two hands and two legs. The important thing is how can we use them to the maximum? In terms of paths [i.e., the geometry of your attacking limbs], they can be used in a straight line, curved line, up, down, round line. They might be slow but, depending on the circumstances, sometimes that might not be slow. And in terms of legs, you can kick up, straight—same thing, right? Physically then, you have to ask yourself, "How can I become very well coordinated?" Well, that means you have to be an athlete using jogging and all those basic ingredients, right?

Absolutely! And as Bruce Lee was—and remains—the pinnacle of martial artists, his conditioning and insights remain the standard-bearers in the industry.

Lee held that all endurance-related activities (and he did plenty of them, from running to cycling to hitting and kicking the heavy bag) should be performed on a progressive basis. As you would expect to increase the resistance on your barbell once your muscular strength reaches a certain level, so too must you increase your endurance demands once your body has reached specific cardiovascular levels. According to Lee:

To achieve this aim, we have two ways; one is running, but you have to increase the distance of your course every day until you are satisfied with it. The second thing to observe is progression; start out slow and then gradually build speed as your conditioning improves. All of this training will lead to a result of increased frequency of breath and heartbeat. And [during intense training] you will feel an unbearable feeling, but you do not have to fear. That point will be the maximum limit of a man's physical energy. If you do not have heart disease, after taking a rest you will soon recover. It is only through this compulsory hard training that one's physical energy can expand continuously.

The idea of progression was paramount to Lee's conditioning system, particularly as it pertained to aerobic conditioning. For example, once Lee mastered the above methods of increasing his running speed and distance, he even incorporated some weight training in his running in order to make the progression even more demanding. According to Lee:

The above methods are only common methods. If you want to go to a higher level, you will have to go through super physical training. That is, climbing a hill with a load on your back. In such instances, the practitioner should wear a specially made strap (like ankle/wrist and waist weights), which can allow some alterations in weight. You can start with eight or ten pounds, then set the course and run as usual—but you must finish your course every day. If you feel that it is getting easier, then add one or two more pounds until you reach twenty pounds. Then the program has finished. This training will strengthen your physical energy, capacity, and endurance.

This was the forerunner to what became known as power walking and heavy-hands exercise, whereby individuals would engage in aerobic exercise but with weights on their limbs or waist in order to continue to increase and improve their physical fitness levels.

Training Tips

While it's true that the best results—not only physically, but as Lee pointed out to Stirling Silliphant, in your work and morality (see page 23)—are obtained when a person refuses to accept limits and instead increases his endurance capacity with each outing, it's also true that you have to start somewhere. In other words, you can't simply jump out of bed, hit the streets, and run until you drop, lest you exceed your physiological limits and end up in the emergency ward in a state of shock.

Lee acknowledged that in order to develop endurance, the activity should be of sufficient intensity and duration to exceed "normal" limits and to push the body functions gradually toward their maximum level. The exercise sessions should result in a higher rate of breathing and should not end until the individual is temporarily "out of breath." Any activity that results in accelerated breathing and pulse rate will develop endurance if sustained for a sufficient length of time.

Exercises to Develop Endurance

Stepping

One of the simplest ways to develop your endurance, by Lee's estimate, was stepping. This is performed by merely stepping up and down from a chair (or bench or stool) to the floor and back. (The chair should be 17 inches high for men, 14 inches high for women). For one minute, lead with the left foot, then change to the right foot for one minute. Then stop, stretch, breathe deeply, and do an arm exercise or an abdominal exercise. Then repeat the routine with the chair. Increase the repetitions as the weeks go along, until you are able to perform it for a full 30 minutes.

Jogging

If one form of exercise could be said to have been Bruce Lee's "passion," it was jogging. He once told *Fighting Stars* magazine: "I really dig exercise. When I'm jogging early in the morning, boy—it's sure refreshing!"

Lee always carried a pair of running shoes with him to ensure that he never missed a day of jogging. Bruce Lee was interested in jogging for several reasons. First, he noted that there are drawbacks to many of the available physical activities and sports, such as expense, convenience, time involved, availability of facilities, required skills, and the regularity of participation. Other activities provide little actual exercise, or the exercise is intermittent, with rest being taken as soon as a person is a little tired or breathless. The result: Very little stress is placed on the body to improve its level of physical fitness, especially to improve the cardiovascular and respiratory systems.

For Lee, the joy of jogging lay in the fact that it was the simplest of exercises. Unlike weight lifting, isometrics, and various calisthenics he performed throughout his life, all of which emphasize muscle building, jogging work to improve the heart, lungs, and circulatory system. Lee was aware that other body muscles were also being worked when he jogged, but he knew the greatest benefit came from improving the efficiency of his heart and lungs. After all, when you're past thirty, bulging biceps and pleasing pectorals may boost your ego, but your life and health depend on how fit your heart and lungs are.

Reasons Why You Should Jog

Whenever people asked Bruce Lee why he spent so much time jogging, he typically answered with one of these eight responses.

1. "It's quick." There are 1,440 minutes in a day. For beginners, jogging takes about 30 minutes three days a week, or only 90 minutes out of 10,080 each week. If you're over thirty and unwilling to spend this minimum time for better fitness, you'd better be prepared to spend even more time being ill.

2. "It's safe." Jogging exercises are gradual. You do not overexert. And you begin at your own level of fitness.

3. "It improves the heart and lungs." Jogging improves the heart, lungs, and circulatory system by gradually expanding their capacity to process oxygen and handle stress. Jogging conditions the rest of you, too, but the benefit comes from the increased efficiency of the heart and lungs. Someday your life may depend on their fitness.

4. "It makes you look and feel better." Exercise stimulates circulation, tones the muscles, and produces a more optimistic outlook. Jogging reduces fat deposits around the hips and thighs, firms sagging muscles, and flattens the abdomen. Lee also viewed jogging as a form of relaxation, telling a reporter in 1972, "Jogging is not only a form of exercise to me, it is also a form

練武風景
灼けつくような日
練武の合間に人なつっこい微笑を見せた。

of relaxation. It is my own hour every morning when I can be alone with my own thoughts." He referred to it again that year in a letter written to a friend: "I hope you are still jogging, which is the only form of relaxation to me nowadays."

5. "It helps you lose weight." Jogging is an aid to losing weight. Through jogging you can reduce the amount of fat and increase the amount of muscle. Jogging plus a healthy diet will guarantee good weight loss.

6. "It will give you a smaller waistline." Jogging helps redistribute weight. In controlled programs, nearly all male joggers reduced the size of their waistline and all female joggers dropped down a dress size.

7. "It builds endurance and confidence." Jogging makes you more fit. You can confidently tackle your

job, increase your workload, or set out to enjoy recreational activity without fear of overexerting your heart.

8. "Lifetime of better health." Exercise should be part of a long-range health program. Regular exercise year in and year out is what counts. Short-term exercise gets short-term results.

How to Jog

Lee believed that how you jog was not as important as the fact that you did jog. Performance is more important than technique. However, certain techniques can affect your jogging performance.

Stand up Straight. Experience with runners proves that for either walking or running, maintaining a good posture is important; it affords the greatest freedom and ease of movement. Good posture means keeping your back as straight as naturally comfortable. Keep your head up, neither forward nor back of the body line. Your buttocks should be "tucked in." In this position, a hypothetical line drawn from the top of your head through the shoulders and hips should be straight, or nearly so. Do not, however, imitate the military brace where it is good form to throw back the shoulders and stick out the chest. If you do, you're likely to get a muscle ache between the shoulder blades and some discomfort in your lower back. And you will use a lot of unnecessary energy by contracting a series of back muscles.

Legs. When you stand up straight, your legs should move freely from the hips. The action is easy, not forced. The lift is from the knees, while the ankles remain relaxed.

Breathing. According to Linda Lee Cadwell, Bruce Lee used to say, "When you are young, you breathe from your abdomen; when you are middle-aged, you breathe from your diaphragm; and when you are old, you breathe from your throat and mouth. In order to remain vital, one should practice breathing from their abdomen." This viewpoint is well-served by running because running requires deep breaths from the diaphragm—not surface breathing—in order to cultivate greater endurance.

The Footwork of Jogging

Heel-to-Toe. The typical jogger lands first on the heel of the foot, rocks forward, and takes off from the ball of the foot. Hitting with the heel first cushions the landing, then distributes the pressure as the foot comes forward. Experience shows that this heel-to-toe footstrike is the least tiring over long distances and the least wearing on the rest of the body. About 70 percent of good long-distance runners use this technique.

Flat Foot. This technique is a variation of the heel-to-toe. Instead of hitting first with the heel, the entire foot lands on the ground at the same time. The wide surface area pillows the footstrike and is easy on the rest of the body. In the flat-foot technique, the foot falls under the knee in a quick, light action. Don't drive the foot down. Just let it pass beneath the body, then quickly pick it up for the next step. About 20 percent of long-distance runners use this technique.

Ball-of-the-Foot. This is the method that Bruce Lee utilized in his one- to two-mile runs. The jogger lands first on the ball of the foot and settles to the heel before taking the next step. Don't be surprised if almost instinctively you start with this method of footstrike, especially if you haven't run since your younger days. The running games you learned as a youngster were almost exclusively sprint games, requiring you to be up on your toes for quick starts. The ball-of-the-foot technique sometimes produces soreness, since the muscles must remain in contraction for a longer period of time than for heel-to-toe or flat foot. For some joggers, this method creates a strain that is not as beneficial as the alternating tension and relaxation of the other methods. A little more bend in the knee with each step may help you to get the full foot down on the ground.

Running can be defined as the performance of many repetitions of an exercise with a small load. Let me explain this by comparing running with lifting weights. If you lift a heavy weight just once, you are moving a heavy load with only one repetition; the training effect produced is an increase in strength. But endurance training does not impose a single, heavy load. In running we move only our own body weight by the action of the legs. We move our legs about a thousand times to run one mile. By running long distances, we obtain many repetitions with a light load, and this increases our endurance. Lee frequently mentioned his running in various letters to friends and in statements to the press:

The Art of Expressing the Human Body

Of course, I run every day. I practice my tools (punches, kicks, throws, etc.). I have to raise the basic conditions daily.

I've just bought a half-acre home in Bel Air on top of a hill—plenty of fresh air—like living out in the country, but tough on the calves running around the hill side.

I'm running every day. Sometimes up to six miles.

Yesterday I drove the car to the field and let Bo [the Lee family dog] run for a while—I ran with her and walked fast around the field a few times.

Out with Bo every day. I drive her to the field instead and run around there.

Running is in my plan today, though I'm sore.

I'm working out on the road more than ever. It's much tougher to run up and down the hill but I like it because I get more out of it. Running uphill is hard but it's good to strengthen your legs and develop your stamina. But it's easier than running downhill! Going down is hard on your legs as you have to keep braking. You don't get too much benefit either.

In running, if you can lift up your knees, the results will be even better.

Every day at 4:00 PM I'll run two miles, paying no attention to the weather. If I really have some important meetings at that time, then I'll do it at another time but on the same day.

The press, of course, made their own observations on Lee's favorite fitness pastime, as in this report from the Hong Kong newspaper *The China Mail:* "Bruce does regular running exercises. He has been in the habit of taking a two-mile run up and down the Waterloo Hill Road area every day around 4 PM. It takes him about 14 minutes."

Beyond Aerobics: Interval Training

Another of Lee's favorite endurance-building techniques was interval training. The principle behind interval training is simply to work hard, ease off, work hard, ease off, and so on.

For example, to train for running a mile, you would run 440 yards in 60 seconds. An interval, say 5 minutes, would then be allowed, during which time you would slow down your pace to a restful jog or walk. At the end of this interval you would run another 440 yards at the same 60-second pace, followed by another 5-minute rest interval, and then another 440 yards, continuing on in this manner for a predetermined number of runs.

Of course, instead of walking and jogging when you do roadwork, you could walk a mile, run a mile, walk a quarter of a mile, sprint 200 yards, and walk a half-mile each day. Then breathe deeply while stretching your chest. Lee once told a reporter: "In the beginning you should jog easily and then gradually increase the distance and tempo, and finally include sprints to develop your 'wind.'"

In fact, Lee prescribed a training program for student Larry Hartsell in which he advocated just this sort of procedure: "Roadwork: Jog (1 minute)—Sprint (keep it up)—Walk (1 minute): in as many sets as you can." (See Chapter 19 for the entire program Lee prescribed.)

Another Bruce Lee student, Richard Bustillo, recalls that Lee's interval training was very demanding indeed:

I ran with him one time and I didn't like the way he ran because, when I run, I like to relax and just jog. I like to get the cardiovascular system going. I used to box before and that's how I used to run; only picking up the pace occasionally. Back when I was training with Bruce, there wasn't much talk of what they now call interval training. Bruce was already doing that before it became popular. And what he used to do, he'd be jogging for a while, and then he'd be sprinting, and then he'd jog; then he'd run backward, and then he'd jog; he'd even do crossovers, bringing his left leg over his right leg—and then he'd jog; he'd do circles for his footwork, and then he'd jog. He ran backward for footwork and coordination because he realized that fighting is not just like jogging; sometimes you've got to turn fast or backpeddle. That's how he applied it, and that's how he ran. That's no fun running! Geez, to me, I like to do things and enjoy things. Man, that was a workout!

18. APPLIED POWER: TRAINING WITH THE HEAVY BAG

I relax until the moment I bring every muscle of my body into play, and then concentrate all the force in my fist. To generate great power you must first totally relax and gather your strength, and then concentrate your mind and all your strength on hitting your target.
—Bruce Lee

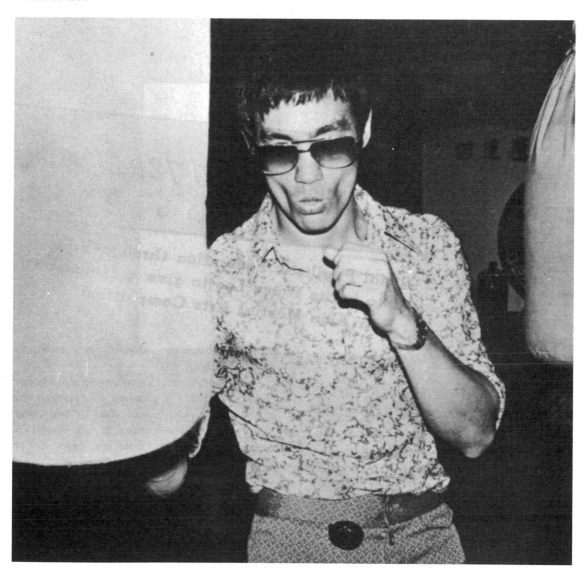

For Bruce Lee, a vital difference existed between strength and power, and this difference involved much more than semantics. He defined strength as "the ability of the body to exert great force."

Power, on the other hand, Lee defined as "the ability to release an explosive force to produce a quick, sudden movement to move the body with maximum effort." He also stated that "power involves the rate of speed at which the force is expressing itself."

In other words, power was the marriage of strength and velocity, and a considerable amount of each had to exist if great power was expected to be unleashed within a given martial art technique.

One of Lee's students, Dan Inosanto, recalled Lee once asking him, "Can you tell me the difference, Dan, when I say that this guy is a strong martial artist and this guy is a *powerful* martial artist?" Inosanto paused before he replied, "I don't know, what is the difference?" Lee's response was: "A man can be *strong*, but if he cannot use that strength *quickly*, he is not *powerful*."

Lee's response is physiologically accurate. For example, in a sport such as track and field, some rookie coaches have discovered that sometimes a fellow who is strong enough to bench press impressive weights can't parlay that strength into a very powerful shot put.

According to film star James Coburn, who was one of Lee's more frequent private students, the power or "strength put quickly into motion" by Lee was almost frightening to witness:

> *I was living on Tower Road. It was kind of a Spanish-style place that had a patio and Bruce and I would train out there. Anyway, Bruce brought over this big, heavy tackle bag . . . football players use them a lot. We hung it up with a big L-iron out there and used it for practicing our side kicks. So I was flicking away with a kick and Bruce said "You're too flicky-flicky! You've got to become involved in the technique!" When punching, he said, "Always lead with the little finger—pow!—it goes out there!" Anyway, he was saying, "Okay now, this is the way to do it," and he kicked this bag, which must have weighed between 100 to 150 pounds. Well, he actually kicked a hole in the middle of it! He broke the chain that was supporting it, and it went flying out into the lawn. I remember that it was filled with rags and there were rags everywhere! I must have been picking up rags for months around there all over the lawn. It was really an astounding thing to see.*

From the standpoint of physics, the factors involved in the generation of such power (P) would include force (F), velocity (V), work (W), distance (d), and time (t). The scientifically inclined among us have defined power in the following formula:

$$W = Fd$$
$$P = W \div t$$
$$\Delta P = Fd \div t$$
$$d \div t = V$$
$$\Delta P = FV$$

Lee, of course, was interested in the application of power from the standpoint of combat. He fashioned a three-point statement about power that encapsulated the areas he felt all serious martial artists needed to consider:

1. Power in attack
2. Power in defense
3. Power in combination.

Learning to Apply Power: The Heavy Bag

One of Lee's favorite pieces of training apparatus was the heavy bag. The heavy bag is not particularly exotic; it typically weighs 70 pounds and can be found in many fitness facilities and, of course, in every boxing gym.

With the heavy bag, Lee could work seriously on improving the devastating power of his striking and kicking techniques. Building strength through weight training was one thing, but being able to have your body apply power—in the right amount and at the right time—was another matter and required special training. After all, Lee reasoned, it isn't knowing *how* that's important, it's *doing*. Even the finest techniques in the world would prove useless without the requisite power to carry them out. Lee once told the readers of *Black Belt* magazine to "hang a heavy bag in your basement and use your legs as you would your hands."

Although Lee later cautioned against *excessive* use of the heavy bag, he still considered it an essential component of his power-training regimen. To those just beginning to train with the heavy bag, Lee offered the following advice: "Start with 3 sets of 50 repetitions of each type of punch, then put them together in combinations. Then work in your kicks individually, then in combination. Finally, work in your hands and your feet in combination." Lee also advised the user to wear bag gloves and/or tape the hands and wrists to prevent injuries.

Although you should train improvisationally, it may help to review some of the heavy-bag training programs that Bruce Lee jotted down. Also included is an account of a videotaped bag session that featured Lee training in his backyard in Bel Air in 1968.

Punching Practice on the Heavy Bag (Monday, Wednesday, Friday)
1. Cross
2. Hook
3. Overhand cross
4. Combinations

Lead Punch (Combination) Practice on the Heavy Bag
1. The one-two
2. The one-two and hook
3. Right-body—right-jaw—left-jaw
4. The one-hook-cross
5. The straight high/low

Kicking Practice on the Heavy Bag (Tuesday, Thursday, Saturday)
1. Side kick—right and left
2. Hook kick—right and left
3. Spin kick—right and left
4. Rear front thrust—right and left
5. Heel kick—right and left

One of Lee's Heavy Bag Punching Routines (Backyard Workout, Bel Air, 1968)
Emphasis: Long Lead Right, Left Cross, Left and Right Hooks
1. Long right lead (high)
2. Right hook (middle)
3. Left cross (high)
4. Right hook (high)
5. Right jab (low—as the bag returns)
6. Feint right jab (medium)
7. Left hook (high)
8. Right hook (medium—as the bag returns)

The Art of Expressing the Human Body

9. Left cross (high)
10. Right lead (high)
11. Left hook (high)
12. Right hook (high)
13. Left hook (high)
14. Right hook (medium)
15. Left hook (medium)
16. Right hook (high)
17. Left cross (high)
18. Right hook (high)
19. Left jab (high)
20. Right hook (high)
21. Left cross (medium)
22. Right hook (medium)
23. Left cross (high)
24. Right hook (high)
25. Bruce backs up, using his footwork to avoid the return of the bag. He allows it to swing toward him and then back away from him fully. As it returns, he stops its swing with his right elbow in a low check, and then brings it up to feint a right jab, and then steps through with a left cross. (As a point of form, as his left hand makes contact with the bag, Bruce's right leg is forward and the thrust is coming up from the torque of his hips from right to left; his left leg is almost perfectly straight.)
26. Right hook (high)
27. Left hook (high)
28. Right hook (high)
29. Stops the bag from swinging, returns to the on-guard position, then fires a right lead.
30. As the bag returns to him, Bruce uses footwork to move back out of range. He assumes the on-guard position briefly, with great sensitivity to the undulations of the bag, then fires a right lead (high).
31. Left cross (high)
32. Right lead (high)

As you can see, Lee used the heavy bag to perfect (and monitor the effects of) different martial art techniques, as well as to gauge which leverage points and kinesiological principles were most likely to result in an increase in his power. According to his former business partner Raymond Chow, of Hong Kong's Golden Harvest Studios, Lee "studied the arts. He really worked at them to find out how a blow was made and how a blow could be made more powerful."

Lee believed the heavy bag to be valuable not only for developing power, but for improving one's timing. Practicing with the bag could teach one to kick at precisely the right moment and at the right distance to deliver the most powerful kick or strike possible.

Pointers on Heavy-Bag Training

Although Lee never wrote a formal treatise on how best to use the heavy bag, certain fragments from his notes and conversations survive and reveal his general approach:

1. *Always keep yourself well covered and never leave yourself open for one moment.*
2. *The power of the punch and kick comes, not as so many people imagine, from the vigor with which the blow is struck, but by correct contact at the right spots at the right moment, and with feet and body correctly in position and balanced.*
3. *Move! Move! Move around the whole time, side-stepping, feinting, varying your kicks and blows to the movement.*
4. *Remember that the body is an integral part of the kick and punch, [it's] not just the leg and arm that deliver it.*
5. *Practice first for form, then for power.*

Lee cautioned against becoming overconfident as a result of heavy-bag training. He was particularly critical of those who would really take time to set up before delivering their power strikes, for he recognized that an opponent is not going to just stand there and allow you the luxury of full preparation. For this reason Lee cautioned against letting your guard down while training on the heavy bag. As he once told his student Daniel Lee: "You can hit a heavy bag that way, but you cannot hit an opponent that way."

Lee also observed in his students (and from personal experience) that too much heavy-bag training cultivated a condition of carelessness in combative awareness: Since the bag never hit you back, you never had to react to a potential counterattack, thus allowing you far more freedom to prepare your strikes and kicks than you would have in a real-life encounter. As Lee once stated: "The one drawback to heavy-bag training is the fact that the bag can't strike you back—which means that you leave yourself open to counterattack—'perfecting faults.'"

Lee also jotted down a short list of things to guard against when training on the heavy bag:
1. Carelessness shown after delivering a blow
2. A definite routine of kicks and blows.

Lee learned one of his favorite heavy-bag techniques from a book written by former world heavyweight boxing champion Joe Louis. The "Brown Bomber," advised that, after hitting the bag while it was stationary, one should try giving it a slight push to start it slowly swinging. Then, when it had started to swing away, Louis advised the trainee to hook sharply with the left or right in the direction of the swing of the bag. Lee liked this, for it caused him to deal with an on-coming or moving force as opposed to simply a stationary target.

Beyond the Heavy Bag

Lee believed that after you cultivated sufficient applied power from your heavy-bag training, you should decrease the amount of time you spend training on it, working instead on some of the other components of technique mastery, such as timing, coordination, distance, speed, and accuracy. He advised Daniel Lee during a phone call in mid-1971:

> *When you use your leg it is much better to use it to kick at the foam pad or something like that. Watch out with the side kick on air kicking [kicking at no target] too much, because it's bad for the knee joint. . . if you snap it too much without [your leg encountering any] resistance at the end. . . . Just think about economical movement.*

Lee also instructed his students to try to cultivate a sense of direct feeling, or, as he put it, "emotional content," with regard to hitting the bag. Don't hit it or push at it mechanically, but really put passion and meaning behind each strike. The best example of this was related to me by Richard Bustillo, one of Lee's Los Angeles students. Bustillo recalls:

> *One time we were training and Bruce was hitting the heavy bag—and he was going wild, like he was pissed off with the heavy bag. He was snorting and really whacking the bag. I think Ted Wong was there and I looked at Ted and he looked at me as if to ask, "Did you piss him off? Did I piss him off, or what?" He was really going at the bag; putting out 100 percent and really whacking the bag. And then he stopped and looked at us and said, "Okay, guys, let's go. Your turn." I asked him, "What was that about?" He said, "That's jeet kune do—you've got to be emotionally involved when you train." And Bruce could turn it on and turn it off whenever he wanted to.*

The heavy bag can be a very valuable tool for learning to apply the power you've gained from your strength-training workouts. In addition to burning off stress, training on the heavy bag will teach you to coordinate the parts of your body into a coherent and dynamic whole, and will teach you about qualities such as rhythm, balance, timing, force production, recoil, and precision. As Lee himself pointed out, "When you are talking about combat, as it is, well then, baby, you'd better learn to train every part of your body!"

Bruce Lee continued to use a heavy bag up until his last workout, and learned much about the potential of his own body from these workouts. We therefore give Lee the last word on the subject to close this chapter: "Use that heavy bag, move, circle it. The only benefit comes from your imagination and your ability to hit with speed and power."

19. INTERVAL TRAINING FOR MARTIAL ARTISTS

Given Bruce Lee's advice that unless a martial artist learns to put kicks and punches together in combinations "and to endure," he is better off hiring a bodyguard or leading a less aggressive life, what training did Lee recommend to cultivate more endurance in punching and kicking? The answer is interval training.

By interval training Lee meant not only jogging, but the punching, kicking, and footwork necessary for combat. So Lee devised a program that enhanced the skills and conditioning necessary for martial artists seeking to improve their chances in combative situations. Bearing in mind that interval training consists of bursts of intense exercise interspersed with brief rest periods, in which the trainee moves from station to station or circuit to circuit to keep his blood pumping and his pulse rate elevated, it is little wonder that, quite apart from the combative enhancement this program cultivates, the health and fitness benefits are also tremendous. If you follow this program for even as little as four weeks you will improve your coordination, agility, endurance, power, speed, rhythm, timing, precision, and muscle tone, and even reduce your body fat levels! Not bad for a 40-minute workout!

Lee practiced this routine himself for a period of time, and also recommended it to his student Larry Hartsell, who was preparing to enter what would become the first-ever kick-boxing

The Art of Expressing the Human Body

(i.e., full-contact) tournament held in the United States. According to Hartsell, the results he enjoyed while employing this routine were spectacular:

> *This was a routine that Bruce did up for me when I was training for the first-ever kick-boxing match in this country back in 1968. It was held in San Francisco, in the San Francisco Civic Auditorium. Bruce told me "Larry, I want you to do this every day, and spar all you can." He said, "Increase your rounds. Do more. Especially when beginning your routine." I trained three months hard on that program for the tournament. I placed second. Bruce trained me for it. I really complained at getting second because I knocked the guy out! I was disqualified in the second round because I hit the guy and boom, boom! I kicked him when he was on all fours. We wore eight-ounce boxing gloves and we could wear boxing shoes and anything went except for groin grabs and eye jabs. The guy I fought was the promoter's boy, a Chinese guy. The third round I knocked him out of the ring and the guy could hardly stand up. He actually came over and said, "You won it." He was a Thai boxer, he studied in the navy. He was living in Thailand. I still beat him.*

The Interval Training Program

Each circuit of the program lasts for 3 minutes, or the length of time of a round of professional boxing. The rest periods (with the exception of the skipping-rope circuit) last only one minute, the length of time a professional boxer is allowed between rounds. Here's the program that Bruce Lee prescribed for Larry Hartsell:

1. Roadwork—jog (1 minute)—sprint (keep it up)—walk (1 minute) in as many sets as you can
2. Skill conditioning
   a. Shadow kick-boxing—3 minutes (1 minute rest); loosen up in good economical form

1). ROADWORK :- JOG — SPRINT — WALK in AS MANY SETS AS YO
[1MIN] [KEEP IT UP] [1MIN]   CAN.

2). SKILL CONDITIONING :-

a). shadow kick-boxing ---- 3 min. (1 MIN REST
(LOOSEN UP IN GOOD ECONOMICAL FORM)

b). shadow kick-boxing ---- 3 min. (1 MIN RES
(WORK HARD :- PUSH YOURSELF - SPEED/POWER)

c). skip rope ----- 5 min. (1½ min. Rest)
(try all footwork)

d). Heavy bag ----- 3 min. — (1 MIN)
(individual punches plus combination)

(e). Heavy bag ----- 3 min — (")
(individual kicks plus combination)

(f) light bag ----- 3 min.
(individual punches plus conditioning)

(g) shadow kick-boxing - 2 min.
(loosen up)

b. Shadow kick-boxing—3 minutes (1 minute rest); work hard: push yourself—speed/power
c. Skip rope—5 minutes (1½ minutes rest); try all footwork
d. Heavy bag—3 minutes (1 minute rest); individual punches, plus combinations
e. Heavy bag—3 minutes (1 minute rest); individual kicks, plus combinations
f. Light bag—3 minutes (no rest indicated); individual punches, plus conditioning
g. Shadow kick-boxing—2 minutes; loosen up.

Depending on how much time you spend on the interval running program, this workout will last anywhere from 32½ minutes to 47½ minutes. Here's the breakdown:

The Art of Expressing the Human Body

Roadwork

Two series of 1-minute jog, 30-second sprint, and 1-minute walk = 5 minutes total

Four series of 1-minute jog, 30-second sprint, and 1-minute walk = 10 minutes total

Six series of 1-minute jog, 30-second sprint, and 1-minute walk = 15 minutes total

Eight series of 1-minute jog, 30-second sprint, and 1-minute walk = 20 minutes total

Skill/Coordination Training

Five 3-minute circuits, one 5-minute circuit, one 2-minute circuit, 5½ minutes rest between circuits = 27½ minutes total training

Lee's Personal Program

In Lee's own version of the program, no mention is made of roadwork; however, although he did not write it down, it is safe to assume from looking at his training schedules from this period that he would have included it at some point during the day. Lee typically did his running early in the morning and his martial art workout either later in the morning or in the mid-afternoon. Here is Lee's personal version of this workout:

1. *Shadow kick-boxing—3 minutes (1 minute complete rest); loosen up, work on good economical form, all types*

2. *Shadow kick-boxing—2 minutes (1 minute complete rest); work harder (speed and more speed)*

3. *Shadow kick-boxing—2 minutes (1 minute complete rest); push yourself (the fastest, but economical)*

4. *Skip rope—5 minutes; try all footwork*

5. *Heavy bag—3 minutes (1 minute rest); all kicks (side, hook, spin, straight)*

6. *Heavy bag—3 minutes (1 minute rest); all punches (hooks, straight, backfist)*

7. *Light bag—3 minutes (1 minute rest)*

8. *Shadow kick-boxing—3 minutes (1 minute rest); loosen up*

The Advanced (Split) Interval Training Program

In time, Lee altered his program so he could perform more concentrated work, specifically on his punches and kicks, over a six-day period. With the new schedule he trained his upper limbs on Monday, Wednesday, and Friday, and his lower limbs on Tuesday, Thursday, and Saturday. Though he did not write down the actual time he spent on each circuit or station, it is safe to assume from his previous workouts that it was a three-minute "round" per station followed by a rest period of one minute.

Punching Development (Monday, Wednesday, and Friday)

1. Skip rope
    a. Loosen up
    b. Fast
    c. Loosen

2. Shadow box
    a. Loosen up
    b. Fast
    c. Thoroughbred
3. Shadow box
    a. Loosen up
    b. Thoroughbred
    c. Unwind
4. Jab
    a. Top and bottom bag
    b. Heavy bag
    c. Focus glove
5. Hook
    a. Heavy bag
    b. Focus glove
6. Cross
7. Spinning blow
8. Biu jee (finger jab)
9. Elbow smash
    a. inward/outward
    b. upward/downward

Kicking Development (Tuesday, Thursday, and Saturday)
1. Skip rope
    a. Warm up
    b. Fast
    c. Loosen up
2. Shadow kick
    a. Loosen up
    b. Fast
    c. Thoroughbred
3. Shadow kick
    a. Loosen up
    b. Thoroughbred
    c. Unwind

4. Side kick
   a. Heavy bag
   b. Glove
   c. Shield
5. Hook kick
   a. Shield
   b. Glove
   c. Heavy bag
6. Spin kick
7. Reverse hook kick
8. Groin kick
   a. Speed
   b. Economy
   c. Coordination
9. Shin/knee kick
10. Shadow kick
   a. Last set only (loosen up)

20. FUELING THE DRAGON (NUTRITION)

When you are a martial artist, you only eat what you require and don't get carried away with foods that don't benefit you as a martial artist.
—Bruce Lee

After seeing the tremendous muscular definition of Lee's body, one could be forgiven for assuming that he was an expert in (among other things) nutrition. The truth is that with everything else Lee was working on and accomplishing throughout his life, he simply did not have time to give the subject any more than a cursory investigation.

Lee never drafted a treatise on nutrition for optimum athletic performance, never once lectured on the subject, nor spent time with nutritional scientists. However, within his personal papers there are substantial notations and literature that, when combined with the recollections of those who knew him best, represent a fair approximation of his beliefs on this subject.

The task fell to Lee's wife, Linda, to assume the responsibility for preparing the food for the Lee household, in addition to concocting the supplemental nutritional formulas for her husband. And she remains the sole authority on Lee's diet. According to Linda, "I was the one who did more research in the field of nutrition because, truthfully, Bruce couldn't boil water—nor did he care to learn. He didn't have that interest or the time to put into that. When I was cooking, he was working out and all those kinds of things, so I just tried my best to provide well-balanced meals that were both healthy and nutritious."

By Linda's recollection, the Lee family didn't make mealtime the primary focus of their lives; eating was simply considered the "fuel" that kept all members of the family on the go. But

The Art of Expressing the Human Body

Linda read many nutrition books, and drew heavily from Adele Davis' books on nutrition, which recommended the use of such foodstuffs as whole grains and the complete avoidance of refined (or processed) foods and simple sugars.

As a result of Linda's research, Lee was able to reap the benefits of a well-balanced and highly nutritious diet, without having to compromise the time he was putting into his training. This is not to suggest that Lee did not pay close attention to what he put into his body. In much the same way that someone wanting a high-performance car wouldn't put anything in its tank but high-octane gasoline, Lee realized that if you wanted a high-performance body, you couldn't fuel it on a steady diet of beer and pizza and expect it to operate at peak efficiency. Without the right "fuel," the engine of your body will perform sluggishly, at best.

This doesn't mean that Lee believed one had to live in a cave on nuts and berries in order to be healthy, but he did realize that you need to take in foods of greater nutritive substance than cola and hot dogs. Linda recalls that:

> *Bruce didn't eat a lot of baked goods, primarily because they were made from refined flour and contained nothing but empty calories. He had no interest in consuming calories that wouldn't do anything for his body. Bruce would eat probably three to five meals a day but he didn't eat large portions, mainly because everything was centered around his working out and fitting that into the day. He might have, depending on how his schedule was on a certain day—and it could have been different on any day—a couple of protein drinks, he might have juice, or go out for a Chinese lunch and then have sort of a normal dinner. Like most people, he ate better if he spread it out over the day. His favorite foods would be almost anything Chinese, and things like spaghetti or pasta.*

A Well-Balanced Diet

According to Linda and others I've spoken to regarding Bruce Lee's views on nutrition, his attitude was that of most reputable nutritional scientists: a well-balanced diet is the fundamental concern governing nutritional intake. However, given that opinions now differ as to what precisely constitutes a well-balanced diet, along with the fact that it is beyond the scope of this book to present an assessment of the prevailing nutritional opinions concerning this subject, I will focus instead on Lee's standards for a well-balanced diet, which simply consisted of his choosing foods that supplied an ample amount of proteins, carbohydrates, and fats.

Complete and Incomplete Proteins

Complete proteins are found in milk, eggs, cheese, meat (including fish and poultry), soybeans, peanuts, peanut butter, and some nuts. Both complete and incomplete proteins are found in wheat. Incomplete proteins are found in corn, rye, beans, peas, lentils, gelatin, and some nuts. The yolk in eggs, incidentally, contains complete proteins, while the white of eggs contains incomplete proteins. Common examples of supplementing incomplete and complete proteins are the use of cereals with milk, bread with cheese, or peas with meat.

Carbohydrates

Starches and sugars are included in the classification of carbohydrates. The name refers to their chemical composition, as they contain carbon, hydrogen, and oxygen. During the process of digestion, starches are converted to sugars so that eventually all carbohydrate foods reach the blood in the form of sugars.

Within the body this sugar is slowly burned, or combined with oxygen (breathed in through the lungs). This oxidation produces the energy that the body needs for its internal process and for muscular activity. Foods that are rich in starch include all the cereal grains (wheat, oats, barley, rice, and rye), cereal breakfast foods, bread, cake, macaroni, and spaghetti while beans, peas, and potatoes are also good sources. Foods that are rich in sugar are molasses, honey, dried fruits (dates, figs, and raisins), jellies, chocolate, and commercial sugar while fresh fruits are also good sources. The bulk of our energy needs should be supplied by starchy foods rather than by sugary foods.

Concentrated forms of sugar (honey, jams, jellies, chocolate, and heavily sweetened desserts) are irritating to the lining of the alimentary tract and have a tendency to ferment, causing gas in the stomach and intestines, while their sweet taste may destroy the appetite for more wholesome and nutritive foods. Starchy foods, on the other hand, can be eaten in comparatively small amounts without digestive disturbances: They do not irritate the alimentary canal, they usually do not ferment, and their bland flavor does not hurt or destroy the normal appetite. However, refined cereals, white bread, polished rice, flour, macaroni, spaghetti, and all cakes and pastry made with white (refined) sugar are much less valuable and much more expensive, because they have been robbed of important nutritive elements.

Fats

Like carbohydrates, fats also supply energy to the body. In fact they are the most concentrated of all energy foods. Since hunger is caused by the contractions of an empty stomach, and fats are slow to leave the stomach, a moderate amount of fat in the diet is valuable for preventing hunger before the next mealtime. On the other hand, too much fat will lead to digestive disturbances.

Fat forms part of every cell in the body. Thin pads of fat protect the nerves; the internal organs are partly supported in position by fat; and a thin layer of fat under the skin rounds out the bodily contours and acts as an insulator to prevent the loss of body heat in cold weather. Certain fatty acids are essential to life; they are found in olive oil, corn oil, peanut oil, cotton-seed oil, cod-liver oil, peanut butter, and egg yolks. The most valuable sources of fat are those that also contain important minerals and food hormones. Such foods include butter, cheese, cream, egg yolks, cod-liver oil, avocados, almonds, butternuts, pecans, Brazil nuts, peanuts, peanut butter, and fat fish (salmon, mackerel, shad, herring, sardines, and tuna).

A Sample Daily Diet

Bruce Lee might start by eating a bowl of muesli or mixed cereal, which consisted of whole grains along with nuts and dried fruit. A modest lunch would then be taken at noon, with dinner following later on in the day. Linda recalls that she often made spaghetti or some other type of pasta for dinner, which would typically be served with a leafy green salad, but that the family more often ate meals consisting of rice, vegetables, and meat, chicken, or seafood. "We didn't have meat all the time," she says, "and, of course, Bruce really preferred to eat Chinese or other Asian food because he liked the variety that it presented as well as the proportion of meat to vegetables. That is to say, that there is often more vegetables than meat in Asian dishes."

Lee felt that Western food overall was rather monotonous, for it was usually restricted to only one entrée, whereas with Chinese food there were usually several—shrimp with vegetables, chicken with vegetables, beef dishes (such as beef in oyster sauce, one of Lee's personal favorites), or other dishes prepared with foods such as tofu (bean curd). Such variety allowed for more balanced nutrition as well as making meals far more enjoyable, allowing you to eat a little bit of everything but not too much of any one thing. Lee considered this the best way to eat.

This is not to suggest that the Lees didn't consume Western food, or even visit McDonald's from time to time with agreeable results. "Bruce was fond of steak," recalls Linda, "and for a while we even made a practice of having liver once a week." Overall, however, Lee much preferred the more balanced approach of the Asian cuisine, which, to his mind, emphasized variety and the proportion of protein to carbohydrates. Lee believed that the typical Western diet placed excessive emphasis on protein and fat. Never particularly fond of dairy products, which he utilized primarily for creating his protein drinks, Lee seldom drank milk and intensely disliked cheese. According to Linda, "Bruce couldn't understand why Western people ate cheese at all."

Because of his active schedule, Lee often consumed nutritious between-meals snacks, including rice soup (*congee*), which Linda prepared by cooking rice to the point it became souplike in consistency. Linda would then add organ meats such as liver, kidney, brains, or heart. Lee was also fond of cooked noodles, particularly Asian noodles, which of course are a wonderful source of carbohydrates, which are so necessary for providing quick a energy boost.

Enter the Supplements

In addition to maintaining a well-balanced diet, Lee also believed heartily in nutritional supplementation. In particular, protein drinks were an important part of Lee's diet. Hardly a day would pass when he wouldn't consume at least one or two high-protein drinks. Once again, it was Linda's domain to create this highly nutritious beverage:

> We used to go down to Bob Hoffman's store in Santa Monica to buy our protein—you can get it anywhere these days. We also mixed noninstant powdered milk into Bruce's protein drink, because, as I had read in Adele Davis's books, noninstant powdered milk was better for you because it was more concentrated. We utilized this either in addition to, or in lieu of, the protein powder we would get at Hoffman's store.

The contents of Lee's high-protein drink varied, but could have consisted of several of these ingredients at any given time:

• Noninstant powdered milk
• Water or juice
• Ice cubes
• 2 Eggs—sometimes with their shells
• 1 Tablespoon of wheat germ or wheat germ oil
• 1 Tablespoon of peanut butter
• Banana for its carbohydrates and potassium (and/or other fruit for flavoring)
• 1 Tablespoon of brewer's yeast
• Inositol
• Lecithin (in granular form)

Linda maintains that she never had a set recipe for preparing the above drink, and cannot infallably recollect exact measurements from over twenty-five years ago. However, depending on what mode of training he was engaged in or what bodyweight he was at, Linda recalls that Lee would be sure to have his protein drink at least once—and usually twice—a day. Bruce Lee wrote his own instructions for maximizing the weight-gain potency of the high-protein beverage: "Add peanuts, eggs (with shells) and bananas into the powder with milk and mix them in a blender. If you really want faster results use 'half and half' instead of ordinary milk."

The Art of Expressing the Human Body

俊九先生.

Thank you for your wonderful gift to my son; he sleeps with the bear nowadays.

Enclosed I'm rushing the ad & informa where you can obtain the gain weight food supplement. Be sure to order it from your Pa. instead of from Lo. Angeles, Calf. as there is a difference in postage.

Add peanuts, eggs (with shells) and ~~bananas~~ bananas into the powder ~~and~~ with milk and mix them in a blender. If you really want faster result use 'half and half' instead of ordinary milk

The postman is here I better mail this.

Talk to you later

Your friend
Bruce Lee

Note that Lee was recommending the above as a "weight-gain" remedy for those who wanted to put on more weight. "Half and half" is much higher in calories for this purpose than regular milk. As a point of fact, Lee himself never used "half and half."

In addition to his protein drinks, Lee took a well-balanced supply of vitamins and minerals. Bruce and Linda frequented the Lindberg Nutrition store in Santa Monica to purchase multipackets of vitamins and minerals (which usually contained seven tablets that, together, provided a well-balanced sampling of the various vitamins and minerals). In 1971, when Lee was filming his first Chinese-language film, *The Big Boss*, in Pakchong, Thailand, he wrote home frequently, often complaining of the lack of proper food. "The food in Bangkok is terrible, especially in Pakchong," he wrote. "This village has no beef and very little chicken and pork. Am I glad to [have] come with my *vitamins*."

Lee, who made sure to take a balanced daily allotment of vitamins and minerals, attributed greatest importance to vitamin C, which he would take extra amounts of at times when he felt his resistance to be lowered as a result of fatigue or stress.

A Sampling of Supplements Taken by Bruce Lee

Energizer "67" (200 tab)

Lecithin granules

Hi Bee Pollen with C

Natural vitamin E

Natural protein

Rose hips (liquid)

Wheat germ oil

Natural protein tablets (chocolate)

Acerola-C (250)

B-Folia (180)

B-Folia (360)

A-Veg (500)

E-Plex (250)

The Value of an Electric Juicer

Concerned with nutritional as well as exercise science, Lee was quick to pick up on the value of an electric juicer. Because he was so active, the primary "fuel" that his body metabolized was carbohydrate and the richest form of carbohydrate, in terms of vitamin and mineral content— in addition to easily metabolized (naturally occurring) starches and sugars—is fruits and vegetables. Among the juices Lee found particularly helpful for his energy level was a mixture of carrots, celery, and apples. Again, we defer to Linda for information on such matters:

> We had a juicer long before they became the rage they are today, and we'd make carrot juice, vegetable juice, and fruit juice. On days when Bruce didn't have his two protein drinks, he might have one protein drink and one juice drink. I guess our most popular juice drink was one that we made mainly from carrots. Carrots would form the largest proportion of the drink, and then apples would be second in proportion. Finally, I would add in some celery. And then often we would throw in some sprigs of parsley, because parsley is so rich in nutrients—but you don't need very much as it does have a distinct taste, so we would just put in a little bit. So, if you wanted to recreate, say, our carrot/apple/celery juice, I would say that half of it should be carrot juice, a third of it would be apple juice, and the rest of it would be celery and parsley—but it's really a matter of your personal taste.

Lee also drank juices extracted from dark green vegetables and other fruits, which he usually combined with carrot juice in order to sweeten the taste. The juice of fresh fruits and vegetables is the richest available food source of vitamins, minerals, and enzymes. In the course of a typical day, a person usually can't eat enough raw fruits and vegetables to nourish the body properly. While this has probably always been true, it is particularly true today, when you need extra nutrients to help your body detoxify more environmental toxins. On most days, you probably can't find the time to eat five pounds of carrots. But you certainly can find the time to drink their nutritional equivalent in a delicious, nutrient-rich glass of juice.

Such a convenient form of super-nutrition was not lost on Lee. Using an electric juicer has become quite popular again—for the very same reasons Lee considered when he first plugged his in over twenty years ago, as seen in this quote from Cherie Calbom and Maureen Keane's book, *Juicing For Life* (Garden City Park, N.Y.: Avery, 1992):

> *Juice allows your body to quickly assimilate the many valuable nutrients found in food. Enzymes are organic catalysts that increase the rate at which foods are broken down and absorbed by the body. Found in plant foods such as fruits and vegetables, enzymes are destroyed when these foods are cooked. This is why fresh raw produce should constitute at least half of your diet. The quick and easy digestion of these foods, made possible by the enzymes will give you greater energy and health.*

Honey and Ginseng
Another carbohydrate drink (although it is so small it barely qualifies as a drink) that helped sustain Lee's energy levels was Royal Jelly; a mixture allegedly made from the honey of queen bees. (It comes in a little glass vial, the top of which has to be cut with a small cutting stone that is provided.) Kareem Abdul-Jabbar recalled that Lee would frequently open one of the little  vials and consume its contents during the filming of *The Game of Death*. Herb Jackson remembers Lee once telling him, "Whenever I have to do a demonstration, I take a little Royal Jelly beforehand and Voom! My energy levels are perfect." According to Linda, "Bruce believed that the Royal Jelly and the ginseng both added to his energy stores and kept his activity levels up. He really appreciated the 4,000-plus years of Chinese experimentation with herbs and teas— and so he felt that if something had worked effectively for so many people for so many thousands of years that they were probably onto something that was very healthful."

The Love of Tea

While Bruce Lee never drank coffee, primarily because he didn't like the taste of it, he remained very fond of tea throughout his life. Linda recalls that Bruce particularly liked tea with honey in it. Whenever he was working, particularly while filming movies in Hong Kong, Linda would make him a large thermos of honey tea to sip in between scenes. She says, "I would prepare it for him by tak-

ing one tea bag of Lipton tea, and making it kind of strong. Then I'd stir in about a tablespoon of honey. Bruce liked the taste of that and we would have it all the time."

Another type of tea that Lee enjoyed was called Li-cha [L-eye-cha] in Chinese—which, literally translated, means, "milk tea." It is a beverage that was often shared by Lee and Linda in the mornings, particularly after they had moved to Hong Kong in 1971. Linda recalls with amusement that Wu Ngan, a man who was Bruce's lifelong friend and frequently was his movie stand-in, and who lived with the Lees in Hong Kong, used to make Li-cha for her and Bruce every morning, and then one day she asked him what was in what she had always considered to be a special kind of Chinese tea. Wu Ngan looked at her in surprise and answered, "Oh, it's Lipton tea, of course!" Li-cha is actually a black tea—almost a red tea—that is allowed to steep until it is quite strong. Milk and sugar are then added, giving it a taste not unlike that of an English tea.

Lee didn't restrict himself to just honey tea or Li-cha, however. Linda recalls that "There are hundreds of kinds of Chinese tea—and Bruce liked most of them." When Lee was working on the set of a film, friends and workers would often provide him with various teas—chrysanthemum being a particular favorite. Apart from the pleasant taste, Lee knew that many health benefits are attributed to various teas, which made them not only good tasting, but good for him as well.

Having briefly touched on what constituted Lee's well-balanced diet, let's take a look at how it would break down on a daily basis by looking at a representative sample of a typical day's eating.

A Day in Bruce Lee's Life: A Typical Diet

Breakfast

Food: A bowl of muesli cereal (Familia was a favorite brand at the time), comprised of whole grains, nuts, and dried fruits, plus 2% milk.

Beverage: Orange juice and/or tea.

Snack

Juice or Protein Drink: Protein powder, noninstant powdered milk made with water or juice, eggs (sometimes with their shells), wheat germ, bananas or other fruit, and even peanut butter were often added. Brewer's yeast was also frequently added.

Lunch

Food: Meat, vegetables, and rice.

Beverage: Tea.

Snack

Juice or Protein Drink: see ingredients for morning-snack protein drink.

Dinner

Food: Spaghetti and salad, or another meal of rice, vegetables, and meat, chicken, or seafood.

Beverage: One glass of 2% milk and/or tea.

Lee believed that people should be aware of the nutrients they consumed on a daily basis. Within the pages of his script for *Enter the Dragon,* Lee made the following annotations about consuming only the calories your body actually needs, rather than simply indulging yourself in the culinary pleasures: "When you are a martial artist, you are a nut; you go to extremes to improve yourself as a martial artist. And one way is to eat only what your body requires and not get carried away with sensual [eating] pleasures." Lee also noted: "When you are a martial artist, you only eat what you require and don't get carried away with foods that don't benefit you as a martial artist."

In summary, Lee believed in staying away from foods with empty caloric content and little nutritive value. He found it especially helpful to avoid refined sugars, excessive fats, fried food, and alcohol.

21. A DAY IN THE LIFE: A LOOK AT HOW BRUCE LEE'S TRAINING METHODS EVOLVED

It is difficult to imagine the amount of research and experimentation that occupied Bruce Lee's brief life. As Lee's former pupil Chuck Norris once noted,

No other human being had ever trained the way Bruce trained—fanatically. He lived and breathed it from the time he got up at six o'clock in the morning until he went to bed at night. He was either working out or thinking about it. His mind was always active, never resting. He was always thinking about what he could do to improve himself or what new inventions were possible. His mind was constantly active.

Not surprisingly, Lee experimented with many different martial art and supplemental training programs. In reviewing a sample of his workout schedules throughout a ten-year period, some interesting developments arise. For one thing, there is a steady shedding process, in which Lee's emphasis shifts from learning new or more techniques, and constant technical practice, to whittling away at the techniques he already had, discarding those he felt were impractical or unnecessary, and simultaneously increasing his supplemental training in an effort to support or bolster the techniques he felt were the essentials of efficient unarmed combat.

The Art of Expressing the Human Body

For example, by looking at his 1963 training records we learn that Lee was working out in what would have to be described as a traditional fashion: He was performing "forms" or a pattern of movements endemic to Wing Chun gung fu, a classical Chinese martial art. He performed sil lum tao (great little idea) and worked out daily on the mook jong (wooden dummy). According to Taky Kimura and Jesse Glover, who knew and studied with Bruce Lee during this period, Lee might work out for three or more hours a day on the wooden dummy and run through the Wing Chun first form several times a day—and then perform punching and kicking exercises.

By 1965, Lee had added the "one-two" (the right jab, left cross) of Western boxing and the backfist (gwa choy) technique to his Wing Chun arsenal. More importantly, he had begun to train with barbells in an effort to develop his forearms, was beginning his cardio program to enhance his endurance, and was engaging in specialization training for his abdomen.

By 1968, Lee had shed sil lum tao (at least as a staple in his own training) and you can see the strong influence of Western boxing (that is, the hook, jab, uppercut, and cross).

By 1970, his workouts were perfect examples of efficient cross-training: weight training for strength, running and cycling for cardiovascular efficiency, stretching for flexibility, the heavy bag for timing and applied power, the speed bag for developing rhythm and timing, and the top and bottom bag for coordination and precision. Further, he had broken down his workouts in order to focus more intensely on each aspect of his martial art, training his hands on Mondays, Wednesdays, and Fridays and his legs on Tuesdays, Thursdays, and Saturdays.

Notice that the classical influences of Wing Chun are now almost totally absent from his training. There is no practice of forms, working out on the mook jong, or air punching. His kicks

also are not restricted to the low-line angles emphasized in Wing Chun, which is not to suggest that Lee had lost or cast aside his knowledge of these methods. They were too firmly embedded in his neuromuscular pathways ever to become inaccessible should he require them. However, his training programs reveal that by the 1970s his area of emphasis had changed to a far more streamlined method of strikes and kicks and increased supplementary training to support the efficient delivery of these techniques.

Circa 1963

    A Personal Training Program for Bruce J. F. Lee

1. Punching
   a. Air punching—3 sets of 50 each
   b. Sand plate—3 sets of 50 each
   c. Hanging bag—3 sets of 50 each
2. Leg stretching
   a. Forward stretch—3 sets of 12 each
   b. Side stretch —3 sets of 12 each
3. Kicking
   a. Straight kick—3 sets of 12 each
   b. Side kick—3 sets of 12 each
   c. Kicking form—3 sets of 12 each
4. Wooden dummy
   a. The classical form of 108
   b. Individual technique training
   c. Training in entering
5. Form practice—sil lum tao, hand techniques, and Wing Chun fist
6. Individual technique practice
7. Sticking hand training
8. Freestyle practice

Circa 1965

    Bruce Lee's Training Schedule

DAY	TIME	ACTIVITY
Monday	10:45 AM–12:00 PM	Forearm
	5:00 PM– 6:00 PM	Stomach
Tuesday	10:45 AM–12:00 PM	Punching
	1:30 PM–2:30 PM	Endurance and agility
	5:00 PM–6:00 PM	Stomach
Wednesday	10:45 AM–12:00 PM	Forearm
	1:30 PM–2:30 PM	Endurance and agility
	5:00 PM–6:00 PM	Stomach
Thursday	10:45 AM–12:00 PM	Punching
	5:00 PM–6:00 PM	Stomach
Friday	10:45 AM–12:00 PM	Forearm
	5:00 PM–6:00 PM	Stomach

DAY	TIME	ACTIVITY
Saturday	10:45 AM–12:00 PM	Punching
	12:00 PM–2:30 PM	Endurance and agility
	5:00 PM–6:00 PM	Stomach
Sunday	10:45 AM–12:00 PM	Off
	5:00 PM–6:00 PM	Off

Technique Training

A.
1. Finger jab
2. Trap and hit
3. Pak sao and straight blast
4. Inside pak sao and strike to opponent's right side
5. Lop sao

B.

1. Pak sao
2. Lop sao
3. Backfist
4. Straight punch to backfist (left and right)
5. Pak sao to backfist
6. Double lop sao
7. Low hit to backfist
8. Low hit to backfist to kick
9. Hit on inside gate
10. Inside gate straight blast
11. Hit low to backfist

Defensive Awareness
1. Stop hit—kick and bill jee
2. Deflect and strike

1. The stop hit or kick
2. The all-purpose striking and/or kicking
3. The four-corner counter
4. The leg obstruction

Classical Techniques
1. Pak sao
2. Lop sao

3. Backfist
4. Low strike to backfist (left and right)
5. Pak sao to backfist
6. Double lop sao and backfist
7. Low punch to backfist, lop sao to backfist
8. Jut sao (pull down opponent's guard and hit)
9. Low strike to backfist to kick
10. Attacking inside gate
11. Inside gate to low backfist
12. Inside kick to straight blast

1. The stance
2. The right punch
   a. From stance
   b. Darts out loosely
   c. Learn broken rhythm
3. The use of the left hand from stance
   a. Straight
   b. Chin down and out of line
   c. Right back for guard also for strategies
   d. No hesitation and shorter
4. The flexible use of kicking (quick resuming to stance, also from mobility)
5. The hook
   a. Tight and short
   b. Looseness and pivot
   c. Protection hand accordingly

   Additional Techniques
1. The high/low (left and right)
2. The one-two

   Combination Techniques
1. Shin kick with pak sao and straight punch
2. Finger jab to low groin strike to straight punch
3. Rear leg kick and finger jab
4. Feint kick to finger jab to straight blast

Circa 1968
   Daily Training
1. Stretching and leg extension

The Art of Expressing the Human Body

- **EVERY DAY**

- A) STRETCHING & LEG EXTENSION

- (B). GRIP POWER.
  - (1) GRIP MACHINE — — — —5 SETS OF 5
  - 2). PINCH GRIP — — — —5 SETS OF 6
  - 3) CLAW GRIP — — — —5 SETS OF
  - 4). FINGER LIFT — — — ALL

- C). CYCLING — — — — — — 10 MILES

- D). BENCH STEPPING. — — — — 3 sets

- E). READING.

- F) MENTAL CHARGE — — — — — THINK ABOU. CHARACTER. EVERY TA THAT COMES!

- 7)- CONSTANT HAND GRIP.

2. Grip power
   a. Grip machine—5 sets of 5
   b. Pinch grip—5 sets of 6
   c. Claw grip—5 sets of as many as possible
   d. Finger lift—all
3. Cycling—10 miles
4. Bench stepping—3 sets
5. Reading
6. Mental charge—Think about character. Everything that comes!
7. Constant hand grip

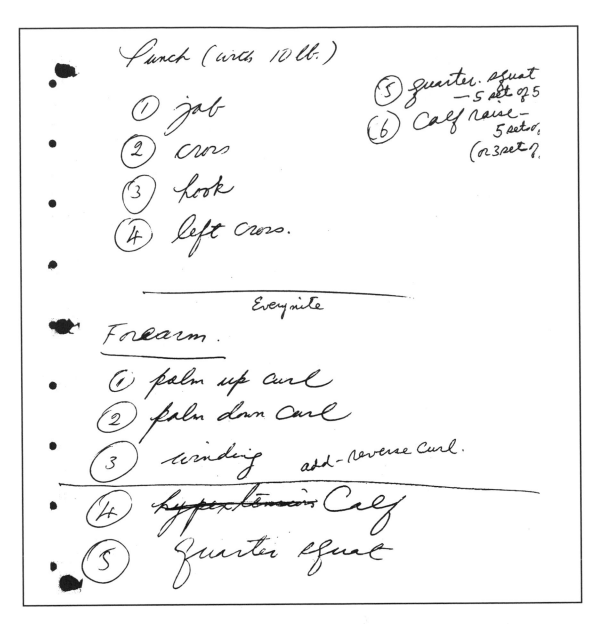

Nightly Training

1. Palm-up curl
2. Palm-down curl
3. Winding
4. Reverse curl
5. Quarter squat—5 sets of 5
6. Calf raise—5 sets of 5 (or 3 sets of 8)

Fist

1. Hook
2. Left cross
3. Finger jab

The Art of Expressing the Human Body

Endurance

1. Jogging

Flexibility/Agility Exercises: Feet

1. Kick
2. Spin kick

Techniques

1. Chi sao
2. Partner trains
3. Hand
4. Sparring
5. Stomach

Monday	Tuesday	Wednesday	Thursday	Friday	Saturday	Sunday
9–9:30 (exer)	9–9:30 (exer)	9–9:30 (exer)	9–9:30 (exer)	9–9:30 (exer)	9–9:30 (exer)	9–9:30 (exer)
9:30–10 (running)	9:30–10 (running)	9:30–10 (running)	9:30–10 (running)	9:30–10 (running)	9:30–10 (running)	9:30–10 (running)

10–11:30 AM—breakfast

11:30 AM—hand toughening—fist and finger and chi sao

12:30 PM—lunch

Monday	Tuesday	Wednesday	Thursday	Friday	Saturday	Sunday
4–5:30 (Hand and elbow)	4–5:30 (Feet and knee)	4–5:30 (Hand and elbow)	4–5:30 (Feet and knee)	4–5:30 (Hand and elbow)	4–5:30 (Feet and knee)	4–5:30 (Hand and elbow)
or	or	or	or	or	or	or
8–9:30	8–9:30	8–9:30	8–9:30	8–9:30	8–9:30	8–9:30

Side Kick

1. Low—left/right
2. High—left/right

Straight Kick

1. Low—left/right
2. Middle—left/right

Hook Kicking (from Right Stance)

1. High—left/right
2. Middle—left/right

1. Straight/side
2. Straight/rear
3. Low side/high side
4. Right—left
5. Left—right

1. Right straight kick (right and left)
   a. Starting
   b. Medium
   c. Near finish

Kicking on the Hanging Padded Board
(Makiwara Pad)

1. Hook kick
   a. Low
   b. Medium
   c. High
2. Side kick
   a. Low
   b. Medium
   c. High
3. Spin kick
4. Reverse kick
5. Forward kick

Left Cross-Stomp Kick

1. The shin straight kick
2. The stop shin
3. The side shin kick

1. The groin kick (with quick retreat)
2. The side thrust kick (with quick retreat)

Roundhouse for Added Angle and Flexibility
The Use of Combination Kicking

1. Combination with one leg
2. Combination with two legs

The Art of Expressing the Human Body

Punching on Padded Board (Hanging)

1. Jab
   a. Punch
   b. Finger
2. Hook
3. Cross
4. Upward hook
5. Palm
6. Elbow

Punch Practice

1. The straight punch
   a. Long
   b. Standard
2. The backfist
3. The finger jab

Lead Punch (Combination) Practice

1. The one-two
2. The one-two and hook
3. Right body—right jaw—left jaw
4. The one-hook-cross
5. The straight high/low

Punching Exercises

1. Straight punch with weight—3 sets
2. Glove straight punching—2 sets
3. Entering straight punching—2 sets
4. Glove elbowing—2 sets
5. Glove hooking—3 sets

Punching Drill (with 10-pound dumbbells)

1. Jab
2. Cross
3. Hook
4. Left cross

The Straight Right Punch

1. High and low
2. Long and short

The Straight Left Punch

1. High and low
2. Long and short

1. The wall pad
2. The heavy bag

Circa 1970–1971

1. Stomach and waist (every day)
   a. Sit-up
   b. Side bend
   c. Leg raises
   d. Flag
   e. Twist
   f. Back bend
2. Flexibility (every day)
   a. Front stretch
   b. Side stretch
   c. Hurdle stretch
   d. Sit stretch
   e. Sliding stretch
   f. Front pulley stretch
   g. Side pulley stretch

	MON.	TUES.	WED.	THURS.	FRI.	SAT.
	7:30 5:30 / 8:00 9:00	7:00 – 9:00	7:00 – 9:00	7:00 – 9:00	7:00 – 9:00	7:00 – 9:00
	a) Stomach b) Flexibility c) Run	a) Stomach b) Flexibility c) cycling	a) Stomach b) Flexibility c) Run	a) Stomach b) Flexibility c) cycling	a) Stomach b) Flexibility c) Run	a) Stomach b) Flexibility c) cycling
	12 – 1 Run	11:00 – 12:00 Weight training	12 – 1 Run	11:00 – 12:00 Weight training	12 12:00 Run	11:00 – 12:30 Weight training
	5:30 – 6:30 Punching	5:30 – 6:30 Kicking	5:30 – 6:30 Punching	5:30 – 6:30 Kicking	5:30 – 6:30 Punching	5:30 – 6:30 Kicking

SECRET

3. Weight training (Tuesday, Thursday, Saturday)
   a. Clean and press—2 sets of 8
   b. Squat—2 sets of 12
   c. Pullover—2 sets of 8
   d. Bench press—2 sets of 6
   e. Good Mornings—2 sets of 8
   f. Curl—2 sets of 8

or

   a. Clean and press—4 sets of 6
   b. Squat—4 sets of 6
   c. Good morning—4 sets of 6
   d. Bench press—4 sets of 5
   e. Curl—4 sets of 6
4. Kicking (Tuesday, Thursday, Saturday)
   a. Side kick—right and left
   b. Hook kick—right and left
   c. Spin kick—right and left

    d. Rear front thrust—right and left

    e. Heel kick—right and left

5. Punch (Monday, Wednesday, Friday)

    a. Jab—speed bag, foam pad, top and bottom bag

    b. Cross—foam pad, heavy bag, top and bottom bag

    c. Hook—heavy bag, foam pad, top and bottom bag

    d. Overhand cross—foam pad, heavy bag

    e. Combinations—heavy bag, top and bottom speed bag

    f. Platform speed bag workout

    g. Top and bottom bag

6. Endurance (stationary cycling)

    a. Running (Monday, Wednesday, Friday)

    b. Cycling (Tuesday, Thursday, Saturday)

    c. Rope skipping (Tuesday, Thursday, Saturday)

The Breakdown of Bruce Lee's Total Fitness Routine

Monday–Saturday (Stomach and Flexibility)

1. Bench leg stretch
2. Sit-up
3. Side leg stretch
4. Leg raises
5. Side bends
6. Hurdle stretch
7. Flag
8. Sitting stretch
9. Twist
10. Split stretch
11. Back bends
12. High kicking

Monday, Wednesday, Friday (Hand Techniques)
Bean Bag

1. Right jab
2. Right jab—foam pad
3. Left cross
4. Right hook

    a. Tight

    b. Loose

    c. Upward

5. Overhand left
6. Combination

Top and Bottom Speed Bag
1. Right jab
2. Left cross
3. Right hook
4. Overhand left
5. Combination
6. Platform speed bag—taper off

Tuesday, Thursday, Saturday (Leg Techniques)
1. Right side pulley stretch
2. Right side kick
3. Right side pulley stretch
4. Left side kick
5. Left side pulley stretch
6. Right leading hook kick
7. Left reverse hook kick
8. Right heel kick
9. Left spin-back kick
10. Left reverse front kick

Tuesday, Thursday, Saturday (Weight Training)

1. Clean and press
2. Squat
3. Bench press
4. Curl
5. Good morning

Bruce Lee's Personal Training Routine (1970–1971)

DAY	ACTIVITY	TIME
Monday	Stomach and flexibility	7:00 AM–9:00 AM
	Running	12:00 PM
	Hand	5:30 PM–6:30 PM and 8:00 PM–9:00 PM
Tuesday	Stomach and flexibility	7:00 AM–9:00 AM
	Weights	11:00 AM–12:00 PM
	Leg	5:30 PM–6:30 PM and 8:00 PM–9:00 PM
Wednesday	Stomach and flexibility	7:00 AM–9:00 AM
	Running	12:00 PM
	Hand	5:30 PM–6:30 PM and 8:00 PM–9:00 PM
Thursday	Stomach and flexibility	7:00 AM–9:00 AM
	Weights	11: 00 AM–12:00 PM
	Leg	5:30 PM–6:30 PM and 8:00 PM–9:00 PM
Friday	Stomach and flexibility	7:00 AM–9:00 AM
	Running	12:00 PM
	Hand	5:30 PM–6:30 PM and 8:00 PM–9:00 PM
Saturday	Stomach and flexibility	7:00 AM–9:00 AM
	Weights	11:00 AM–12:00 PM
	Leg	5:30 PM–6:30 PM and 8:00 PM–9:00 PM

22. DAYS IN THE LIFE: EXCERPTS FROM BRUCE LEE'S PERSONAL TRAINING DIARIES

Some guys may not believe it, but I spent hours perfecting whatever I did.
—Bruce Lee

During 1968, Bruce Lee kept a meticulous record of every workout he had and every private lesson he taught. These have proven to be invaluable testaments to his daily commitment to a lifestyle emphasizing the development of health and fitness.

Fortunately, Linda Lee Cadwell has kept all of Bruce's day-timer diaries. These provide us with a time capsule of sorts, going back to a time before Lee became one of the biggest stars in the world (which he was in 1973). They allow us to take a look at the training methods and degree of commitment required for him to become such a fitness specimen and master martial artist.*

It is evident from Lee's day-timers and from a letter he wrote to longtime friend and student George Lee that he made a fitness "resolution" as he headed into 1968. George Lee had evidently manufactured some high-quality punching bags for Bruce to use, which Bruce had mounted on a fence in his backyard. Bruce made mention of this in his letter to Lee: "Your wall punching bags have definitely helped in my daily training. I've started the training on Christmas eve—my 1968 resolution. I now train an average of two-and-a-half hours a day, including hand exercises, leg exercises, running, isometrics, stomach exercises, sparring exercises, free-hand exercises. Your training equipment all helps in my program. Thanks."

So that you can see for yourself the level of Lee's dedication to training (note the entry on March 2 where he performed 2,000 punches that day!), two months' worth of Lee's daily workouts, commencing January 1, 1968, and running through until March 2, 1968, are provided as Lee recorded them in his day-timer diaries.

*The contents of Bruce Lee's day-timers will be published as volume seven of the Bruce Lee Library.

Excerpts from Lee's Day-Timers for 1968

Monday, January 1, 1968
9:20–9:30 AM
Warm up (leg & stomach)
9:30–9:49 AM
Running

The Art of Expressing the Human Body

12:00–12:45 PM
Punch: 500
Finger jab: 300
3:00–3:55 PM
1. Leg squat
2. Leg stretching
   a. Pulley
   b. Stand
3. Hook kick
   a. Left & right
   b. Front & rear
7:30–7:50 PM
Finger jab—100
Punch—200
9:00–9:30 PM
Sit-up—4 sets
Side bend—4 sets
Leg raise—4 sets
Total: 2 hrs, 59 minutes

Tuesday, January 2, 1968
9:20–9:25 AM
Warm up (waist, legs, stomach)
9:27–9:41 AM
Run
11:30–12:35 PM
Punch—500
Finger jab—400
3:00–3:45 PM
Squat

Punching
1. Weight—3 sets
2. Light bag—20 minutes
3. Heavy bag—3 sets
(emphasizing left cross)
5:15–5:45 PM
Sit-ups—5 sets
Side bends—5 sets
Leg raises—5 sets

8:20–8:24 PM
Forearm (isometric)
Total: 2 hrs, 53 minutes

Wednesday, January 3, 1968
7:00–9:00 AM
Gung fu workout
(Sticking hand—all present)
9:00–9:15 AM
Warm up (waist, leg, stomach)
9:20–9:50 AM
Punch (back fist)—500
Skip rope—3 sets
10:00–10:30 AM
Finger jab—500
11:05–11:15 AM
Run
3:05–4:00 PM
1. High kick stretching (left & right)—4 sets

2. Side leg stretching (left & right)—4 sets
3. Pulley hip extension—3 sets
4. Right leading hook kick
   a. heavy bag—3 sets
   b. paper—3 sets
5. Rear left hook kick
   a. heavy bag—3 sets
   b. paper—3 sets
4:15–4:35 PM
Stomach & waist
3 exercises of 4 sets each

Thursday, January 4, 1968
10:35–10:45 AM
Warm up
11:15–12:20 PM
Punch (left)—500
Punch (right)—500
12:53–1:07 PM
Run
3:05–3:25 PM
Punching, weight, paper
Skip rope
10:05–10:53 PM
Sit-up—4 sets
Leg raise—4 sets
Side bends—4 sets
Forearm/wrist (isometrics)

Friday, January 5, 1968
Warm up
9:25–10:13 AM
Punch
(right)—500
(left)—500
11:00 AM
Chuck Norris
(chi sao practice)
4:10–5:00 PM
Leg stretching

The Flying Side Kick

Pulley & stand (hip)
Straight & side
Work on left side kick
8:30 PM
Sit-up—5 sets
Leg raise—5 sets
Side bend—5 sets
Forearm/wrist (isometric)

The Stop Kick

Saturday, January 6, 1968
9:10 AM
Warm up
10.40 AM
Punch—500
(middle knuckle bleeding)
Finger jab—500
Ted [Wong] came over
Running downtown
Dinner in Chinatown with Cheree's [Linda's school friend's] parents

Sunday, January 7, 1968
10:00 AM
Punch—500
Finger jab—500
Leg stretching
Ted [Wong] over
Chi sao practice
11:30 AM–12:00 PM
Forearm (isometric)
9:10–9:55 PM
Stomach & waist
Sit-up—5 sets
Side bend—5 sets
Leg raises—5 sets
Stop by Chinatown gym

Monday, January 8, 1968
9:35–10:40 AM
Warm up

Punch—500

Finger jab—500

10:50 AM

Run (with weight)

5:15 PM

Side bends—5 sets

Leg raises—5 sets

Sit-up—5 sets

8:45–9:30 PM

Stretching

• pulley, stance

Straight & side (left and right)

Hook kick

• right leading

• left rear

Forearm (isometric)

Mike Stone called

Tuesday, January 9, 1968

10:00–11:00 AM

Punch—500

Finger jab—500

11:30 AM

Forearm/wrist (isometric)

Squat & stance (isometric)

11:45–12:15 PM

Stomach

Sit-up—4 sets

Leg raises—5 sets

Side bends—4 sets

3:55 PM

Run (with weights)

10:00 PM

Skip rope—3 sets

Punch

1. Weight

2. Light bag

3. Heavy bag

(emphasizing left punch & overhand left)

The Left Hook

Wednesday, January 10, 1968

10:00–11:10 AM

Leg stretching

    a. Stand—3-ways stretch

    b. Pulley—straight & side

    c. Kicking exercises

11:15 AM

Skip rope—3 sets

Forearm/wrist (isometrics)

Squat/stance (isometrics)

11:45–12:20 PM

Stomach

Leg raises—5 sets

Sit-up—5 sets

Side bends—5 sets

3:15 PM

Run (with weight)

5:20–5:45 PM

Punch—500

7:30 PM

The Right Lead Punch

Mito [Uyehara], Ted [Wong], [Richard] Bustillo, Herb [Jackson]—workout

Thursday, January 11, 1968

10:45–11:25 AM

Skip rope— 4 sets

Light bag—5 sets

(emphasizing general striking)

11:55 AM

Forearm/wrist (isometric)

Squat/stance (isometric)

12:15–12:35 PM

Finger jab—500 reps

1:45–2:18 PM

Punching—500 reps

One-legged squat—2 sets

2:45–3:00 PM

Punching (supplemental)—500 reps (total = 1,000)

3:15 PM

Running (with weight)

10:00 PM
Stomach
Sit-up—5 sets
Leg raises—5 sets
Side bends—5 sets

Friday, January 12, 1968
9:30–10:50 AM
Stretching
    a. Straight
    b. Side
    c. Knee
    d. Pulley (side)
    e. Pulley (straight)
Skip rope—4 sets
11:00 AM–12:00 PM
Stomach
Leg raises—6 sets
Sit-up—6 sets
Side bends—6 sets
12:15 PM
Forearm/wrist (isometric x 2)
2:20 PM
Finger jab—450
Punch—500
3:20 PM
Run (with weight)
8:00 PM
Single leg squats—2 sets
Squat/stance (isometrics)
Punch (supplemental)—300

Saturday, January 13, 1968
10:00 AM
Punch—500
Stretching
    a. Straight
    b. Side
    c. Knee

The Spinning Back Kick

Pulley
   a. Straight
   b. Side
Punch (supplemental)—500
Stomach—2 sets
Forearm/wrist (isometric)

Sunday, January 14, 1968
9:30 AM
Punch—500
Finger jab—100
Skip rope—4 sets
Light bag striking (right & left—emphasize left)
Running
Gung fu workout
(knuckle bleeds)
Ted, Sam [girlfriend], Linda, went to show
10:00 PM
Ted [Wong]—chi sao

Monday, January 15, 1968
11:45 AM
Leg stretching
Stand
   a. Straight
   b. Side
   c. Knee
Pulley
   a. Side
   b. Straight
3:45 PM
Stomach
   a. Leg raise—5 sets
   b. Side bends—5 sets
   c. Sit-up—5 sets
4:45 PM
Running
Squat/stance (isometric)
Punch (supplemental)—500 (total 1,000)
Forearm/wrist (isometric)

The Hook Kick

Tuesday, January 16, 1968

10:00 AM

Punch—500

11:00 AM

Stomach

    a. Side bend—5 sets

    b. Leg raises—5 sets

    c. Sit-ups—5 sets

12:00 PM

Forearm/wrist (isometric)

3:45 PM

Running

4:30 PM

Stance/squat (isometric)

Squat—2 sets

Punch—500

Finger jab—350

Single leg squat—2 sets

9:30 PM

Heavy bag (overhand left emphasis)

Punch (supplemental)—500

The Outside Crescent Kick

Wednesday, January 17, 1968

10:55–12:05 PM

Stretching

Stand

    a. Straight

    b. Side

Pulley

    a. Side

    b. Straight

Skip rope—4 sets

12:15 PM

Stomach

    a. Leg raises—5 sets

    b. Side bends—5 sets

    c. Sit-ups—5 sets

1:45 PM

Punching—400

(middle knuckle hurt)

Finger jab—4 sets

Forearm/wrist (isometric)

Stance/squat (isometric)

2:40 PM

One-legged squat—2 sets

3:30 PM

Running

7:30 PM

Photo shoot: Chinatown gym (Ted [Wong] and Dan [Inosanto])

Thursday, January 18, 1968

11:00 AM–12:40 PM

Stomach

1. Sit-up—5 sets

2. Side bends—5 sets

3. Leg raises—5 sets

Skipping rope—5 sets

Light bag (one-two)—3 sets

Heavy bag (overhand)—3 sets

3:20 PM

One-legged squat—2 sets

Forearm/wrist (isometric)

Stance/squat (isometric)

3:45 PM

Running

(rest knuckles for one day)

5:30 PM

Dinner—The Gee

Gung fu workout

The Reverse Hook Kick

Friday, January 19, 1968

11:00 AM

Punch—500

12:00–2:30 PM

Chi sao—Chuck Norris

9:00 PM

Stomach

Side bends—5 sets

Leg raises—5 sets

Sit-up—5 sets

The Art of Expressing the Human Body

Forearm/wrist (isometric)

Stance/squat (isometric)

One-legged squat—2 sets

Leg stretching

Stand

1. Straight

2. Side

3. Knee out

Punch (supplemental)—500

Total = 1,000 punches

(blister on second knuckle)

Saturday, January 20, 1968

3:30 PM

Running (footwork advancing)

5:00 PM

Stomach

1. Sit-up—5 sets

2. Side bends—5 sets

3. Leg raises—5 sets

Forearm/wrist (isometric)

Stance/squat (isometric)

One-legged squat—2 sets

Leg stretching (hip)

Pulley

   a. Side kick

   b. Straight kick

   (3 sets each)

Finger push-ups—3 sets

Punch—350

Sunday, January 21, 1968

10:00 AM

Running

Ted [Wong]—chi sao

Light bag—3 sets

(left cross)

Heavy bag—3 sets (overhand left)

1:30 PM

Promotion test at school

Punch—350
Stomach
1. Sit-up—5 sets
2. Side bends—5 sets
3. Leg raises—3 sets
Punch (supplemental)—650
Total (punches) = 1,000
Forearm/wrist (isometric)
One-legged squat—2 sets
Stance/squat (isometric)

Monday, January 22, 1968
10:00 AM
Leg stretching
   a. Stand
1. Straight
2. Side
3. Knee
   b. Pulley
1. Side (hip)
2. Straight (hip)
Stomach
1. Side bends—5 sets
2. Sit-ups—5 sets
3. Leg raises—5 sets
2:45 PM
Punch—500
4:00 PM
Stance/squat (isometric)
4:05 PM
Running
10:00 PM
One-legged squat—2 sets
Forearm/wrist (isometric)

Tuesday, January 23, 1968
10:00 AM
Punch—500
Stance/squat (isometric)

The Side Kick

The Art of Expressing the Human Body

Skip rope—4 sets

Leg raises—6 sets

3:26 PM

Forearm/wrist (isometric)

3:35 PM

Light bag

1. Left cross

2. One-two

3:48 PM

Running/sprinting

(blister on right foot)

Stomach

Sit-up—3 sets

Stance/squat (isometric)

4:00 PM

Mike Stone—chi sao

Wednesday, January 24, 1968

8:30 AM

Punch—500

9:15 AM

Punch (supplemental)—500

10:40 AM

Stance/squat (isometric)

Single leg squat—2 sets

Stomach

1. Leg raises—6 sets

2. Sit-up—6 sets

3. Side bends—6 sets

11:30 AM

Leg stretch (stand)

1. Straight

2. Side

3. Knee stretch

Leg stretch (pulley)

   a. Side

   b. Straight

Light bag

1. One-two

2. Left cross

2:00 PM
Dr. Wong
Mito, Ted, Herb, Arnold Wong, George, Gee, Linda
Gung fu workout
Chi sao

Thursday, January 25, 1968
Chi sao (distance)
1:00 PM
Joe Lewis
Run (jog)
Stomach
Sit-up—6 sets
Leg raises—6 sets
Side bends—6 sets
One-legged squat—2 sets
Forearm/wrist (isometric)
Stance/squat (isometric)
Light bag
1. One-two-three—3 sets
Heavy bag
1. Overhand
2. Cross (high-low)—3 sets

Friday, January 26, 1968
9:45 AM
Punch—500
11:10 AM
Leg stretching
Stand
   a. Straight
   b. Side
   c. Knee
Pulley
   a. Straight
   b. Side
Stomach
1. Sit-up—6 sets
2. Leg raises—6 sets
3. Side bends—6 sets

The Right Cross

The Art of Expressing the Human Body

2:00 PM
Forearm/wrist (isometric)
Stance/squat (isometric)
3:05 PM
Run/sprint (3 miles)
6:00 PM— 6:50 PM
Flight #645 (Oakland)
James Lee's surprise party

Saturday, January 27, 1968
(Oakland)
Running
Ted, James, & family

Monday, January 29, 1968
11:00 AM
Punch—1,000 reps
3:00 PM
Stomach
1. Leg raises—6 sets
2. Sit-up—6 sets
3. Side bends—6 sets
Single-legged squat—2 sets
4:00 PM
Wrist/forearm (isometric)
Stance/squat (isometric)
9:15 PM
Leg stretching
    a. Front stretch (left)
    b. Side stretch (both)
    c. Knee spread (right)
Tuesday, January 30, 1968
11:00 AM
Punch—500
3:30 PM
Punch (supplemental)—350
4:15 PM
Stomach
    a. Sit-up—6 sets
    b. Leg raises—8 sets

The Right Hook

    c. Side bends—6 sets
3:00 PM
Doctor checkup (canceled)
5:30 PM
One-legged squat—2 sets
Stance/squat (isometric)
Wrist/forearm (isometric)

Wednesday, January 31, 1968
10:30 AM
Joe Lewis #2
3:00 PM
Black Belt magazine meeting
(Gung fu, karate, judo, kendo, aikido)
Punch—500
Light bag
1. Left cross
2. One-two-three
7:00 PM
Chuck Norris—Ted Wong

Thursday, February 1, 1968
(Brandon's birthday)
3:00 PM
Punch—800
3:50 PM
Stomach
1. Sit-up—6 sets
2. Leg raises—6 sets
3. Side bends—6 sets
10:00 PM
Forearms/wrist (isometric)
One-legged squat—2 sets
Stance/squat (isometric)
Skipping rope—3 sets

Friday, February 2, 1968
11:00 AM
Stomach training

The Art of Expressing the Human Body

1. Side bend—6 sets
2. Leg raises —6 sets
3. Sit-ups—6 sets
5:00 PM
One-legged squat—2 sets
Completion of translating *The Peng Pu Chuan*

Saturday, February 3, 1968
12:00 PM
Stomach
Sit-up—6 sets
Side bends—6 sets
Leg raises—6 sets
3:30 PM
Light bag—3 sets
    a. One-two
    b. One-two-three-two
4:00 PM
Punch—400
Heavy bag—left body blow
9:00 PM
One-legged squat—2 sets

Sunday, February 4, 1968
11:00 AM
Stomach
1. Leg raises—8 sets
2. Sit-up—6 sets
3. Side bends—6 sets
Footwork—timing/rhythm
3:00 PM
Punch—500
Hook kick—from long distance
Punch (supplemental)—350

Monday, February 5, 1968
1:00 PM
Punch—600
4:30 PM
Light bag training

5:00 PM

Stomach

1. Leg raises—6 sets

2. Side bends—6 sets

3. Sit-ups—6 sets

Punch (supplemental)—300

One-legged squats—2 sets

Black Belt picked up book

Tuesday, February 6, 1968

Punch—500 reps

Stomach

1. Sit-up

2. Leg raises

3. Side bends

(6 sets each)

Punch (supplemental)—500 reps

Punch (supplemental)—500 reps

Total (punches)—1,500

Car repaired

Wednesday, February 7, 1968

12:00 PM

Little Joe

2:00 PM

Punch—500

Punch (supplemental)—500

Total: 1,000

3:00 PM

Stomach

    a. Sit-up—6 sets

    b. Leg raises—6 sets

    c. Side bends—6 sets

Thursday, February 8, 1968

Punch—500

Talked to Lou Pitte

Ted [Wong] came over

The Art of Expressing the Human Body

Sunday, February 18, 1968
8:15–9:00 PM
Flight #742
(missed plane, standby for 9 PM)
Punch—500

Monday, February 19, 1968
Rest
Punch—500
Mike Stone called

Tuesday, February 20, 1968
Punch—500

Wednesday, February 21, 1968
Punch—800
Mito, Ted, Herb (workout)

Thursday, February 22, 1968
Punch—2,000
100 (left)

Friday, February 23, 1968
Punch—1,000
200 (left)

Sunday, February 25, 1968
Punch—500 (right)
200 (left)
Boy Scout appearance?
(canceled)

Monday, February 26, 1968
12:00 PM
Lunch—Arnold Wong
Punch—500 (right)
Punch—200 (left)
Mike Stone called

Tuesday, February 27, 1968
3:00–3:45 PM
Flight #342
Punch—500 right
Punch—200 left

Wednesday, February 28, 1968
Punch—1,000
Joe Lewis called

Thursday, February 29, 1968
9:00 AM
Little Joe
12:30 PM
Lunch—Fitzsimon
(call Jay—get together next week)
Punch—1,000
Print card

Saturday, March 2, 1968
Steve McQueen called
2:30 PM–5:00 PM
Steve's house
Punch—2,000
Punch— 500 (left)

The Art of Expressing the Human Body

23. A COMPENDIUM OF BRUCE LEE'S PERSONAL TRAINING ROUTINES

Use your own ideas on creating new ways to improve the function of the body in Gung Fu—the hell with conventional methods and opinions.
—Bruce Lee

Lee's already considerable activity levels essentially doubled once he moved to Hong Kong with his family in 1971. Upon arrival he weighed between 135 and 140 pounds; by the time he finished shooting *Enter the Dragon* he weighed 125. Some have tried to make a correlation between his weight loss and eventual death, but this is unfounded. The fact is that Lee lost between 10 and 15 pounds over a period of two years, and during these years he lived in the extraordinarily humid climate of Hong Kong, and significantly increased his activity—for example, he staged dozens of fight scenes for the films he shot from 1971 to 1973, and would choreograph hundreds of "takes" before deciding which scenes were usable.

The multiple takes and fight-scene choreography alone would be equivalent (at least) to several classes a day of today's popular "karaerobics," "box-out," and other cardiovascular and fat-burning activities. But Lee also ran two miles a day in Hong Kong's humidity, seven days a week, rain or shine. And he performed his usual jeet kune do training, which, as he told American journalist Alex Ben Block in August of 1972, required "about two hours a day" in addition to "special weight-training exercises." Such an increased level of activity cannot help but result in weight loss—if only through water loss alone. In fact, such weight loss is a common occurrence among superathletes in various sports, though it is seldom addressed. As authors Gabe Mirkin and Marshall Hoffman noted in *The Sportsmedicine Book*:

> *On a hot day, Philadelphia pitcher Larry Christenson and soccer star Kyle Rote, Jr. can lose twelve pounds; tennis player Butch Buchholz, ten pounds; and basketball stars Calvin Murphy, five pounds, and Paul Silas, seventeen pounds. In the 1968 Olympic marathon trials, Ron Daws lost nine pounds, or 6 percent of his body weight, despite drinking fluids every two miles. Most of this weight loss is due to sweat.*

In comparison, Lee's weight loss over a period of two years doesn't appear as dramatic, particularly when he was just as physically active as these athletes, if not more so.

One might be tempted to ask "Wouldn't all of this activity quickly lead to overtraining?" In fact this very question was posed to Lee in 1970 by his student Bob Bremer. Lee's response was "I'd rather be overtrained than undertrained." It's important here to put Lee's response in context: He was not talking about weight training, per se, for he knew of its systemic-draining effects and recommended that it only be performed every other day; what Lee and Bremer were referring to was Lee's martial art or technique training and his cardiovascular and flexibility training. And all of these can and should be performed daily by athletes who want to become more proficient in their particular skill or craft. In martial art, it takes hundreds of thousands of repetitions of a punch or a kick in order to lay down the neuromuscular pathways necessary to develop complete proficiency in delivering such techniques efficiently and reflexively. Unlike boxing, Lee's art of jeet kune do has far more than four techniques (i.e., the jab, cross, uppercut, and hook) to perfect. In fact, in his notebooks "Commentaries on the Martial Way,"* under the heading "A Jeet Kune Do Weapons Arsenal," Lee lists the following 127 techniques:

- 10 different side kicks
- 4 leading straight kicks
- 1 groin kick
- 2 rising kicks
- 1 step back straight kick
- 11 hook kicks
- 3 foot sweeps
- 5 spinning back kicks
- 5 heel kicks (performed both stiff-legged and bent)
- 8 reverse straight kicks
- 1 leading right finger jab
- lead right hand strikes
- 6 right hooks
- 5 left crosses
- 4 right back fists
- 4 right quarter swings
- 2 uppercuts
- 3 pivot point strikes
- 13 elbow strikes
- 4 knee thrusts
- 4 head butts

*See volume three of the Bruce Lee Library, *Jeet Kune Do: Commentaries on the Martial Way* (Boston: Charles E. Tuttle, 1997), pp. 70–85.

The Art of Expressing the Human Body

- 2 hook throws (one with an arm drag, another without the arm drag)
- 2 left foot sweeps (one executed from a right stance, the other from a left stance)
- 2 right foot sweeps (one from a left stance, the other from a right stance)
- 2 kick backs (one from a right stance, the other from a left stance)
- 2 single leg tackle and trips (one from a standing position, the other from a lying position)
- 1 double leg tackle (to a double leg and spine lock turn over)
- 2 outside armpit locks (from a left stance and a right stance)
- 2 wrist locks (one a cross wrist lock, the other an elbow wrist lock)
- 1 lying cross arm bar lock (after hook throw)
- 1 reverse wrist lock (to double arm lock)
- 3 chokes
- 1 hair pulling (for infighting control)
- 1 foot stomp (for infighting to hurt)
- 1 skin pinching (to hurt)
- 1 ear pulling (for control)
- 1 groin grab

These techniques represent what Lee was researching and practicing in 1970; some of these were later discarded, others maintained, and still more would be examined over the next three years of his life. Now imagine how you could possibly acquire proficiency in all of these techniques by undertraining.

As we have seen, Lee spent thousands—if not hundreds of thousands—of hours researching and trying out new exercise routines, theories, systems, and methods. The cornerstones of Lee's training belief were experimentation and a refusal to become a slave to any one approach. Lee believed that the moment one locks in to one way of doing anything, the potential for true learning, growth, and development is shut down. Therefore, Lee employed and experimented with many different training methods throughout his lifetime. Fortunately, he also wrote down many of the training programs he employed at various stages of his martial art career. If we are careful to look at them as Lee did, that is, as different approaches or signposts to help lead us in the direction of our own self-improvement and body awareness, then they can offer us many worthwhile benefits in the areas of strength, coordination, agility, speed, and total fitness. What follows are all of the workout programs—both in martial art and supplemental training—that Bruce Lee saw fit to commit to paper during the course of his life.

Fundamentals and Flexibility
Exercise Fundamentals
1. Depending on the need
2. The basics are flexibility and agility
3. We do not need split!
4. Running
5. Shadow sparring

Flexibility Routine 1

1. High kick and rear stretch
2. Side leg raise
3. Forward bend
4. Elbow touching
5. Waist twisting
6. Alternate splits on chair
7. Leg stretch (front, side)
8. Sitting bends
9. Stride stretch

Flexibility Routine 2

1. Leg stretching (straight and side)
2. Forward bend
3. Back bend (Roman chair)
4. Groin stretch

Coordination and Precision Routines

A Top and Bottom Bag Routine

1. Right jab
2. Left cross
3. Right hook
4. Overhand left
5. Combination
6. Platform speed bag—taper off

A Focus Glove Routine

1. Right lead (from starting position)
2. Right jab
3. Left cross
4 Right uppercut
5. Left cross
6. Right body hook
7. Left cross
8. Right cross
9. Transition
10. Low left cross
11. High left hook
12. Right body hook

The Art of Expressing the Human Body

13. High right hook

14. Left overhead cross

Stamina/Agility Routines

Stamina/Agility Training

1. Alternate splits—3 sets of 20

2. Jumping squat—3 sets of 10

3. 3 sets of one minute each

Agility/Endurance

1. Jumping squat

2. Alternate split

3. Rope skipping and footwork

4. Punch and kick combination (techniques, speed, and power)

5. Stomach training

    a. Bent-leg sit-up

    b. Leg raises

    c. Side twist

    d. Frog kick

    e. Isometric squeeze

Endurance Exercises

1. Running

2. Shadow fighting

3. Bicycling

Calisthenics Routines

Morning Calisthenics

1. Straight leg stretch

2. Sit-up

3. Side stretch

4. Leg raises

5. Side bend

6. Hurdler's stretch

7. Flag

8. Sit stretch

9. Twist

10. Hamstring stretch

11. Back bend

(一) STOMACH EXERCISES   一九六五年 十月 十五日
1) Waist Twist ——— 4 SETS OF 70
2) SIT UP TWIST ——— 4 SETS OF 20
3) LEG RAISES ——— 4 SETS OF 20
4) LEANING TWIST ——— 4 SETS OF 50
5) FROG KICK ——— 4 SETS OF

(二) FOREARM EXERCISES
1) UNDERHAND WRIST CURL ——— 4 SETS OF 17
2) OVERHAND WRIST CURL ——— 4 SETS OF 12
3) LEVERAGE BAR CURL (A) ——— 4 SETS OF 15
4) " " " (B) ——— " " " "
5) REVERSE CURL ——— " " " 6
6) WRIST ROLLAR ——— 4 COMPLETE WINDINGS
7) LEVERAGE BAR TWIST ——— 3 SETS OF 10

(三) PUNCHING EXERCISES
1) STRAIGHT PUNCH WITH WEIGHT — 3 SETS OF
2) Glove straight punching — 2 SETS OF
3) ENTERING " " " — " " "
4) Glove elbowing ——— " " "
5) Glove hooking ——— 3 SETS OF

(四) STAMINA/AGILITY TRAINING
1) Alternate splits — 3 SETS OF 20
2) Jumping squat — 3 SETS OF 10
3) Skip Rope ——— 3 SETS OF MIN

(五) GRIP TRAINING
EVERY CHANCE — DAILY

Basic Fitness Routines

 1. Alternate splits
 2. Push-up
 3. Run in place
 4. Shoulder circling
 5. High kicks
 6. Deep knee bends
 7. Side kick raises
 8. Sit-up (twist)
 9. Waist twisting
10. Leg raises
11. Forward bends

General Fitness

1. Stomach and waist—sit-up, leg raises, twist
2. Endurance (plus agility)—running, skipping, hopping
3. Grip and forearm—grip machine, reverse curl, underhand wrist curl, overhand wrist curl

Sequence 1

1. Basic fitness
2. Kicking
3. Punching
4. Form
5. Isometric
6. Endurance
7. Grip and forearm

Fitness Program

1. Alternate splits (agility, leg, endurance)
2. Waist twisting (external obliques)
3. Run in place (agility, endurance, leg)
4. Shoulder circling (flexibility)
5. High kicks (flexibility)
6. Side kick raise (flexibility)
7. Leg stretch (straight/side)—waist twisting
8. Sit-up (rectus abdominus—upper)
9. Leg raises (rectus abdominus—lower)

The Jun Fan Gung Fu Institute Fitness Program
1. Alternate splits
2. Waist twisting (3 times to each side)
3. Run in place
4. Shoulder circling
5. High kicks (knee stiff and locked)
6. Side kick raises
7. Bent-knee sit-ups
8. Waist twisting (one time to each side)
9. Leg raises
10. Forward bend (3 times to front, left, front, right)

Chinatown School Warm-Up Program 1
(alternate each double set, back and forth, until 2 sets of each have been completed)
1. Alternating splits and shoulder rolls—2 sets
2. Running in place and waist twisting—2 sets
3. Bent-knee sit-up and shoulder circling (double/single)—2 sets
4. 4-count leg raises and breathing exercises—2 sets
5. Alternating touching leg raises and breathing exercises—2 sets
6. Straight high kicks and side leg raises—2 sets
7. Jumping squats (or jumping jackknives) and breathing exercises— 2 sets

Chinatown School Warm-Up Program 2
1. Alternating splits—2 sets
2. Shoulder rolls—2 sets
3. Running in place—2 sets
4. Waist twisting—2 sets
5. Straight high kicks—2 sets
6. Shoulder circling—2 sets (double and single)
7. Side leg raises—2 sets
8. Breathing exercise—2 sets
9. Alternating jackknives—2 sets
10. Breathing exercises—2 sets
11. 4-count leg raises—2 sets
12. Breathing exercise—2 sets
13. Bent-knee sit-up—2 sets
14. Breathing exercise—2 sets
15. Jumping jackknives—2 sets
16. Stretching exercise—2 sets

The Jun Fan Calisthenics Program

1. Stomach
    a. Sit-up (hand in front; behind head; arm in air)
    b. Jack
    c. The complete leg raise
2. Push-ups
    a. Wide arm (clapping 1, 2)
3. ¼ squats
    a. ½ squats
4. Burpee
    a. Two-count
    b. Four-count (including standing up)
    c. Four-counts and jumping, lying
5. Back
    a. Dorsal raise (one leg; alternate arm and feet [sides, overhead]) rocking
6. Jump and reach
    a. Tack jump
    b. Pike jump
    c. Straddle pike jump
7. Lying lateral trunk exercises
    a. Bent knees
    b. Stiff two-legged
    c. Single crossover
    d. Double crossover
8. Kicks (all directions)
    a. Front
    b. Side
    c. Behind
    d. Groin stretch
        1. With knees bent
        2. Stiff-legged
    e. Lifting knee
    f. Controlled (slow motion)
        1. Knee leveling
        2. Actual slow kicks
9. Flexibility stretch
    a. Leg
10. Step-ups

The Art of Expressing the Human Body

Basic Fitness Exercises

A. Basic fitness exercises

1. Alternate splits
2. Run in place
3. Jumping squat
4. Push-up

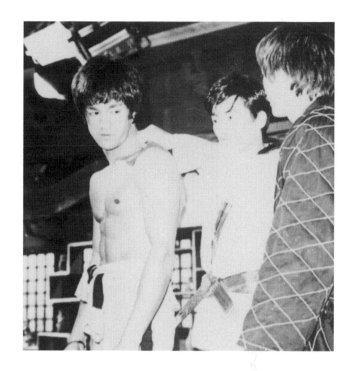

Everyday Opportunities

1. Stairs
2. Standing one-legged (when putting shoes on)
3. Walk
4. Quiet awareness

B. Waist

1. Waist twist
   a. Stick
2. Side bend
3. Forward and backward

C. Stomach

1. Sit-up
2. Leg raises

D. Shoulder

1. Roll
2. Circling and swing

E. Leg

1. Knee turning
2. High kick

Preparational Exercises

1. Alternate splits
2. Shoulder circling

1. Sit-up
2. Breathing slimmer

1. Run in place
2. Waist twisting

1. High kick
2. Leg raises

1. Jumping squat
2. Shoulder circling

Fitness Exercises
1. Stomach
    a. Sit-up
    b. Leg raises
    c. Waist twisting
2. Shoulder
    a. Rotating
    b. Swinging
3. Leg
    a. High kicking (flexibility)
    b. Leg swinging
4. Agility (general)
    a. Split alternating
    b. Stationary running
    c. Jumping squat
    d. Push-up

Power/Speed Routines
    a. Bag punching—heavy, light, paper (and mask for finger jab)
    b. Isometric training—outward pressure
    c. Weight training
1. Squat
2. Bench press

Isometric Routine
    The Basic Eight Isometric Exercises
1. Press lockout
2. Press start
3. Rise on toes
4. Pull
5. Parallel squat
6. Shoulder shrug
7. Deadlift
8. Quarter squat

    Tensolator (Bullworker) Routine
Chest
    a. Compression
    b. Twisting

The Art of Expressing the Human Body

Arm
    a. Bow and arrow
    b. Vertical compression
    c. Biceps—standing, kneeling
    d. Forearm

Shoulder
    a. Behind the head compression
    b. Above-head compression
    c. Door corner press

Stomach
    a. Sitting pulling downward
    b. Kneeling compression
    c. Oblique compression

Back
    a. Kneeling pulling downward
    b. Vertical compression on thigh
    c. Behind buttock compression
    d. Lean over compression
    e. Deadlift

Leg
    a. Stiff-legged outward stretch
    b. Knee outward stretch
    c. Sitting calf press down
    d. Knee squeezing inward on grip
    e. Lifting instep upward

Circulation exercise

Weight-Training/Bodybuilding Routines

General Weight-Training Routine

1. Clean and press
2. Squat
3. Curl

Weight Training
    a. Legs
      • Squat
      • Calf raise
    b. Grip
      • Forearm
      • Grip

Training schedule

1). Stomach and waist — (everyday)
  a). sit-ups.   d). flag.
  b). side bend   e). twist
  c). leg raise   f). back bend.

2). Flexibility (every day)
  a). front stretch   d). sit stretch
  b). side stretch   e). sliding stretch
  c). hurdle stretch   f). front pully stretch – A

3). Weight Training (TUES. THURS. SAT.)
  a). clean and press – 2 sets of 8 d). bench press – 2 sets of 6
  b). squat – 2 sets of 12 e). good morning – 2 sets of 8
  c). pull over – 2 sets of 8 f). curl – 2 sets of 8

1) clean & press — 4 sets of 6   5) curl — 4 sets of 6
2) squat — 4 sets of 6
3) good morning — 4 sets of 4
4) Bench press — " " 5   SECRET

4). KICKING :– (TUES. THURS. SAT.)
  1) side kick — right & left
  2) hook kick — " "
  3) spin kick — " "
  4) rear front thrust " "
  5) Heel kick — " "

5). PUNCH (M. W. FRI.)
  1) jab — speed bag, foam pad. top & bottom bag
  2) cross — foam pad. heavy bag, top and bottom
  3) hook — heavy bag, foam pad. "
  4) over hand cross — (foam pad, heavy bag)
  5) combinations — (heavy bag) top & bottom, speed bag.
  6) platform speed bag workout out —
  7) top and bottom bag.

5). Endurance —
  1) running – (M. W. FRI.).
  2) cycling (TUES. THUR. SAT.).
  3) rope skipping (TUES. THUR. S
    SECRET

c. All-around power

- Squat
- Deadlift
- Bench press

The Jun Fan Weight-Training Routine

A. Leg

1. Squat
2. Calf raise

B. Grip

1. Forearm
2. Grip

1. Calf
2. Press
3. Isometrics

SECRET
MORNING.
1). straight leg stretch   5). side bend.   9) twist
2). sit up   6). hurdle stretch   10). hamstring stel.
3). side stretch   7). flag.   11). back bend.
4). leg raises   8). sit stretch

KICKING :—

1). side pully stretch
2). front pully stretch
1). side kick — right   } pad.
2). side kick — left.
3). hook kick — right - pad
4). hook kick — left.
5). spin kick — heavy bag.
6). heel kick — pad.
7). rear front thrust — (swinging heavy bag) or pad.

WEIGHT TRAINING
1). clean & press
2). squat
3). Bench Press / Curl
4). Good morning.
5). Curls /

One of Lee's Heavy-Bag Punching Routines

Note: Spend one to two minutes per drill. Drill only on two to three drills a night (on "hand" days). Always do drill 1 plus another drill or another two drills.

Drill	Technique
1	Single jab or double jab
2	Right jab (low) to right hook or right jab
3	Right jab (inside) to right hook (outside)
4-a	Right jab to right back fist
4-b	Right jab (outside), right jab (inside) to left hook (low)
5-a	Right jab (high) to right jab or hook
5-b	Right jab (high) to right jab (low) to right hook (outside)
6	Right jab (high) to left cross (high) or left hook
7	Right jab (high) to left cross (low)
8	Right jab (low) to right hook (high) to left cross (high)
9	Right jab (outside high) to left cross/hook (inside high) to right hook (low)
10	Right jab (high) to left cross (high) to right hook (high)
11	Right jab (high) to left cross (low) to right hook (high)
12	Right jab (high) to left cross (low) to left hook
13	Left cross (low) to right jab (low) to left hook (high)
14	Right jab (low) to right hook/jab (high) to left cross/hook (low)
15	Right jab (low) to left cross (high) to right hook (high) to left hook (low)
16	Right jab (high) to left cross/hook (high) to right hook (high) to left cross/hook (high) to right hook (low)

The Art of Expressing the Human Body

17   Right jab (high/inside) to right jab (high/center) to right hook (high/outside) to left cross/hook (low)

18   Right jab (low) to right hook (high) to left cross (low) to right hook (high)

19   Right jab (high) to right hook (high) to left cross (high) to right hook (low)

20   Right jab (high) to right jab (medium) to right hook (high) to left hook/cross (inside low)

21   Right jab (low) to right hook (high) to right jab (low) to left cross/hook (high)

22   Jik chung (straight blast)

23   Feint left (don't hit) and strike with right (high and low)

24   Feint left (low) to hook left (high)

25   Right jab (center) to left hook/cross (inside/high) to right hook (high)

26   Right jab (center) to right hook (high/outside) to left hook (high/inside)

1. Heavy bag—long right, long left, left/right punching (hooks)

2. Paper—long right, long left, left/right punching (straight)

3. Kicking
   a. Group 1—SI/SI/BA
   b. Individual—groin/knee/shin
   c. 2 men kicking

Power Training (Supplementary)

1. Isometric training
   • Upward forward force
   • Side kick and straight kick

2. Weight training

All-Around Power Routine
   a. Squat
   b. Deadlift
   c. Bench press

Sequence Training Routine (For Total Fitness)
Sequence 1a (Mon., Wed., Fri.)

1. Rope jumping

2. Forward bend

3. Cat stretch

4. Jumping jack

5. Squat

6. High kick

Sequence 1b (Mon., Wed., Fri.)
Forearm/Waist

1. Waist twisting

2. Palm-up curl

3. Roman chair

4. Knee drawing

5. Side bending

6. Palm-down curl

Sequence 2a (Tues., Thurs., Sat.)

1. Groin stretch

2. Side leg raise

3. Jumping squat

4. Shoulder circling

5. Alternate splits

6. Leg stretch—AB

Sequence 2b (Tues., Thurs., Sat.)

1. Leg raises

2. Reverse curl

3. Sit-up twist

4. Leverage bar twist

5. Alternate leg raise

6. Wrist-roller

General (Overall) Development

1. Arm

   a. Clean and press

   b. Curl

2. Shoulder

   a. Press behind neck

   b. Upright rowing

3. Leg

   a. Squat

4. Back

   a. Rowing

5. Chest

   a. Bench press

   b. Pullover

Abdominal Routines

  Stomach Exercises

1. Waist twist—4 sets of 70

The Art of Expressing the Human Body

2. Sit-up twist—4 sets of 20

3. Leg raises—4 sets of 20

4. Leaning twist—4 sets of 50

5. Frog kick—4 sets of as many as possible

Stomach/Waist Exercises (2 Sets)

1. Roman chair sit-up

2. Leg raises

3. Side

Running

Forearm-/Grip-Training Routines

Forearm Exercises

1. Underhand wrist curl—4 sets of 17

2. Overhand wrist curl—4 sets of 12

3. Leverage bar curl (A)—4 sets of 15

4. Leverage bar curl (B)—4 sets of 15

5. Reverse curl—4 sets of 6

6. Wrist-roller—4 complete windings

7. Leverage bar twist—3 sets of 10

Grip Training

1. Every chance—daily

1. Gripping machine—5 sets of 5

2. Pinch gripping—5 sets of 5

3. Claw gripping—5 sets of 5

Finger Lifts

1. All five (left and right)

Wrist Training

1. Barbell rotation—5 sets of 5

2. Leverage bar—3 sets of 10

3. Extended leverage bar—3 sets of 5

Forearm Training

1. Palm-up curl

2. Reverse curl

1. Reverse curl—3 sets of 10

2. Palm-up wrist curl—3 sets of 12

3. Palm-down wrist curl—3 sets of 12

4. Wrist-roller—wind up and down once

(*Note:* Carry sponge gripper and use daily as much as possible)

1. Reverse curl—3 sets of 10

2. Palm-up wrist curl—3 sets of 12

3. Palm-down wrist curl—3 sets of 12

4. Wrist-roller—wind up and down once

1. Reverse curl—3 sets of 10

2. Flexor wrist curl (B or D)—3 sets of 10

3. Extensor wrist curl (B or D)—3 sets of 10

4. Wrist-roller—as much as you can

(*Note:* B = barbell, D = dumbbell)

All-Around Forearm Exercises

Finger—finger lift

Grip—pinch grip, claw grip, gripping machine

Forearm—palm up, palm down, reverse curl

Wrist—leverage bar, barbell rotation

A Personal Training Program for Bruce J. F. Lee

1. Punching

   a. Air punching—3 sets of 50 each

   b. Sand plate—3 sets of 50 each

   c. Hanging bag—3 sets of 50 each

2. Kicking

   a. Leg stretching

1. Forward stretch—3 sets of 12 each

2. Side stretch —3 sets of 12 each

   b. Straight kick—3 sets of 12 each

   c. Side kick—3 sets of 12 each

   d. Kicking form—3 sets each

3. Wooden dummy

   a. The classical form of 108

   b. Individual technique training

   c. Training in entering

4. Form practice—sil lum tao, hand techniques, and Wing Chun fist

5. Individual technique practice

The Art of Expressing the Human Body

6. Sticking hand training

7. Freestyle practice

Footwork Routine (Freelance Set 1—Shadow Boxing)

Consists of All Footwork

 1. Step and slide shuffle advance

 2. Step and slide shuffle retreat

 3. Slide shuffle advance

 4. Slide shuffle retreat

 5. Push shuffle advance

 6. Push shuffle retreat

 7. Step through

 8. Step back

 9. Circle right

10. Circle left

11. Curving right

12. Curving left

13. Replace step

14. Heel and toe sway

15. Pendulum shuffle

16. Lead step (three ways)

17. Triangle pattern (two ways)

18. Rocker shuffle

Training for Kicking

Warm-Up

 a. Side pulley stretch

 b. Front pulley stretch

1. Warm-up

 a. The letting out of water

 b. Knee

2. The whip

3. The sideways whip

Training Drills for Kicking

1. Side kick—right (on pad)

2. Side kick—left (on pad)

3. Hook kick—right (pad)

4. Hook kick—left (pad)

5. Spin kick—heavy bag

6. Heel kick—pad
7. Rear front thrust—swinging heavy bag (or pad)

Freelance Set 2

Consists of:

Jik tek (straight kick)

O'ou tek (hook kick)

Juk tek (side kick)

Hou tek (rear kick)

Juen tek (spin kick)

Qua tek (inverted hook kick)

The following kicks from a:

1. By-jong
2. Slide shuffle
3. Step and slide shuffle
4. Pendulum shuffle
5. Step through and back

Side Kick

1. Low—left/right
2. High—left/right

Straight Kick

1. Low—left/right
2. Middle—left/right

Hook Kicking (From Right Stance)

1. High—left/right
2. Middle—left/right

1. Straight/side
2. Straight/rear
3. Low side/high side
4. Right—left
5. Left—right

1. Right straight kick (right and left)
   a. Starting
   b. Medium
   c. Near finish

Kicking on the Hanging Padded Board (Makiwara Pad)

1. Hook kick
   a. Low
   b. Medium
   c. High
2. Side kick
   a. Low
   b. Medium
   c. High
3. Spin kick
4. Reverse kick
5. Forward kick

Left Cross-Stomp Kick

1. The shin straight kick
2. The stop shin
3. The side shin kick

1. The groin kick (with quick retreat)
2. The side thrust kick (with quick retreat)
Roundhouse for added angle and flexibility

The Use of Combination Kicking

1. Combination with one leg
2. Combination with two legs

Punching on the Hanging Padded Board

1. Jab
   a. Punch
   b. Finger
2. Hook
3. Cross
4. Upward hook
5. Palm
6. Elbow

Punch Practice

1. The straight punch
   a. Long
   b. Standard

2. The backfist
3. The finger jab
Bring string and glove (or paper—sound effect)

Lead Punch (Combination) Practice
1. The one-two
2. The one-two and hook
3. Right body—Right jaw—Left jaw
4. The one-hook-cross
5. The straight high/low

Punching Exercises
1. Straight punch with weight—3 sets
2. Glove straight punching—2 sets
3. Entering straight punching—2 sets
4. Glove elbowing—2 sets
5. Glove hooking—3 sets

Punching Drill (with 10-pound dumbbells)
1. Jab
2. Cross
3. Hook
4. Left cross

The Straight Right Punch
   a. High and low
   b. Long and short

The Straight Left Punch
   a. High and low
   b. Long and short
1. The wall pad
2. The heavy bag

Technique Training
A.
1. Finger jab
2. Trap and hit
3. Pak sao and straight blast

The Art of Expressing the Human Body

4. Inside pak sao and strike to opponent's right side

 5. Lop sao

B.

 1. Pak sao

 2. Lop sao

 3. Backfist

 4. Straight punch to backfist (left and right)

 5. Pak sao to backfist

 6. Double lop sao

 7. Low hit to backfist

 8. Low hit to backfist to kick

 9. Hit on inside gate

10. Inside gate straight blast

11. Hit low to backfist

Self-Defense Techniques 1

   a. Collar grasp (left and right hand)

   b. Collar grasp—left or right push

   c. The shove

   d. Behind

Self-Defense Techniques 2

 1. The collar grasp (left or right hands)
    (push—left or right hand)

 2. The shove (two hands—or after being shoved—kick)

 3. The right straight

   a. The right swing

   b. The right uppercut

   c. The right twisting curve

 4. The left jab

   a. The left hook

   b. The left upper cut

   c. The left swing

   d. The left twisting curve

Defensive Awareness

1. Stop hit—kick and bill jee

2. Deflect and strike

1. The stop hit or kick

2. The all-purpose striking and/or kicking

3. The four corner counter

4. The leg obstruction

Classical Techniques

1. Pak sao

2. Lop sao

3. Backfist

4. Low strike to backfist (left and right)

5. Pak sao to backfist

6. Double lop sao and backfist

7. Low punch to backfist, lop sao to backfist

8. Jut sao (pull down opponent's guard and hit)

9. Low strike to backfist to kick

10. Attacking inside gate

11. Inside gate to low backfist

12. Inside kick to straight blast

1. The stance

2. The right punch

   a. From stance

   b. Darts out loosely

   c. Learn broken rhythm

3. The use of the left hand from stance

   a. Straight

   b. Chin down and out of line

   c. Right back for guard also for strategies

   d. No hesitation and shorter

4. The flexible use of kicking (quick resuming to stance, also from mobility)

5. The hook

   a. Tight and short

   b. Looseness and pivot

   c. Protect hand accordingly

Additional Techniques

a. The high/low (left and right)

b. The one-two

Combination Techniques

1. Shin kick with pak sao and straight punch

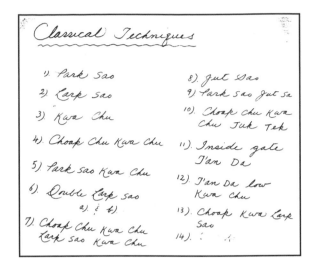

The Art of Expressing the Human Body

2. Finger jab to low groin strike to straight punch

3. Rear leg kick and finger jab

4. Feint kick to finger jab to straight blast

Private Lesson

1. Shin/knee stop kick

2. The all purpose right hand strike (close distance)

3. The moving out of line, sudden change of level, and snap back with counters

4. The rear kick

1. Hard and soft

2. What to judge in selection

3. Common characteristic

4. Form?

5. Styles

Specialized Technique Training

1. General
   a. Stop finger jab
   b. Stop shin kick
   c. The four corners

2. Classical

3. Self-defense

Bruce Lee's Training Schedule

Day	Time	Activity
Monday	10:45 AM–12:00 PM	Forearm
	5:00 PM–6:00 PM	Stomach
Tuesday	10:45 AM–12:00 PM	Punching
	1:30 PM–2:30 PM	Endurance and agility
	5:00 PM–6:00 PM	Stomach
Wednesday	10:45 AM–12:00 PM	Forearm
	1:30 PM–2:30 PM	Endurance and agility
	5:00 PM–6:00 PM	Stomach
Thursday	10:45 AM–12:00 PM	Punching

Day	Time	Activity
Thursday	5:00 PM–6:00 PM	Stomach
Friday	10:45 AM–12:00 PM	Forearm
	5:00 PM–6:00 PM	Stomach
Saturday	10:45 AM–12:00 PM	Punching
	12:00 PM–2:30 PM	Endurance and agility
	5:00 PM–6:00 PM	Stomach
Sunday	10:45 AM–12:00 PM	Off
	5:00 PM–6:00 PM	Off

Daily Training

Every Day

A. Stretching and leg extension
B. Grip power
   1. Grip machine—5 sets of 5
   2. Pinch grip—5 sets of 6
   3. Claw grip—5 sets of as many as possible
   4. Finger lift—all
C. Cycling—10 miles
D. Bench stepping—3 sets
E. Reading
F. Mental charge—Think about character. Everything that comes!
G. Constant hand grip

Every Night

1. Palm-up curl
2. Palm-down curl
3. Winding
4. Reverse curl
5. Quarter squat—5 sets of 5
6. Calf raise—5 sets of 5 (or 3 sets of 8)

Fist

1. Hook
2. Left cross
3. Finger jab

Endurance

1. Jogging

Flexibility/Agility Exercises: Feet

1. Kick
2. Spin kick

Techniques

1. Chi sao
2. Partner trains

Hand

Sparring

Stomach

Monday	Tuesday	Wednesday	Thursday	Friday	Saturday	Sunday
9–9:30	9–9:30	9–9:30	9–9:30	9–9:30	9–9:30	9–9:30
(exer)	(exer)	(exer)	(exer)	(exer)	(exer)	(exer)
9:30–10	9:30–10	9:30–10	9:30–10	9:30–10	9:30–10	9:30–10
(running)	(running)	(running)	(running)	(running)	(running)	(running)
10–11:30 AM—breakfast						
11:30 AM—hand toughening—fist and finger and chi sao						
12:30 PM—lunch						
4–5:30	4–5:30	4–5:30	4–5:30	4–5:30	4–5:30	4–5:30
(Hand and elbow)	(Feet and knee)	(Hand and elbow)	(Feet and knee)	(Hand and elbow)	(Feet and knee)	(Hand and elbow)
or	or	or	or	or	or	or
8–9:30	8–9:30	8–9:30	8–9:30	8–9:30	8–9:30	8–9:30

Animal Qualities

1. Tiger—cat stretch, stretching, bend crawl, neck turning stare, hand stretch
2. Ape—jumping, dodging
3. Crane—air movement, one-legged movement
4. Bear—isometric

Sparring Practice

1. Sticking hand
2. Freestyle

Gung Fu Practice

1. Punching—straight, hook, cross, back fist
2. Kicking—side, straight, hook, combination
3. Form—the three forms

Putting It All Together: The Bruce Lee Workout

1. Stomach and waist (every day)
   a. Sit-up
   b. Side bend
   c. Leg raises
   d. Flag
   e. Twist
   f. Back bend
2. Flexibility (every day)
   a. Front stretch
   b. Side stretch
   c. Hurdle stretch
   d. Sit stretch
   e. Sliding stretch
   f. Front pulley stretch
   g. Side pulley stretch
3. Weight training (Tuesday, Thursday, Saturday)
   a. Clean and press—2 sets of 8
   b. Squat—2 sets of 12
   c. Pullover—2 sets of 8
   d. Bench press—2 sets of 6
   e. Good mornings—2 sets of 8
   f. Curl—2 sets of 8
or
   a. Clean and press—4 sets of 6
   b. Squat—4 sets of 6
   c. Good morning—4 sets of 6
   d. Bench press—4 sets of 5
   e. Curl—4 sets of 6
4. Kicking (Tuesday, Thursday, Saturday)
   a. Side kick—right and left

    b. Hook kick—right and left

    c. Spin kick—right and left

    d. Rear front thrust—right and left

    e. Heel kick—right and left

5. Punch (Monday, Wednesday, Friday)

    a. Jab—speed bag, foam pad, top and bottom bag

    b. Cross—foam pad, heavy bag, top and bottom bag

    c. Hook—heavy bag, foam pad, top and bottom bag

    d. Overhand cross—foam pad, heavy bag

    e. Combinations—heavy bag, top and bottom speed bag

    f. Platform speed bag workout

    g. Top and bottom bag

6. Endurance (stationary cycling)

    a. Running (Monday, Wednesday, Friday)

    b. Cycling (Tuesday, Thursday, Saturday)

    c. Rope skipping (Tuesday, Thursday, Saturday)

The Breakdown of Bruce Lee's Total Fitness Routine

Monday–Saturday (Stomach and Flexibility)

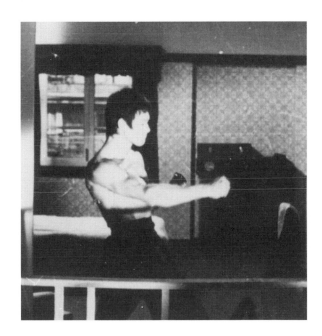

1. Bench leg stretch
2. Sit-up
3. Side leg stretch
4. Leg raises
5. Side bends
6. Hurdle stretch
7. Flag
8. Sitting stretch
9. Twist
10. Split stretch
11. Back bends
12. High kicking

Monday, Wednesday, Friday (Hand Techniques)

Bean Bag

1. Right jab
2. Right jab—foam pad
3. Left cross
4. Right hook

    a. Tight

    b. Loose

c. Upward

5. Overhand left

6. Combination

Top and Bottom Speed Bag

1. Right jab

2. Left cross

3. Right hook

4. Overhand left

5. Combination

6. Platform speed bag—taper off

Tuesday, Thursday, Saturday
(Leg Techniques)

1. Right side pulley stretch

2. Right side kick

3. Right side pulley stretch

4. Left side kick

5. Left side pulley stretch

6. Right leading hook kick

7. Left reverse hook kick

8. Right heel kick

9. Left spin-back kick

10. Left reverse front kick

Tuesday, Thursday, Saturday
(Weight Training)

1. Clean and press

2. Squat

3. Bench press

4. Curl

5. Good morning

The Art of Expressing the Human Body

Bruce Lee's Personal Training Routine

DAY	ACTIVITY	TIME
Monday	Stomach and flexibility	7:00 AM–9:00 AM
	Running	2:00 PM
	Hand	5:30 PM–6:30 PM and 8:00 PM–9:00 PM
Tuesday	Stomach and flexibility	7:00 AM–9:00 AM
	Weights	10:00 AM–12:00 PM
	Leg	5:30 PM–6:30 PM and 8:00 PM–9:00 PM
Wednesday	Stomach and flexibility	7:00 AM–9:00 AM
	Running	12:00 PM
	Hand	5:30 PM–6:30 PM and 8:00 PM–9:00 PM
Thursday	Stomach and flexibility	7:00 AM–9:00 AM
	Weights	11:00 AM–12:00 PM
	Leg	5:30 PM–6:30 PM and 8:00 PM–9:00 PM
Friday	Stomach and flexibility	7:00 AM–9:00 AM
	Running	12:00 PM
	Hand	5:30 PM–6:30 PM and 8:00 PM–9:00 PM
Saturday	Stomach and flexibility	7:00 AM–9:00 AM
	Weights	11:00 AM–12:00 PM
	Leg	5:30 PM–6:30 PM and 8:00 PM–9:00 PM

Everyday Opportunities for Exercise

1. Take a walk whenever you can—like parking the car a few blocks away from your destination.
2. Avoid taking the elevator; climb the stairs instead.
3. Cultivate your quiet awareness by imagining an opponent attacking you while you are sitting, standing, lying down, etc., and counter that attack with various moves (simple moves are the best).
4. Practice your balance by standing on one foot to put your clothes or shoes on—or simply stand on one foot whenever you choose to.

I did it this way, I trained my hands every Monday, Wednesday, and Friday—and my legs on the alternate days.

24. TRAINING ROUTINES DESIGNED BY BRUCE LEE FOR HIS STUDENTS

A popular misconception has endured throughout the years that Bruce Lee devised unique and different training programs for each of his students. Not only would such a practice have been tremendously time-consuming (and impossible with Lee's busy schedule), but also unnecessary, for Lee's research into human physiology revealed that we all share a common physiology and, consequently, a similar response to the stimulus of exercise.

Lee's own notes dispell this misconception. In some instances, he would list three or more students' names, and, on the same page, he would prescribe for them identical training programs to cultivate power, flexibility, bodybuilding, and forearm enhancement. Why? Again, because he realized that the stimulus that resulted in the response of a more powerful punch, a stronger forearm, and an increase in flexibility or strength was universal—applicable for himself or any of his students.

From superathlete Kareem Abdul-Jabbar to world champion martial artist Joe Lewis to Lee's students Daniel Lee, Pete Jacobs, Bob Bremer, Jerry Poteet, and Steve Golden, both the core curriculum of martial art techniques and the attendant supplemental training programs were nearly identical.

While it's true that Lee would look upon each student individually to discern in which areas they most needed improvement (and then prescribed the appropriate supplemental training exercises accordingly), his antidote to each individual's particular martial or fitness deficiency was drawn from the same source—that is, the same supplemental training programs that Lee himself had devised and, in most cases, followed himself.

This chapter presents several training routines that Lee designed for his students and indicates the fundamental physical-fitness aspects that each program helped to cultivate.

Kick-Boxing Training Routine

1. Roadwork

Jog (1 minute)—Sprint (keep it up)—Walk (1 minute) in as many sets as you can

2. Skill conditioning

    a. Shadow kick-boxing—3 minutes (1 minute rest) (*Note:* loosen up in good economical form)

    b. Shadow kick-boxing—3 minutes (1 minute rest) (*Note:* work hard—push yourself—speed/power)

    c. Skip rope—5 minutes (1½ minutes rest) (*Note:* try all footwork)

    d. Heavy bag—3 minutes (1 minute rest) (*Note:* individual punches plus combinations)

    e. Heavy bag—3 minutes (1 minute rest) (*Note:* individual kicks plus combinations)

    f. Light bag—3 minutes (*Note:* individual punches plus conditioning)

    g. Shadow kick-boxing—2 minutes (*Note:* loosen up)

Supplementary Exercises for Flexibility

 1. Forward bend
 2. Stride stretch
 3. High kick
 4. Side leg raise
 5. Elbow touching
 6. Waist twisting
 7. Alternate splits on chair
 8. Sitting bends
 9. Leg stretch—straight, side
10. Arched bridge position

 1. High kick and rear stretch
 2. Side leg raise
 3. Forward bend
 4. Elbow touching
 5. Waist twisting
 6. Alternate splits on chairs

Training Program For Dan Inosanto

Everyday before getting out of bed do :—

Group A
(everyday)

1) full body stretch---5 times, maintaining stretch 3 sec. rest 2 sec.
2) arch back------------five times
3) leg tensing---------12 times, 3 sec. tensing, 2 sec. rest
4) abdominal tensing---10 times, 3 sec. tensing, 2 sec. rest
5) sit up touch toes---five times
6) bent leg raises-----five times

Isometric Power Training (to build up basic requirements)

Group B
(M.W.F.)

1) low pull
2) middle pull
3) high pull
4) chin level press
5) middle press

6) curl
7) reverse curl
8) chest squeeze
9) abdominal tensing
10) middle squat

Isometric functional power training (for more forceful application)

Group C
(T.Th.S.)

1) upward/outward
2) punch penetration---low, middle, high
3) straight kick-------low, middle, high
4) side kick----------low, middle, high

Kicking & Punching (for more explosiveness)

A) _Kicking---flexibility training_

Group D
(M.W.F.)

1) front leg stretching---3 sets of 12
2) side leg stretch-------3 sets of 12
3) high front kicking-----3 sets of 12
4) side leg raising-------~~3 sets of 12~~ **4 sets of 12**

B) ----- _power training_

1) front kick thrust------3 sets of 12
2) side snap kick---------3 sets of 12
3) front toe kick---------3 sets of 12
4) ~~Roundhouse~~ **Kick...2 sets of 12**

C) _Punching_

hanging paper

1) lacing ----------------~~4~~ **4** sets of 20
2) right stance----------~~3~~**2** sets of 20
3) entering right punch--~~3~~**2** sets of 20
4) left hand strike------**3** sets of 20
5) bag punching-----------
6) **Right + left punching - 2 sets of 20**
(~~right stance~~) + **LEFT STANCE**

Abdominal Exercises

Group E
(T.Th.S.)

1) waist twisting---------4 sets of 100
2) sit up twist----------4 sets of 15
3) leg raises-----------4 sets of 15

7. Leg stretch (front, side)

8. Sitting bends

9. Stride stretch

Basic All-Around Power Routine

1. Press lockout

2. Press start

3. Rise on toes

4. Pull

5. Parallel squat

6. Shoulder shrug

7. Deadlift

8. Quarter squat

1. Isometric
   a. Press lockout
   b. Press start
   c. Rise on toes
   d. Pull
   e. Parallel squat
   f. Shoulder shrug
   g. Dead weight lift
   h. Quarter squat

2. Heavy squat

   Take three very deep breaths—all the air you can cram into your lungs. Hold the third breath and squat. Bounce back up as hard and fast as possible. Breathe out forcibly when you're almost erect. Use heavy weight—repeat from 12 to 20 repetitions.

The Chinatown School, at College Street, Los Angeles, 1969

   Punches

1. Straight punch—the three ranges

2. Bent-arm punch—the three ranges

   Kicks

1. Straight kick—the three ranges

2. Hook kick—the three ranges

3. Side kick—the three ranges

Bodybuilding Training Routines

Sequence 1	Sequence 2
a. Squat	a. Press behind neck
b. Bench press	b. Rowing
c. Pullover	c. Neck
d. Deadlift	d. Upright rowing
e. Two-arm curl	e. Side bend

Forearm/Grip Training

Do the following exercises with complete extension and contraction by maintaining a good grip on the bar at all times. For better results, thicken the bar by wrapping something around it; above all, never cheat on any exercises—use the amount of weight that you can handle without undue strain.

1. Reverse curl—3 sets of 10
2. Overgrip curl—3 sets of 10
3. Undergrip curl—3 sets of 10
4. Wrist-roller—3 sets of one trip up and down
5. Leverage bar twist—3 sets of 10

1. Reverse curl
2. Flexor curl
3. Extensor curl
4. Wrist-roller
5. Leverage bar twist

1. Reverse curl—3 sets of 10
2. Flexor wrist curl (barbell or dumbbell)—3 sets of 10
3. Extensor wrist curl (barbell or dumbbell)—3 sets of 10
4. Wrist-roller—as much as you can

1. Reverse grip—3 sets of 10
2. Overgrip curl—3 sets of 10
3. Undergrip curl—3 sets of 10
4. Wrist-roller—3 sets of one trip up and down
5. Leverage bar twist—3 sets of 8

The "Wake-Up" Routine

Everyday before getting out of bed do:

1. Full-body stretch—5 times, maintaining stretch 3 seconds, rest 2 seconds
2. Arch back—5 times
3. Leg tensing—12 times, 3 seconds tensing, 2 seconds rest
4. Abdominal tensing—10 times, 3 seconds tensing, 2 seconds rest
5. Sit-up, touch toes—5 times
6. Bent-leg raises—5 times

Isometric Power Training (To Build Up Basic Requirements)

Monday, Wednesday, Friday

1. Low pull
2. Middle pull
3. High pull
4. Chin-level press
5. Middle press
6. Curl
7. Reverse curl
8. Chest squeeze
9. Abdominal tensing
10. Middle squat

Isometric Functional Power Training (For More Forceful Application)

Tuesday, Thursday, Saturday

1. Upward/outward
2. Punch penetration—low, middle, high
3. Straight kick—low, middle, high
4. Side kick—low, middle, high

Kicking and Punching (For More Explosiveness)

Monday, Wednesday, Friday
Kicking—Flexibility Training

1. Front leg stretching—3 sets of 12
2. Side leg stretch—3 sets of 12
3. High front kicking—3 sets of 12
4. Side leg raising—4 sets of 12

Power Training

1. Front kick thrust—3 sets of 12

The Art of Expressing the Human Body

2. Side snap kick—3 sets of 12

3. Front toe kick—3 sets of 12

4. Hook kick—2 sets of 12

   Punching

1. Facing—4 sets of 20

2. Right stance—3 sets of 20

3. Entering right punch—3 sets of 20

4. Bag punching—3 sets of 20

5. Right and left punching—2 sets of 20
   (right and left stance)

   Tuesday, Thursday, Saturday

   Abdominal Exercises

1. Waist twisting—4 sets of 100

2. Sit-up twist—4 sets of 15

3. Leg raises—4 sets of 15

APPENDIX A. BRUCE LEE'S VITAL STATISTICS

Height: 5' 7½"

Weight: 135 (*Note:* By the time he made *Enter the Dragon*, Lee's weight was down to 125 pounds.)

Waist size: high 30"; low 26"

*Measurements**

Body Parts

Chest (start): relaxed 39"; expanded 41½"

Chest (after): relaxed 43"; expanded 44¼"

Neck (start): 15¼"

Neck (after): 15½"

Left Biceps (start): 13"

Left Biceps (after): 13¾"

Right Biceps (start): 13½"

Right Biceps (after): 14¼"

Left Forearm (start): 11"

Left Forearm (after): 11¾"

Right Forearm (start): 11¾"

Right Forearm (after): 12¼"

Left Wrist (start): 6¼"

Left Wrist (after): 6¾"

Right Wrist (start): 6½"

Right Wrist (after): 6⅞"

Left Thigh (start): 21"

Left Thigh (after): 22½"

Right Thigh (start): 21¼"

Right Thigh (after): 22½"

Left Calf (start): 12¼"

Left Calf (after): 12⅞"

Right Calf (start): 12½"

Right Calf (after): 13"

By the time of *Enter the Dragon*, Bruce Lee had lost considerable body fat: His chest measurement was down to 33½ inches (normal) and 38 inches (expanded), at a body weight of 125 pounds, and his waist was only 26 inches.

(*based on a 1965 bodyweight of 140 lbs)

The Art of Expressing the Human Body

APPENDIX B. BRUCE LEE'S "MUSCLE MACHINE": THE RETURN OF THE MARCY CIRCUIT TRAINER

Bruce Lee used his Marcy Circuit Trainer exercise machine up until the day he died—July 20, 1973. After his death, Bruce's widow, Linda Lee Cadwell, realizing that it would be unnecessary, difficult, and expensive to move the machine from Hong Kong back to California, donated the machine to Bruce's former secondary school, La Salle College, in Kowloon. And so the Marcy Circuit Trainer remained at La Salle College until 1995.

While researching this book, I contacted La Salle, hoping that Linda may also have donated one of Bruce's workout programs for the machine, which they might share with me. At the very least I hoped they might be able to take a picture of the machine that I could include in the book. On May 1, 1995, Brother Patrick at La Salle College responded: "I'm afraid we cannot be of much help to you in your quest for the Bruce Lee materials. Yes, his Circuit Trainer machine was left to our Primary School but had to be dismantled a few years ago in order to make room for reconstruction and renovation. The dismantled parts are now kept in a storeroom here in La Salle College. . . . Should you feel I can be of any further assistance, just fax or phone."

Brother Patrick's last statement seemed to invite a follow-up fax. Plus, the thought of such a significant item of Lee's lying dismantled in a storeroom over a period of several years did not sit particularly well with me. I wrote back to Brother Patrick, informing him that I was sorry to hear that Bruce's exercise machine has been dismantled. "If you plan to put it together soon," I

wrote, "would it be possible to obtain a photograph of it? Or, if you are planning on making additional room in your storage facility and would like to sell it, please keep me in mind, as I would be interested in purchasing it."

Then came the shock of a lifetime. I came home late one evening to find a return fax from Brother Patrick: "Despite my best efforts, I have not been able to unearth anything in the line of photos or charts about Bruce. . . . Now as regards the Training Machine which had to be dismantled, you are very welcome to take it and there is no need at all for payment. In fact, it is a pity to see it rusting away in the storeroom. Let me know if I can be of further help."

His response left me shocked—and delighted! I immediately called Linda Lee Cadwell to let her know that, after a period of some twenty-two years, Bruce's exercise machine was coming home! I knew Linda would be as excited as I was about the news. I also felt an obligation to let her know that even though La Salle College had given me the machine, I recognized that its real owner had been her husband, and although Linda had given it away in 1973, if she wanted it back, I would be obliged to return it to her possession.

Linda *was* very interested in the news. She asked me only one question: "Are you planning on selling it, John?" "No," I replied—quite sincerely—"I want to restore it, train on it, and some day pass it on to my children." My response seemed to please her. "Well, in that case, why don't you keep it?" Linda said. I was ecstatic.

At this stage, I had no idea how much the machine might have deteriorated (or even if it had deteriorated), nor how much work would be involved in its restoration. And there was the not-so-small-matter of finding a way to pay for the shipping of this "free" machine. As most writers will readily attest, unless your name happens to be John Grisham, what little money a writer makes is usually long ago spoken for, and I certainly had none to spare.

Enter Ted Wong

I pondered this dilemma for many weeks. During that time, I received a phone call one night from my sister Jane Loftus informing me that my father had passed away. He was eighty-five years old, and while his passing was not completely unexpected, it caught us by surprise. I returned home to Canada for the funeral, and during my absence, Ted Wong happened to call my house. Upon learning from my wife about my father's death, Ted asked when I would be returning, and shortly after I arrived home, he called again. I'm always delighted to talk with Ted, who is one of the kindest and most sincere people I've ever encountered. (I've found this to be the case among all the men in Bruce's "inner circle" of friends. Men such as Taky Kimura, Herb

The Art of Expressing the Human Body

Jackson, Dan Inosanto, Daniel Lee, and Ted are all straightforward, honest men of integrity and sterling character.) On this night, Ted's voice sounded more serious than usual. "John, I'm sorry to hear about your Dad," he began. "I know that with a new baby on the way (our third child, Brandon) and everything else you're doing, times are probably pretty tough on you financially." I concurred, adding that things were, as the saying goes, "tough all over" and that while I appreciated his concern, he needn't worry about things. "Well, I would like to stop by your house," he said, "if you don't mind."

I looked forward to seeing Ted and, having just left the somberness of my father's funeral, I welcomed the change in conversation. To my surprise, though, Ted had a specific purpose for that evening's visit. He presented me with a check, and insisted that I take it. "I think Bruce would have wanted you to have that machine," he said, quite earnestly. "There were times during my friendship with Bruce when he was strapped financially and I wished I could have helped him then, but I wasn't in a position to," he explained. "Now I am in a position to do something for you, and for Bruce. I think he would want his machine restored and protected. And don't bother paying me back. I want to do this. I'm just glad to see Bruce's Marcy Machine come home."

I didn't know what to say. I still don't. I had never been the recipient of such kindness or generosity before. I learned a lot about Ted Wong that night—and about the caliber of Bruce Lee's friends. I accepted his offering because I wanted that machine more than anything else in the world—but also out of respect for him; I knew that this was something Ted felt very strongly about.

The Return of the Dragon's Circuit Trainer

Several weeks later, on the evening of August 15, 1995, the ocean liner *Seabreeze* pulled into harbor in San Francisco with, among other things, a cargo that had traversed the same Pacific Ocean route some twenty-three years before. After clearing U.S. Customs, I received word that my "delivery" would be arriving at my door on the evening of September 13, 1995. I quickly called Ted to let him know. Ted, in turn, notified Herb Jackson (these were the same two men who had been in Hong Kong with Bruce Lee when the machine first made its away across the ocean). At 10:00 PM on September 13, they were standing in my driveway awaiting its return.

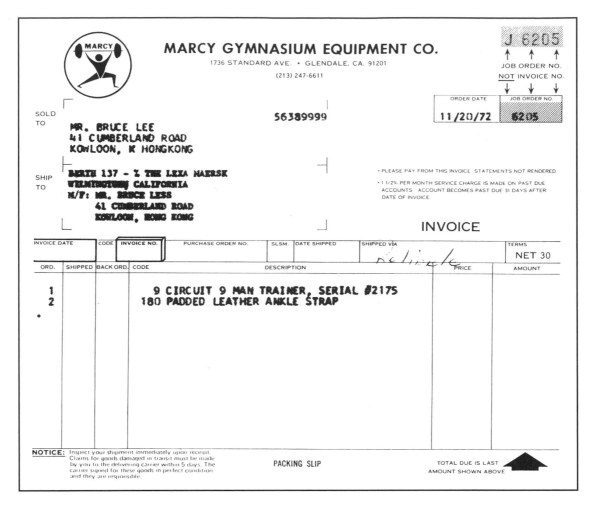

When the huge transport truck pulled in and opened its cargo door, all of us jumped up to help unload the machine. We were overcome with wonder: What would it look like? Would it still be functional? How badly had it rusted? Herb and Ted began banging away on the big pine and plywood crate. Herb—seventy-two years old—outworked all of us that night, hammering the spikes out of the crate and tearing off the protective plastic cover.

When the lid was finally opened, we looked inside and saw the dismantled parts that, collectively, had once been responsible for building the most impressive physique of the twentieth century. Yes, there was some serious rust and even some paint obscuring the original chrome of the machine. Nevertheless, there could be no mistaking that this was *the* machine. I checked the parts I could identify with the quick glimpses of the machine that had appeared in the video "Bruce Lee: The Man/The Legend" and in a Japanese television special that featured this same machine (then on loan from La Salle College) to commemorate the release of Lee's last film *The Game of Death* in 1978.

There were the pulley handles that Bob Wall told me Bruce had used so feverishly while training for *Enter the Dragon;* there was the detachable knee-up station, part of which was visible in "Bruce Lee: The Man/The Legend"; and there was the lat pull-down unit that Bruce had employed in the development of his tremendous latissimus dorsi muscles, resulting in his

The Art of Expressing the Human Body

never-equaled "V"-shape. More importantly, the lat pull-down unit had a factory sticker on it which read "Marcy Circuit Trainer, Model CT-9-M" and the serial number "2175"—confirming that this was the very machine that had belonged to Bruce Lee. The Marcy Circuit Trainer, Bruce Lee's "muscle machine," was finally—after a period of some 22 years—home at last.

Postscript

With the help of Ted Wong and Herb Jackson I have completely reassembled Bruce's machine. Missing because of the ravages of time are the original bench press bench and roughly 140 pounds of weights from the shoulder press station. Apart from that (and the rust!) the machine is in excellent shape. Herb and I have been working on removing the rust, stripping the paint (which was not on the unit when Bruce used it), restoring the chrome, and greasing the pulleys.

Sometimes I look at the Marcy Circuit Trainer and wonder what it must have been like sitting in Bruce's home in Kowloon Tong, when he came home exhausted after a hard day's work at Golden Harvest Studios. I envision him not being able to walk past that lat pull-down bar without taking hold of it, sitting down, and banging out a dozen or so repetitions—if only to relieve the stress of the day.

Once it was finally reassembled, I felt Ted Wong deserved the honor of being the first one to work out on it. I've since used it myself and have had some of the best workouts of my life. My sincerest hope is that some day, when an admiring gym teacher asks my sons or daughter why they are in such good health, they'll be able to reply, "because we work out daily on Bruce Lee's Circuit Trainer!"

NOTES ON SOURCES

In writing this book, I was fortunate to be able to discuss Bruce Lee's approach to fitness with many people who worked closely with Lee during his life. In addition, Linda Lee Cadwell provided access to Bruce Lee's extensive library of books on physical culture, development, and nutrition as well as to written materials in the Bruce Lee Archives. By paying special attention to his marginal notes and to passages he had underlined and highlighted, I gained further insight into his beliefs, philosophy, and approach to total health and fitness. Listed below are the sources upon which I relied most extensively. Readers who wish to pursue this subject in greater depth are encouraged to seek out the published sources.

Interviews

Kareem Abdul-Jabbar
Jon T. Benn
Sharon Bruneau
Richard Bustillo
Linda Lee Cadwell
Lou Ferrigno
Leo Fong
Jesse Glover
Larry Hartsell
Dan Inosanto
Herb Jackson
Wally Jay
Allen Joe

Taky Kimura
Gene LeBell
George Lee
Joe Lewis
Andre Morgan
Lenda Murray
Hayward Nishioka
Jhoon Rhee
Bob Wall
Van Williams
Ted Wong
Bolo Yeung

Printed sources

Unpublished writings by Bruce Lee*

- Annotations of "Longstreet" screenplay, June 22, 1971
- [Chinatown jeet kune do class schedule], n.d. (Dan Inosanto Papers)
- "Commentaries on the Martial Way," vols. 1 and 7
- "General Development," notes, ca. 1968
- "General Notes on Martial Way," n.d.
- "Heavy Bag Drills," paper written for Los Angeles Jeet Kune Do School, n.d.
- "Isometric," n.d.
- "Jun Fan Calisthenics Program," October 10, 1971
- "Jun Fan Gung Fu Institute Fitness Program," notes, ca. 1967
- "The Jun Fan Method," notes, n.d.
- "Kicking," notes, ca. 1970
- Letters to George Lee, December 19, 1965, and June 25, 1966 (George Lee Collection)
- Letter to James Lee, August 6, 1965
- Letters to Linda Lee, ca. 1973, and June 16, 1967
- Letter to Mito Uyehara, August 11, 1972
- "Non-Classical Sets of Jeet Kune Do (Chinese Boxing)," n.d.
- "Private Lesson," ca. 1969
- "Simplicity Is the Key," notes, ca. 1967
- [training fundamentals], notes, n.d.

• training programs:

"The Basic Fitness Program," notes, n.d.

from choreography notes for *Enter the Dragon*], 1973

"Every Day," notes, n.d.; "Morning," notes, ca. 1970; "Every Night," notes, n.d. (Dan Inosanto Papers)

"Flexibility," stretching routines, n.d.

forearm development, maximizing (Daniel Lee Papers)

forearm routines (personal), n.d.

forearm program recommended to Daniel Lee, n.d. (Daniel Lee Papers)

written for Larry Hartsell in preparation for first North American kick-boxing tournament, ca. 1968 (Larry Hartsell Papers).

written for Dan Inosanto, ca. 1968. (Dan Inosanto Papers)

written for Daniel Lee, ca. 1968. (Daniel Lee Papers)

written for Daniel Lee, Pete Jacobs, Bob Brenner, and Jerry Poteet, n.d.

"Morning," notes, ca. 1970

personal programs, various dates

tensolator routine, October 10, 1971

"Training Schedule," notes, ca. 1970

"Weight Training," notes, ca. 1970

* Unless noted otherwise, all unpublished materials are in the Bruce Lee Archives and the Bruce Lee Library.

Books about Bruce Lee, Those Containing Passages Annotated by Lee, and Books Consulted by the Author

Barrs, John. *Bodybuilding: The Official Training Textbook of the British Amateur Weight-Lifters Association*. London: Vigour Press, (n.d.).

Bowerman, William J., and W. E. Harris, with James M. Shea. *Jogging*. New York: Grosset & Dunlap, 1967.

Bruce Lee Jeet Kune Do Club. *Reminiscence of Bruce Lee*. Hong Kong: Bruce Lee Jeet Kune Do Club, 1978.

Clouse, Robert. *Bruce Lee: The Biography*. Burbank, Calif.: Unique Publications, 1988.

———. *The Making of* Enter the Dragon. Burbank, Calif.: Unique Publications, 1987.

Cooper, Kenneth H. *The New Aerobics*. New York: Bantam, 1970.

Corrigan, Brian, and Alan R. Morton. *Get Fit the Champion's Way*. London: Souvenir Press, 1968.

Cureton, Thomas Kirk, Jr. *Physical Fitness and Dynamic Health*. New York: Dial Press, 1965.

Gironda, Vince. *The Vince Gironda Workout Bulletin*. (n.p., n.d.).

Glover, Jesse. *Bruce Lee: Between Wing Chun and Jeet Kune Do*. Self-published, 1976.

Hoffman, Bob. *Functional Isometric Contraction*. York, Pa: Bob Hoffman, 1964.

Hyams, Joe. *Zen in the Martial Arts*. New York: Bantam, 1979.

Inosanto, Dan. *A Guide to Martial Arts Training with Equipment*. Burbank, Calif.: Know Now, 1980.

Johnson, David G., and Oscar Heidenstam. *Modern Bodybuilding: A Complete Guide to the Promotion of Fitness Strength and Physique*. New York: Faber Popular Books, 1958.

Lee, Linda. *Bruce Lee: The Man Only I Knew*. New York: Warner Books, 1975.

Louis, Joe. *How to Box*. Philadelphia: David McKay, 1948.

The Muscles of the Body and How to Develop Them. London: Athletic Publications, (n.d.).

Miller, William H. *How to Relax: Scientific Body Control*. New York: Smith & Durrell, 1945.

Mirkin, Gabe, and Marshall Hoffman. *The Sportsmedicine Book*. Boston: Little, Brown, 1978.

Morehouse, Laurence E., and Augustus T. Miller, Jr. *Physiology of Exercise*. St. Louis: C. V. Mosby, 1963.

Morehouse, Laurence E., and Philip J. Rasch. *The Scientific Basis of Athletic Training*. Philadelphia: W. B. Saunders, 1958.

Norris, Chuck, with Joe Hyams. *The Secret of Inner Strength: My Story*. New York: Charter Books, 1988
Paschall, Harry B. *Muscular Arms and Shoulders*. Moortown—Leeds: John Valentine, 1953.
Peebler, J. R. *Controlled Exercise for Physical Fitness*. Springfield, Ill.: Charles C. Thomas, 1962.
Pickens, Richard, ed. *The NFL Guide To Physical Fitness*. New York: Randon House, 1965.
Raye, Zelia. *Rational Limbering*. London: Imperial Society of Teachers of Dancing, 1929.
State, Oscar. *Weight Training for Athletics*. London: Amateur Athletic Association, (1955?).
Trevor, Chas. T. *Training for Great Strength: An Introduction to the Science of Strength and Bodybuilding by Means of Progressive Weight-lifting*. London: Mitre Press, (n.d.).
Uyehara, Mito. *Bruce Lee: The Incomparable Fighter*. Santa Clarita, Calif.: Ohara, 1988.
Van Huss, Wayne, et al. *Physical Activity in Modern Living*. Englewood Cliffs, N.J.: Prentice-Hall, 1960.
Wallis, Earl L. and Gene A. Logan. *Figure Improvement and Body Conditioning Through Exercise*. Englewood Cliffs, N.J.: Prentice-Hall, 1964.
Webster, David. *The Complete Physique Book*. London: Arlington Books, 1963.
Williams, Jesse Feiring, and Eugene White Nixon. *The Athlete in the Making*. Philadelphia: W. B. Saunders, 1932.

Magazines, newspapers, and articles

Interviews with Bruce Lee

• "Bruce Lee Talks Back," in January 1968 issue of *Black Belt*
• Taped telephone conversation with Daniel Lee, ca. 1971 (Daniel Lee Collection)
• August 15, 1972, issue of *New Nation* (Singapore newspaper)
• Plane, Mike, "Super Star Bruce Lee: An Acclaimed Phenomenon," in August 1973 issue of *Fighting Stars* magazine
• Stom, Mitch, "Bruce Lee's Training Methods," in 1968 *Yearbook* of *Black Belt* magazine

"Abdominals, Part. 2" *Florida Weight Man* (n.d., ca. 1967)
Anderson, Paul, "Squatting for Power," in *MD Magazine* (n.d.)
Berger, Richard A., "An Application of Research Findings to Weight Training." (publication unknown)
Corcoran, John, "One-on-One with Stirling Silliphant," in January 1993 issue of *Martial Arts Legends*
Inosanto, Dan, "Bruce Lee: The Little Dragon Remembered," in September 1985 issue of *Inside Kung Fu*
"Interviewing Bruce Lee: Bruce Lee Tells Us the Secrets of Combat," in *Bruce Lee and Jeet Kune Do* magazine, no. 10 (1977)
Todd, Terry, as told to John Grimek, "Mighty Mitts." (publication unknown), ca. 1966
Pearl, Bill, "Fabulous Forearms." (publication unknown), ca. 1966
[Running habits article] in *The China Mail*, July 25, 1972
Vasilieff, Val, "Developing a Muscular Mid-section" (publication unknown), ca. 1968
Weider, Joe, "Some Championship Secrets on Chest Development," in *Muscle Builder* magazine, (n.d., ca. 1965)

Printed sources—Ephemera

• Gironda, Vince. "The Vince Gironda Workout Bulletin," n.d.
• "Grip, Wrist and Forearm Developer Instructions"
• Regulations of the Jun Fan Institute, which were distributed to jeet kune do students.
• Suggested circuit training routine sent with Marcy Circuit Trainer; excerpted from John E. Nulton, *Overload Circuit Training*. Glendale, Calif.: Marcy Gym Equipment, 1969.

INDEX

abdomen: exercises for, 81–84; muscles of, 44, 80–84, routines for, 220–21

Abdul-Jabbar, Kareem, 18, 65, 128, 169, 236

adduction, unilateral horizontal arm, 71

aerobics. *See* cardiovascular training

agility/stamina routines, 210

Application of Measurement to Health and Physical Education, The (Clarke), 27–28

arm(s), 15, 47–48; adduction, unilateral horizontal, 71; exercises for, 113–17

Asian cuisine, 165

back, 14, 49–50; bend, 137; exercises for, 105–112; lower, exercises for, 109–111, 136; thrust (standing), 122; upper, exercises for, 105–109

backfist (gwa choy) technique, 173

bar, leverage, 62, 90

barbells, 39–45, 92; curls with, 53–54, 89–90; presses with, 98; squats with, 49, 52

bean curd (tofu), 165

behind-neck pull-down, 108

bench press, 50, 53, 71, 101–102, 103

bend: forward, 58

biceps, 41-44, 113

Big Boss, The (film), 52, 64, 167

bilateral alternate hip extension, 71

Black Belt (magazine), 151, 202, 204

Block, Alex Ben, 207

bodybuilding, 32; routine, core tenets of, 52; training routines, 240. *See also* routine(s); training; weight training; workout(s)

boxing, Western, 173

breathing: in curl, 48; in rowing, 49; in squat, 49

Bremer, Bob, 236

Brewer's yeast, 171

"Bruce Lee: The Man/The Legend" (video), 248

Buchholz, Butch, 207

Bustillo, Richard, 73–74, 148, 155, 192

cable crossover, unilateral, 104

cable machine, 77–78

Cadwell, Linda Lee, 15, 17, 18, 24, 55, 66, 85, 145, 162–63, 168–69, 186, 245, 246

calf: exercises for, 123–24 raise, 45, 71, 76–77; stretch, 136

calisthenics: Jun Fun Gung Fu Institute program, 214; routines, 211

carbohydrates, 164

cardiovascular system, 24; efficiency activity (running), 72; training and, 139–48

cat stretch, 58

chest, 14, 50; exercises for, 101–12

chi sao (sticking hand), 38, 55

chin-up: overhand, 108; palms-up, 113

China Mail, The, 147

Chinatown School warm-up programs, 213

Chinese Connection, The (film), 52

Chinese Gung Fu—The Philosophical Art of Self Defense (Lee), 128

Chow, Raymond, 153

Christenson, Larry, 207

circle, dumbbell, 43, 115

circuit training, 57, 68–72; timing of, 68; variables in, 68. *See also* routine(s)

Clarke, H. H., 27

clean and press, 47–48, 52, 98

Clouse, Ann, 19

Clouse, Robert, 19

Coburn, James, 18, 150

coordination, routines for, 210–211

crossover, unilateral cable, 104

curl(s), 48; alternate cable, 71; barbell, 53–54, 89–90, 113–14; breathing in, 48; concentration for, 42, 114; incline 42; palm-down, 60; palm-up, 59; reverse, 62, 77, 87; standing cable, 114–15; two-hand, 43; wrist, 44; wrist, reverse, 44, 90; Zottman, 46, 89

Davis, Adele, 163, 166

Daws, Ron, 207

deadlift, 71, 75–69, 111–12

decline press, 102

deep-knee bend, 58

deltoids, 47–48, 95, 97

diet: daily (typical), 165-66, 170–71; reduced-calorie, 83; supplements to, 166–68; well-balanced, 164–66

dumbbell, 92; circle, 43, 115; flyes, 104; kick-back, 117; lateral raise standing, 99–100; press, 103

endurance, exercises for, 142–43, 211

Enter the Dragon (film), 26, 64, 65, 67, 207, 248

Enter the Dragon routine for martial artists, 73–79

exercise(s): for abdomen, 81–83, 78; for back (lower), 109–11; for back (upper), 105–109; basic fitness, 215–16; for biceps, 113–15; for chest, 101–104; compound, 46; for endurance, 142–43, 211; for flexibility, 131–38; forearm, 85–94; fundamentals of, 209–10; good morning, 53, 109–11; heavy hands, 141; leg-training, 119–22; neck and shoulder, 95–100; opportunities for, 235; resistance, advantage of, 28–29; for triceps, 115–17. *See also* routines; workout(s)

running, 15, 140–41; as cardiovascular-efficiency activity, 72. See also jogging

Sandow, Eugene, 25
Schwarzenegger, Arnold, 18, 19, 64
seated exercise(s): calf raise, 124; groin stretch, 134; leg press, 70, 122–23; leg thrust machine, 76; shoulder press, 71, 78–79, 99
sequence training routine, 219–20
serratus muscles, 80
shoulder(s), 48–49, 78–79; circling and, 61; flexibility training for, 138; and neck, exercises for, 95–100; press, 71, 78–79; shrug, 37. See also deltoids
side bends, 60, 82–83
side leg raise, 60–61
side stretch, 136
sil lum tao, 173
Silas, Paul, 207
Silliphant, Stirling, 23, 139, 142
sit-up, 44, 81; twist, 62
sparring practice, 232
speed, 21; increasing, 27–28, 29; routine for, 216
splits, alternate, 61
Sportsmedicine Book, The (Mirkin and Hoffman), 207
squat, 41-42, 58, 119-20; with barbell, 49, 52; breathing, 119–20; breathing during, 49; jumping, 61 119; parallel, 37; quarter, 38; straddle, 120–21
Stallone, Sylvester, 19
stamina/agility routines, 211
standing: back thrusts, 122; barbell press, 98–99; calf raise, 71; hip stretch, 134; leg thrust machine, 76; pulley stretch, 135; unilateral horizontal arm adduction, 71; wrist roller, 72
static contractions. See isometric(s)
Steinhause, Arthur, 56
stepping, 142
steroids, anabolic, 35
sticking hands (chi sao), 38, 55
Stone, Mike, 199, 205
straddle squat, 120–21
strength: pursuit of, 26–34; and shape routine, 52–54
Strength and How to Obtain It (Sandow), 25
strength training: aspects of, 31–32; research on, 32; value of, 28
stretch(es): beginner, 131; calf, 136; groin, 60; hamstring, 132; hurdler's, 133; lower back, partner, 136; lunging, 135; reflex, 130; seated groin, 134; side, 136; standing hip, 134; standing pulley, 135; thigh, 135–36
stretching post, 127
submaximal loads, 32

Tanny, Vic, 22
tea, 170
technique training, 226–29

thigh, 76; stretch for, 135–36
toes, rise on, 37
top and bottom bag routine, 210
training: bodybuilding, 240; forearm/grip, 91–93, 221–22, 240–41; heavy bag, 149–55; interval, 147–48, 157–61; isometric power, 241–42; kick-boxing, 237; methods, 15; for muscularity, 64–72, 92; record, 32; student, 236–43; technique, 226–29; types of, 27. See also circuit training; routine(s); weight training; workout(s)
trapezius, 97
triceps, 41–43, 113; push-down, 72, 116; raise, 116–17
twist, 81–82; waist, 59

unilateral hip and knee flexions, 123
unilateral horizontal arm adduction, 71
upper back, exercises for, 105–109
upright row, 97, 115
Uyehara, Mito, 192, 200, 205

velocity. See speed
vitamin C, 168

waist twisting, 59
wake-up routine, 241
walking, power, 141
Wall, Bob, 67, 85, 248
warm-up programs, 213
Way of the Dragon, The (film), 21, 52, 58, 61, 64, 65, 95, 105, 128
Weider, Joe, 64
weight loss, 207
weight training: 28, 32; in bodybuilding routines, 217–18; and isometrics, differences between, 33–34; in Jun Fan Gung Fu Institute routine, 218
Wheeler, Flex, 20
Wing Chun system of gung fu, 55, 173
Wong, Arnold, 200, 205
Wong, Ted, 21, 44, 65–66, 192, 194, 196, 197, 200, 202, 204, 205, 246–47, 249
workout(s): Bruce Lee, 232–33; duration of, 28–29; principles of, 14. See also routine(s); training
wrestler's bridge, 96–97
wrist(s): flexibility training for, 137; roller, 63, 86–87; wrestling, 85

Yale University, 28
Yang-tze (a.k.a. Bolo Yeung), 67
Yarrick, Ed, 39
Yates, Dorian, 20
yin-yang symbol, 24
York, Penn., 35, 82
York Barbell Club (Penn.), 82

Ziegler, John, 82